Eyewitness Accounts of the Thirty

Eyewitness Accounts of the Thirty Years War 1618–48

Geoff Mortimer
Lecturer in German
St Edmund Hall, Oxford

First published 2002 by
PALGRAVE
Houndmills, Basingstoke, Hampshire RG21 6XS and
175 Fifth Avenue, New York, N.Y. 10010
Companies and representatives throughout the world

PALGRAVE is the new global academic imprint of
St. Martin's Press LLC Scholarly and Reference Division and
Palgrave Publishers Ltd (formerly Macmillan Press Ltd).

ISBN 0–333–98404–8

This book is printed on paper suitable for recycling and made from fully managed and sustained forest sources.

A catalogue record for this book is available from the British Library.

Library of Congress Cataloging-in-Publication Data
Mortimer, Geoff, 1944–
    Eyewitness accounts of the Thirty Years War 1618–48/
    Geoff Mortimer.
        p. cm.
    Includes bibliographical references and index.
    ISBN 0–333–98404–8
        1. Thirty Years War, 1618–1648 – Personal narratives. I. Title.
D270.A2 M67 2002
940.2′4′0922–dc21

                                                            2001056137

10   9   8   7   6   5   4   3   2   1
11   10   09   08   07   06   05   04   03   02

Printed and bound in Great Britain by
Antony Rowe Ltd, Chippenham, Wiltshire

Contents

List of Illustrations

Map

Plates

Sources, References and Translations

Sources

All the eyewitness accounts referred to in this book have been published, albeit in many cases in the nineteenth century or even earlier, and all quotations are drawn from these publications. Some of the original manuscripts have been consulted, but a number are no longer extant, having either disappeared long ago or been lost in the aftermath of the Second World War.

References and quotations

The author–date system is used within the text to identify works cited, and to give the page references for quotations. The relevant full publication details are listed alphabetically by first author in the Bibliography.

Because of their very large number, quotations from eyewitness accounts are identified only by a code and page number thus: (Di.193). These codes are given with the relevant entry for the published text in the Bibliography, and with the map and list of authors on pages 199–201.

Where there is more than one quotation in a sentence, the references are placed at its end. Subject to the needs of clarity, in other cases where two or more quotations from the same source occur consecutively in a paragraph the references are grouped together, and if these all have the same page number it is given only once. References follow the quotations and are given in the order in which they appear in the preceding text.

Translations, spelling, names and dates

All translations from German are my own, and I have sought to render the meaning accurately in good modern English rather than attempting to capture the style or literacy level of the individual authors. Latin interpolations have been left untranslated, with the meaning given only when this is neither obvious nor unimportant.

In the main text recognised English versions of names of people and places have been used where they exist. In quotations names have been retained in the German form but spelling has been modernised if it is quite clear who or where is meant, whereas if there is any possible doubt the author's original spelling has been retained. Quotations from authors who wrote in English follow the spelling and capitalisation of the published editions. Dates within quotations are as given by the authors, but otherwise are 'new style'.

Units of measurement and money

At the time of the Thirty Years War Germany was not a single country, but comprised a large number of political entities of various types and greatly differing sizes, united only by their nominal allegiance to the Holy Roman Empire. Many of these were able to issue their own money, while units of measurement were frequently determined by local custom and practice rather than by wider regulation. The eyewitnesses often mention sums of money and prices or quantities of food and drink, which presents a problem as the original terms will probably be unfamiliar to the reader while equivalents may be tendentious or suggest spurious accuracy.

Where quantities are involved it is desirable to give at least some idea of whether a little or a lot was implied. Thus the many and varied volume measures used for dry foodstuffs, particularly grain, have been divided into smaller and larger ones and translated by the old British terms 'bushel' and 'quarter' respectively (the latter, a little under 300 litres, being about eight times the former). Measures of wine and beer have likewise been translated as 'quart', a term actually in use in seventeenth-century Germany, 'keg' – a small barrel of unspecified size, and 'tun' – a very large barrel holding almost 1000 litres. For weights, 'pound' and 'hundredweight' are reasonable equivalents if not viewed too precisely, while if 'wagon-load' seems vague it is in fact how the relevant term was defined at the time. For precious metal 'half-ounce' provides a workable conversion, while 'ell' is the same word as an old British cloth measure of rather over a metre. *Stunde* (hour) as a measure of distance has been converted roughly into miles. Land areas are particularly difficult, with a *Morgen*, for example, being the amount of land a man and a team of horses or oxen could plough in a morning. Opinions about this varied, and in the early nineteenth century Baden fixed it as 3600 square metres but Hesse preferred 2500. Things were no clearer in the seventeenth century, so it has been loosely translated as an acre, while other measures have been correspondingly converted.

Translation is effectively impossible for money. Not only did coins with the same names have different values in different places, but those values also varied with time. Inflation was one of the burdens of war for much of the period, and it was rampant during the 1620s, when private mints, coin-clipping and debasement of the precious metals used added to the problems. Hence the original terms for money have been retained in the text and all that can be done here is to rank them roughly by size.

The Reichstaler was an Imperial coin and in theory the same across the Holy Roman Empire, and it was often used as a basis for exchange of local currencies. Any coin referred to simply as a taler was probably of local issue, and if so almost certainly worth less, and perhaps much less, than a Reichstaler. Taler, gulden or florin were common names for the larger units of currency, while kreuzer, batzen or groschen were typical smaller units.

Some rulers also issued a coin known as a kopfstück, literally meaning one with his head on it, while coins such as ducats came in from outside Germany, probably with the armies.

Acknowledgement

The substance of Chapter 14 has previously been published in the journal *German History*, and I am grateful for permission to reprint it here.

G.M.

1
What Happened in the Thirty Years War?

In 1912, when Ricarda Huch first published her account of the Thirty Years War (1618–48), she called it simply *The Great War in Germany*. Her original title, quickly changed following the world conflict of 1914–18, typifies the long-standing view of the Thirty Years War as a seminal event, and until the twentieth century the most terrible, in German history. Among more recent British and German historians one calls the war 'an unprecedented catastrophe for the German people', another notes its significance as 'the trauma of the German nation, whose effects are still felt in the twentieth century' and a third characterises the effect it created on the population as 'a war syndrome of violence, hunger and disease, which encroached upon all aspects of life, seemed unending, and became everyday reality' (Parker, 1984, p. 215; Schmidt, 1995, p. 81; Burkhardt, 1992, p. 238). These comments also reflect an enduring perception among the general public in Germany, as illustrated by a survey in Hesse in 1962 in which respondents rated the Thirty Years War and the accompanying plague as the greatest disaster in German history, ahead of both World Wars, the Third Reich and the Black Death (Krusenstjern and Medick, 1999, p. 34).

The war has been repeatedly portrayed as a period of prolonged devastation during which armies marched and fought the length and breadth of Germany for 30 weary years, taking and retaking towns, eating the countryside bare and leaving behind a trail of rapine and plunder from which an exhausted economy and people took many decades, even centuries, to recover. Ergang, who has traced the growth of this popular image of the war in his well-argued but little-known book, *The Myth of the All-Destructive Fury of the Thirty Years War* (1956), says that it developed in the early nineteenth century, in place of more moderate portrayals in histories written by Pufendorf in the seventeenth and Schiller in the eighteenth centuries. He attributes the view of the conflict as a cataclysm to the Romanticists, with their interest in fanciful tales of terror, and its initial propagation to their repopularisation of Grimmelshausen's near-contemporary novel, *Simplicius Simplicissimus*, while he ascribes its later and wider publicising in large measure to Gustav Freytag's mid-nineteenth-century populist historical work *Pictures from the German Past*. Sensational accounts of sadistic torture, murder and cannibalism form part of the resultant enduring image of the war, Ergang notes, but he also quotes claims by many respectable historians that Germany lost two-thirds or even three-quarters of her population, adding that such estimates were still being repeated in the mid-twentieth century.

A reaction to the most extreme accounts has led some, notably Steinberg, to a categorical 'rejection of the traditional picture of the Thirty Years War as an unmitigated disaster', and what, echoing Ergang, he calls 'the fable of wholesale ruin and misery' (Steinberg, 1966, pp. 91, 2–3). More recent historians strive to present a balanced view, in which they stress that atrocities, though in many individual instances well documented, were not necessarily commonplace, pointing instead to the relatively orderly extraction of heavy taxes and military contributions as the true burden of war. The impact of the conflict differed greatly from place to place, however, so that an overview of its effects on the populace has been hard to achieve. The extremes are illustrated by Franz's assessment that Hamburg flourished during the war, experiencing a 50 per cent population increase in the first half of the seventeenth century, whereas Roeck notes that Augsburg was 'one of the hardest-hit cities in the Empire; ... the population loss was at least half, and probably as much as 60 per cent' (Franz, 1979, p. 9; Roeck, 1991, p. 299). Similar variations also occurred at local level. Franz identifies population movements of up to 50 per cent in either direction, district by district, in the Lippe region, and numbers of houses destroyed or abandoned by the end of the war ranging from 25 to 75 per cent, area by area, in the Weimar – Jena part of Saxony (Franz, 1979, pp. 13, 33). It is currently generally agreed that the population of Germany as a whole fell significantly during the war period, with figures of around one-third being the most commonly quoted, but this average tends to obscure local extremes (Vasold, 1993).

One response to this problem has been an increasing emphasis on local studies in academic research into the Thirty Years War. This is not new *per se*. Franz's work is itself based on a large number of local studies, mostly from the first half of the twentieth century, while research into the effects of the war on particular towns or areas has been carried out by local or amateur historians over a much longer period. Nevertheless the level and depth of more recent work represents a qualitative change, while the shift in focus from the bigger picture to the detail reflects growing interest in the concept of microhistory. In their introduction to the papers from a recent conference, significantly subtitled 'The Thirty Years War in Close-up', Krusenstjern and Medick summarise the method adopted:

> This attempts to get closer to the social and everyday experience of the Thirty Years War from the perspective of a new local and regional, or microhistorical, approach. ... Through precise focusing on the limited

field of observation of a local or regional community, of a life history, or of a particular incident, it becomes possible to study and depict the war as an interrelationship of actions, events and structures shaped by violence, and caused, experienced and suffered by human beings. (Krusenstjern and Medick, 1999, pp. 26–7)

The range and scope of research of this kind is illustrated by recent collections of articles published by Kroener and Pröve (1996), Lademacher and Groenveld (1998) and by Krusenstjern and Medick (1999). Many of these studies extend beyond the Thirty Years War, however, while the focus of most recently published work, although increasingly local, still tends to be wider than the individual soldier or civilian.

Access to the actual experience and perception of war at the personal level is not easy, although the problem does not at first sight appear to be lack of information. The Thirty Years War was the first great conflict in which the printing press had free rein, and events both major and minor are widely reported in contemporary newspapers, pamphlets and broadsheets, often providing graphic descriptions in which sensationalism and propaganda are barely distinguishable – which is exactly the problem in evaluating them. Official records, although plentiful in town halls and archives of former principalities up and down Germany, likewise cannot necessarily be taken at face value. Accounts of events and conditions written by individuals for their landlords, or by towns and villages for the local ruling court, indeed anything intended for contemporary officialdom, are potentially suspect, as although probably not without a basis in fact the material may have been selected, exaggerated and crafted to an extent which cannot now be assessed. Thus 'the first local narratives of death and destruction in the Thirty Years War were usually supplications for a reduction in the tax burden or billeting of troops', while the 'lack of truth in the outrageous demands for damages' and pleas of poverty from towns hit by the war has been demonstrated from the actual state of municipal finances as shown in their records (Theibault, 1993, p. 275; Benecke, 1972, p. 245).

Eyewitness personal accounts, not intended for publication and written for private purposes rather than for the authorities, offer an alternative source of information about the war as experienced by ordinary people. They too present problems of interpretation, as probably imperfect representations of the author's not necessarily accurate perception, but they are at least less likely to contain deliberate deception or to have been consciously shaped to particular practical ends. Such accounts range from more or less contemporaneous day-to-day diaries to recollections written much later, up to 30 or 40 years after the events described. Some were written as private notes or in household record books, while others were inserted into parish or municipal registers, and they range stylistically from self-centred memoirs to impersonally-written chronicles of community experiences. A surprising number are extant although little known, and many have been edited and published, mostly in the journals of local historical societies, reflecting what has previously been mainly a local interest.

It has to be recognised that such texts do not necessarily provide a typical picture, even when a large number are examined. Personal accounts are by definition individual, while limiting study to examples which focus on the war is itself selective. Limited literacy and expensive materials also restricted the range of those able to write extended accounts of their experiences, largely excluding the lower socio-economic classes, while the chances of their manuscripts surviving the intervening centuries are greater for authors such as clerics or officials with access to some form of archive. Of the 72 accounts forming the original basis of this study 21 were written by Lutheran pastors and 9 by Catholic priests, monks or nuns. A further 16 authors were from the professional classes, including officials, and 12 were soldiers. The balance of 14 includes 4 farmers or wine-growers, some of whom may have been relatively well-off, albeit of limited education, but the remaining 10 were from the artisan class. These include 2 bakers, 2 millers, a shoemaker, a cloth-finisher and a copper engraver, as well as an innkeeper, a steward and a court chorister, while 3 or 4 of the soldiers were probably originally from this social level. Thus while the sample is by no means statistically representative it does draw upon quite a broad cross-section of the literate population (Mortimer, 1999).

Steinberg, when attempting to reinterpret the war and to revise the traditional picture of the conditions it created, sought to discount eyewitness reports, arguing that their authors 'all belonged to the same class of educated professional men – clerks, priests, officials, lawyers – who were hardest hit by the vicissitudes of the times. ... Whatever may have befallen the citizens of a town and the peasants of a village, the men who wrote the town chronicles, the monastic annals, the parish registers, were those who had to tell a tale of personal grievance and personal loss' (Steinberg, 1966, p. 95).

There is of course an element of truth in this, but it is equally evidently not the whole truth, as the range of occupations of authors above indicates. There are indeed accounts exhibiting this personal bias – that of the Naumburg official Johann Georg Maul is a long lament over his own financial losses – but they are balanced by many others which give a wider view. Moreover the lower orders present essentially the same picture as the professional men. Although the details of their experiences and the forms of their texts vary, the description of the war given by the peasant farmer Kaspar Preis does not differ in the fundamentals from that of the aristocratic landowner Christoph von Bismarck, while the same is true of accounts from different villages near Ulm, those of the shoemaker Hans Heberle and the pastor Johannes Schleyss. Much the same representation of the war emerges even from the accounts of men who did rather well out of it, such as Augustin von Fritsch, who rose from the ranks to become an ennobled colonel, Captain Jürgen Ackermann, who set himself up as a landowner with his spoils of war, or Hans Conrad Lang, apprenticed as a cloth-finisher but who became a military supplies contractor. Hence while eyewitness personal accounts may not present the whole truth they do provide a valid perspective on it. They offer a means of assessing the experiences of individuals and communities to set against the later 'myth of the all-destructive fury', as well as suggesting how the authors themselves related these personal and local experiences to a contemporary perception of the war as a whole.

The course of the war

Although this book is not directly concerned with the military and political history of the war, some knowledge of the framework of events and issues is necessary to put the personal accounts into context. The expert may wish to skip the rest of this chapter (which is of necessity reduced to essentials) but others may find it helpful in summarising a confusing and to non-Germans usually little understood war.

To begin at the beginning, Steinberg challenged the validity of the very concept of a Thirty Years War, arguing that the wars (plural) of 1618 to 1648 were merely part of a longer series of wars in Europe, and that the Thirty Years War was thus an artificial entity created by historians, whereas contemporaries neither viewed it nor described it as such (Steinberg, 1966, pp. 1–2). Repgen largely demolished this latter argument, citing examples from the Westphalia peace negotiations in which the war is spoken of in the singular and referred to as having spread itself over almost 30 years. He also quotes Richelieu in 1631, the record of Swedish negotiating aims of 1636, and the German poet Gryphius's well-known sonnet of the same year, all of which use terminology which directly implies a single war in progress since 1618. Repgen rounds off his case by noting publications soon after the peace which treat the conflict as an entity with the description 'Thirty Years War', such as the *Kurtze Chronica,* first published in 1648 in Strasbourg under the title *Concerning the Thirty-Year German War...which began Anno 1618 and through God's Grace came to an end Anno 1648* (Repgen, 1982). I have also published a number of references from eyewitness personal accounts which confirm the same perspective among the wider population of Germany both during and soon after the war period (Mortimer, 2001a).

Nevertheless there is something to be said for Steinberg's thesis, in that the war in Germany between 1618 and 1648 passed through four distinct phases. The first of these, the Palatine phase, started with a rebellion in Bohemia, where the largely Protestant nobility and gentry were facing pressures stemming from the Counter-Reformation and from their Catholic Habsburg ruler, the Holy Roman Emperor Matthias. These tensions came to a head on 23 May 1618, when two unfortunate Imperial councillors were hurled from the castle windows in the celebrated defenestration of Prague, the event which is traditionally regarded as beginning the Thirty Years War. The Bohemians and the Habsburgs mobilised their supporters, and a period of complicated political manoeuvring followed. In March 1619 Emperor Matthias, who was also king of Bohemia, died, and the ultra-Catholic Austrian Archduke Ferdinand of Styria immediately succeeded him on the Bohemian throne, having been elected as king-designate by the Bohemian Estates in 1617. The Bohemians then sought to displace this unwelcome Habsburg king and to find an alternative, leading to their deposition of Ferdinand in August 1619 and their election of Frederick V, the Calvinist Elector Palatine, in his place four days later. Meanwhile the Imperial election was proceeding, so that less than a week after being deposed as king in Prague Ferdinand was elected Holy Roman Emperor Ferdinand II in Frankfurt. Manoeuvring continued during the following year, as Frederick attempted to secure his new position as king of Bohemia by military means, but this ended with his total defeat at the battle of the White Mountain in November 1620. The 'Winter King', as he was now mockingly called, fled, totally dispossessed, as Habsburg Spanish forces invading from the Netherlands had already occupied his Rhineland Palatinate. This made the Dutch of the United Provinces, long in conflict with Spain, his natural allies, and six months later, armed with their money to pay armies under Christian of Brunswick and the mercenary general Mansfeld, and with support from the margrave of Baden-Durlach, he was able to reopen hostilities and seek to recover his principality. This met with little success, and in the next two years Frederick's allies and hired generals were successively defeated, mainly by the forces of the Catholic League, headed by Maximilian, duke of Bavaria, and under the generalship of Tilly. A crushing defeat at the battle of Stadtlohn in August 1623 finally forced Frederick out of the war, leaving Imperial and Catholic power apparently decisively reasserted.

This led to the second or Danish phase of the war, in which Christian IV, king of Denmark, theoretically acting in his capacity as duke of Holstein and hence a prince of the Empire, took upon himself the role of defender of the Protestant faith. Christian secured election as president of the Lower Saxon Circle of the Empire, and in June 1625 he invaded Germany with a substantial mercenary army. To meet this challenge Wallenstein, a minor Bohemian nobleman, was commissioned to raise an army which would for the first time place substantial forces directly under Imperial rather than Catholic League control. Wallenstein was a Catholic who had become immensely wealthy from speculation in the aftermath of the defeat of the Protestant rebellion in Bohemia, and armed with the emperor's approval, together with his own money and organising talents, he quickly created a powerful army and an equally powerful position for himself. In the following two years Christian IV and his few allies were driven back, and first Lower Saxony and then Jutland were occupied by Wallenstein and Tilly. The issue was settled in September 1628, when Wallenstein's defeat of the Danes at the battle of Wolgast forced Christian to flee back to Denmark and sue for terms, leading to the peace of Lübeck in July 1629. Once again the Imperial and Catholic party was dominant.

Emperor Ferdinand II chose to use this position of strength to escalate the religious and political struggle by issuing his Edict of Restitution in March 1629. This required return to the Catholic church of all lands within the Empire which had been secularised since 1552, as a longer-term consequence of the Reformation. These were numerous and extensive, including not only landed abbeys, monasteries and convents but also bishoprics with large temporal possessions and powers. The edict also allowed ecclesiastical princes, all Catholic, the same powers as already held by secular princes to impose religious conformity on their subjects, and banned all forms of Protestant religion other than Lutheran, most notably Calvinism. As well as aiming at the militant recatholicisation of significant areas this also implied a substantial attack on the lands and revenues, and hence the practical power, of the Protestant princes who had been the main beneficiaries of the secularisations of the previous three-quarters of a century. At the same time the promulgation of this edict on the emperor's authority alone, without following the complex and legalistic procedures of the Holy Roman Empire, implied a considerable extension of Imperial power. This created alarm which extended far beyond Germany.

In these circumstances Gustavus Adolphus, king of Sweden, was able to assume the mantle of the defender of Protestantism, and to initiate the third or Swedish phase of the war by invading Germany, landing at Peenemunde, near Stettin, in July 1630. Gustavus, a seasoned campaigner in contrast to the incompetent Christian IV, quickly consolidated his position in northern Germany, assisted by the emperor's ill-timed dismissal of Wallenstein in August 1630, under pressure from the Catholic princes at an electoral meeting in Regensburg. In the following year, building upon French financial support and his own military successes, Gustavus drew first Brandenburg and then Saxony into alliances, before inflicting a decisive defeat on the Catholic League army at Breitenfeld, near Leipzig, in September 1631. By the end of the year the Swedes had taken Mainz and were on the borders of Bavaria, while their Saxon allies had captured Prague. In spring 1632 the Swedes occupied Bavaria, including Munich, after again defeating the League forces at the battle of Rain, following which Tilly died of his wounds. Meanwhile the emperor had turned to Wallenstein again, commissioning him to raise a fresh army, and in this calamitous situation he restored him to full power as Imperial generalissimo. This new threat, together with stretched communications and uncertain allies in his rear, prompted Gustavus to withdraw northwards, meeting Wallenstein first in a protracted but inconclusive confrontation outside Nuremberg, and finally at Lützen, near Leipzig, in November 1632. Although it cost the Swedish king his life the battle itself was indecisive, and it was followed by a full year of relative inactivity, during which Imperial fears grew about Wallenstein's ambitions, intentions and suspect contacts with the Saxons and Swedes. These culminated in a strange half-rebellion and counter-rebellion at Pilsen and Eger, in western Bohemia, ending with the Imperially sanctioned assassination of Wallenstein in February 1634. At the end of the following campaigning season the fortunes of war changed, and forces under the emperor's son, the later Emperor Ferdinand III, inflicted a devastating defeat on the Swedes at Nördlingen in September 1634.

From here the conflict drifted into the fourth and final phase of general European war. Swedish reverses led to the defection of her main allies in the spring of 1635, as first Saxony and then Brandenburg came to terms with the emperor through the peace of Prague. Ferdinand II was forced in return to suspend the Edict of Restitution for 40 years, a face-saving formula for its abandonment, and he died two years later, in February 1637. Meanwhile France was gradually forced into direct involvement in the war against Habsburg power, which she had long sought to pursue in surrogate manner through financial support of the Dutch against the Spanish and of the Swedes against the emperor. In May 1635 France declared war on Habsburg Spain, and in March of the following year the Habsburg emperor declared war on France. This wider conflict continued for a further 12 years, during which most of the fighting took place in Germany and troops were frequently recruited there or marched through to support campaigning in the adjoining areas of France, Italy and the Netherlands. In this period mercenary armies marched and countermarched across Germany in a confusing series of campaigns and changes of fortune, even after peace negotiations had begun in Westphalia in 1643. The peace conference dragged on for over five years, as each military success or defeat shifted bargaining positions, but the tide of war turned gradually but decisively against the Imperial party. After successive defeats in 1645 by the Swedes at Jankov and the French at Allerheim the emperor finally recognised the inevitability of making such concessions as were necessary to end the war, but even so the peace of Westphalia was not signed until 24 October 1648.

Apart from short breaks and winter pauses in campaigning there was military activity somewhere in Germany, sometimes localised and sometimes widespread, throughout the period from 1618 to 1648, whereas for some time before 1618 and for some time after 1648 there was relative peace, or at least absence of open warfare on a significant scale. The Thirty Years War is thus very much a German concept. Other wars which became interlinked with it began earlier, like the Dutch struggle with Spain, or went on long afterwards, like the Franco-Spanish war. Poland too was at war for much of the period, with the Swedes, the Turks or the Russians, but these conflicts were largely independent of the war in Germany. Conversely the Transylvanian attacks on the emperor in the east, first under Bethlen Gabor and later under Rákóczi, were made in nominal alliances with the various Protestant forces, although the Transylvanians proved fickle allies. France and Spain, before open war between them began in 1635, had long confronted each other at one remove in northern Italy and the Swiss cantons, in the wars over the succession to the dukedoms of Mantua and in the long struggle for control of the Val Telline, the strategic link in the military route from Spain via Spanish Italy to the Spanish Netherlands. Habsburg connections involved the emperor in these southern conflicts, just as Spain was diplomatically, financially and often militarily involved in the emperor's wars with his Protestant opponents. Conversely Protestant solidarity never extended to real cooperation between the Baltic powers of Sweden and Denmark, whose long-standing rivalry led to war in 1643–45. All these were linked with the war in Germany, as the various parties sought by means of subsidies and shifting alliances to turn the battles of others to their own advantage. All have to be considered in a comprehensive political and military history of what is, as much for convenience as for any other reason, termed the Thirty Years War. This is the basis for Steinberg's argument that it was not a single war, and that by extension it did not last for just 30 years, although viewed in a purely German context the name is demonstrably valid and appropriate.

The issues

If the political and military history of the war is complicated, the underlying issues are no less complex and interrelated, while individual participants all had their own, often mixed, motives for involvement. The most obvious starting point is religion. The ostensible issue underlying the revolt in Bohemia was religious freedom, or at least the freedoms of the largely Protestant nobility and gentry which had been wrung from Emperor Matthias following his de facto supersession of his brother Rudolf II in 1608, concessions which Matthias confirmed in a Letter of Majesty of July 1609. Attempts to claw back these concessions in the last years of Matthias's life, which would have effectively revoked these Protestant freedoms, precipitated the crisis which found its most dramatic expression in the defenestration which initiated open revolt.

By the early seventeenth century the Reformation had penetrated much further into many of the Habsburg and neighbouring lands than their subsequent solidly Catholic history suggests. Protestants of various persuasions were either a majority or a substantial and influential minority, particularly among the nobility, not only in Bohemia but also in Hungary, Transylvania and much of north Italy. Worse still from the Habsburg point of view, the same was true in much, if not most, of their hereditary lands centred around Austria. For some time the Catholic religion and the Catholic emperors had been on the defensive, as indicated by Matthias's concessions in Bohemia. Ferdinand, however, was not disposed towards religious compromise. Personally devout and heavily influenced by his Jesuit education, advisers and confessor, he saw it as not only his duty but also his route to personal salvation to win back lost ground for Catholicism in his domains. Ferdinand had amply demonstrated his zeal for the Counter-Reformation in his capacity as archduke of Styria before his designation as successor to his cousin Matthias, and his accession to the Imperial throne was viewed with apprehension by Protestants throughout the Empire, particularly in lands under direct Habsburg rule such as Bohemia.

Despite this, during the first phase the war was not overtly one of religion, but at least technically a matter of suppression of rebellion against a legitimate Habsburg ruler in Bohemia. Religion was of course used as a rallying cry, with the Protestants looking to their co-religionists for help, and such allies as Frederick, the elector Palatine and temporary king of Bohemia, was able to mobilise were essentially Protestant. Nevertheless the staunchly Lutheran but equally staunchly constitutionalist elector of Saxony, Johann Georg I, not only did not support him but joined in the military campaign against him, for which the emperor gave him a lien on the neighbouring Imperial territory of Lusatia as a guarantee for his expenses. The religious element in the war increased in the second phase, with the entry of Christian IV of Denmark as the self-appointed defender of Protestantism against the Imperial threat. Even so only some minor Protestant German princes joined him; the more significant ones, notably Saxony and Brandenburg, did not. What really placed religion in the forefront was Ferdinand's exploitation of his strong position after the defeat of Christian IV to impose his Edict of Restitution upon the Empire in 1629. This inevitably drove the leading Protestant princes into opposition and made them natural, although still hesitant, allies when Gustavus Adolphus in turn invaded Germany in 1630. Although he may also have had other motives, Gustavus was personally devout and committed to the Protestant cause, and during the two years when he led one party and Ferdinand the other religion was close to the centre of the issue. After Gustavus's death Swedish political interests superseded religious motives, and although the Catholic–Protestant divide remained through to 1648 international politics increasingly governed the war, while territorial and financial questions dominated the peace negotiations.

It is sometimes thought that the troops fought for their faith while the leaders fought for their own advantage. This is certainly unduly charitable to the majority of the troops, most of whom were mercenaries and many of whom were not unduly fussy about which side they fought for. Wallenstein was notably tolerant about the private religion of his soldiers, but few of the commanders made much distinction in practice, and it was normal after a successful engagement to recruit, usually compulsorily, as many of the defeated enemy's men as possible, irrespective of their nationality or religion. Most of the soldiers, like most of their officers, seem to have fought for a living and for the prospect of booty. Arguably many of the leading political figures did much the same, although it is not necessary to be too cynical about the sincerity of their faith simply because they were often able to make their religious and material objectives coincide. The most embarrassing position throughout the war was that of France, for whom religion and politics pulled in opposite directions. Because she was confronted by and feared being surrounded by Spanish and Imperial, albeit Catholic, Habsburg power, which also limited her own expansionist ambitions, Catholic France was forced to support the Protestant party, entering into an alliance and providing financial support for the militantly Protestant Gustavus Adolphus and eventually having to fight for many years alongside the Swedes in Germany.

Material advantage (or fear of material loss) was certainly a major consideration for participants in the war. Whatever Gustavus's original motives for invading Germany may have been, after his death the Swedes were determined to secure adequate compensation for their efforts in the form of territory in Germany as the price for peace. This determination, and the fact that anything given to the Swedes had to be taken from a prince of the Empire, who then had to be compensated elsewhere, was long an obstacle to the commencement of serious peace talks, and then a major cause of their protracted nature. But the Swedes were far from alone. Christian IV's Protestant zeal did not preclude ambitions to acquire the secularised bishoprics of Bremen, Verden and Osnabrück for his sons, which indeed he partially achieved before his invasion of 1625. France too, combining security considerations with expansionist aims, took advantage of the opportunity to lay hold of Alsace and a number of other nearby Imperial territories, gains which were confirmed by the peace of Westphalia. German princes were as eager as foreigners to take what they could get. Johann Georg of Saxony gained a permanent hold on Lusatia, as the emperor's dire finances never allowed him to pay the expenses against which he had pledged it early in the war. Maximilian of Bavaria similarly secured possession of the Upper Palatinate (in north-eastern Bavaria, physically remote from but then belonging to the Rhineland principality), although since the lands in question were confiscated from the elector Palatine rather than being an Imperial fief the transfer was more dubious. Much of Maximilian's political manoeuvring over many years, which considerably complicated the course of the war, was centred on his determination not to be parted from his gains. As well as land these included the new dignity of an elector of the Holy Roman Empire, which Ferdinand II was induced, in abuse if not in excess of his Imperial powers, to confer upon him. The elector of Brandenburg's designs on Pomerania, to which he had at least the basis of a legal claim on the death of the last duke, were obstructed by Swedish ambitions; the eventual result was a compromise, Pomerania being divided and Brandenburg gaining a mixed bag of territories spread across north Germany as far as Cleves, on the Dutch border. Even the emperor, ultimately the biggest loser, was on the lookout for opportunities when circumstances permitted.

Although the main motivation for the Edict of Restitution was religious, Ferdinand was by no means blind to the opportunity which the restored bishoprics and their associated temporalities would provide for suitable scions of the house of Habsburg.

The military men too were on the make. Colourful independent generals were a feature of the war, among the most notable being the perennial mercenary Ernst von Mansfeld, the quixotic aristocrat Christian of Brunswick, known as the mad Halberstadter, and the resolute soldier and ally of the Swedes Bernard of Weimar. Their ambitions to carve personal principalities from the toils of war were never realised, whereas the most remarkable, Wallenstein, achieved princely status and possessions before succumbing to intrigue and death. In addition to the vast estates in northern Bohemia which he bought up in dubious circumstances and from which he drew his title of duke of Friedland, Wallenstein secured the duchy of Sagan in Silesia and the immensely valuable duchy of Mecklenburg, together with the status of a prince of the Empire, as rewards and repayments of debt from Ferdinand II. Mecklenburg was lost again in the changing fortunes of war, but most of the remainder of Wallenstein's estates were later distributed to those of his generals who had helped to secure his downfall and death. Tilly, in contrast, rather pathetically complained that despite a lifetime of loyal military service he had never managed to acquire an appanage for himself.

Material ambitions spread all the way through the ranks. The colonels were the key men, entering into contracts with one side or the other to raise regiments which were then their personal property, and from whose pay, provisioning, equipping and employment they expected to make a personal profit. The prospect of booty was an attraction at all levels, but at its most basic the war became the only means of livelihood for many, officers and men alike, who had few possessions and few other skills to offer. As an issue in the war this should not be under-estimated. For a man like Mansfeld, his army was his principality, and it could only exist as long as he could find employment for it, so that his need provided the opportunity for others to pursue their war aims. Such generals and the colonels below them were careful with their key possessions, and were reluctant to expose their forces to the chance of battle unless absolutely necessary, and preferably then only when they had achieved significant numerical superiority. This is one reason for the endless marching, countermarching and manoeuvring for position which dominated the Thirty Years War, while major battles were relatively few and far between over this long period. Moreover the very existence of armies created the need for constant campaigning, to keep them on the move so that they could live off the land, while the need to garrison and control territory in order to extract 'contributions' from the populace, the ultimate means by which the war was financed, created a vicious circle in which ever more troops were needed. Campaigning was determined as much by supplies as by strategy, particularly in winter, when the aim was to quarter the armies on enemy rather than friendly territory in view of the economic damage they would cause. Thus the existence and material needs of the armies fed and prolonged the war, and indeed the peace conference too; the question of how to achieve and finance demobilisation was a major issue in negotiations, and required two years' effort after the peace treaty to resolve.

Underlying all the politics of the Thirty Years War was the question of Imperial power. Internally this was a matter of the balance between the so-called German liberties of the princes of the Empire, who were becoming increasingly absolutist in their own territories, and the central authority of the Imperial crown, which was in theory elective but which had become almost hereditary in the house of Habsburg. For the rest of Europe a weak Empire with power diffused among a large number of principalities was much preferable to a stronger Imperial authority which might create sufficient unity for Germany to become a threat to its neighbours. Gustavus Adolphus had already experienced Imperial involvement against him in his war with Poland before he decided to invade Germany. With Wallenstein becoming duke of Mecklenburg and his army besieging Stralsund in 1628 Gustavus may have had good cause to see Sweden's security threatened by Imperial control extending to the Baltic coast. For France, with Spain to the south and the Spanish Netherlands to the north, any growth of Imperial power in Germany increased the prospect of Habsburg encirclement, although she would not have been happy to see a strong Germany even without a Habsburg emperor, and certainly not one under Protestant Swedish control. French policy was effectively, if not intentionally, directed as much at keeping the war going and preventing either side from gaining a clear advantage as at assisting her nominal allies, partly explaining some apparently mutually incompatible manoeuvres and her maintenance of close contact with Maximilian of Bavaria throughout her period of alliance with the Swedes.

Maximilian, who like Johann Georg of Saxony was one of the few rulers in power throughout the war, also provides the best example of the resistance inside the Empire to extensions of Imperial power. In view of Ferdinand's religious policy the concerns of the Protestant princes are easy to understand, but while Maximilian too favoured the Catholic Counter-Reformation, although through less confrontational means than the Edict of Restitution, he was equally anxious to ensure that the German liberties and princely powers – his liberties and his powers – were not eroded by the emperor. This was the basis of his hostility to Wallenstein and the Imperial army, as he much preferred Catholic policy to be underpinned by the armies of the Catholic League, controlled by the princes rather than by the emperor, particularly as he himself stood at the head of the League. It does not necessarily invalidate this general attitude that Maximilian was only too ready to benefit directly from Ferdinand's arguably *ultra vires* actions in ceding him the Upper Palatinate and electoral status; the unifying thread in the twists and turns of his policy over the years was his desire to ensure that the emperor did not emerge constitutionally or politically strengthened in relation to the princes. The other leading secular princes shared this attitude, although some of the ecclesiastics, several of whom were Habsburg relatives or nominees, were more amenable. Significantly, only the Catholic electors were present in person at the electoral meeting in Regensburg in 1630, and it was they who curbed Ferdinand at the peak of his military success, forcing the dismissal of Wallenstein and the partial disbandment of the Imperial army just as Gustavus invaded.

Whether Ferdinand actually aimed at such an extension of Imperial power is a different question. Pursuit of religious objectives seems to have been his primary consideration, and to have motivated his most high-handed action, the Edict of Restitution. His confiscations of Mecklenburg and the Upper Palatinate in order to confer them respectively upon Wallenstein and Maximilian, along with the electoral title, can be interpreted as practical responses to difficult, even desperate, political and financial situations rather than as calculated arrogation of power to the person of the emperor. Nevertheless neither Ferdinand nor his advisers can have been blind to the implications of these moves, and certainly the princes were not slow in pointing out their impolitic, if not illegal, nature. Here perception is important. Whatever was actually the case, princes inside and beyond the Empire thought that the emperor might be trying to extend his powers and to move the Empire towards the more unified nation-state structure which France and Spain had achieved. Preventing this was one of the motives for the conflict, and ruling it out for the foreseeable future was one of the consequences of the peace of Westphalia.

2
Sources, Authors and Texts

Eyewitness personal accounts, written for private purposes rather than for the authorities, and not (with a few exceptions) intended for publication, provide a direct link with individual experience and perception of the Thirty Years War. Further definition is necessary, however, as potentially relevant sources extend from a limited number of quite specific accounts of the author's experience of the war to a much larger number of wider-ranging contemporary texts in which the war is occasionally mentioned or some isolated incident is described. Krusenstjern's invaluable bibliographic register of personal writing from the age of the Thirty Years War spans this range and lists over 230 examples (Krusenstjern, 1997). A limited number of these cover the whole war period, but most deal with only a part and some with only a few months, while many commence years or decades before the war began or extend correspondingly far beyond its end. For present purposes the preferred texts are those which can meaningfully be described – even if not fully defined – as eyewitness personal accounts of the war.

The terms 'eyewitness' and 'personal account' are important criteria, although not ones to be drawn too narrowly. The essential question is whether the author wrote from direct experience and personal knowledge, rather than deriving information from the press, from his own research, or from the reports of others, particularly others not well known to him. This does not imply that the writer need have witnessed every incident reported (although there is an important distinction between such direct testimony and even the most local hearsay) but that he should have had a clear link, close in space and time, to the source of the information. There is an obvious difference between including a neighbour's report of being robbed outside the village and incorporating rumours of events in distant cities. Many writers do introduce such extraneous information but the point is that this should be digression rather than the substance if their texts are to be useful. The concept of a personal account thus derives from the writer's standpoint in relation to his material rather than implying that he is himself the central figure in the narrative, which may indeed be quite impersonal in style and yet still serve the purpose. (NB. Although 'his or her' is not used repeatedly here it should be understood where the context requires, as some of the writers were women.)

The most valuable accounts are those which, deliberately or de facto, make the war their principal theme, either throughout or for significant periods, and in which the reactions of individuals or communities to war are explicitly or implicitly recorded. In some cases it is clear either from the writer's own statement or from the text that he set out specifically to describe his own or his neighbourhood's experience of war, even though he may have deviated from time to time or have continued writing after the end of the war. In other cases the experience of war has imposed itself upon a text originally commenced for another purpose or in another form, perhaps as a private diary, housebook or chronicle, while entries in church registers or municipal records sometimes also became accounts of the war. The precise format is less important than the nature of the resulting record. More problematic are texts in which the war features, but in a less central role. In long-running personal diaries war-related incidents may be recorded as they occur, although the main emphasis lies elsewhere, perhaps on the author's personal life or business affairs. Such accounts can provide factual information which is relevant in other contexts but they tend not to be characterisations of the war as such.

Taking the war as the principal subject suggests that the author sought to give some breadth to his picture of the experience rather than focusing upon isolated and perhaps arbitrarily selected or remembered details, but many accounts are restricted to a single event or a short period of time. At the other extreme a few authors, such as the soldier Augustin von Fritsch, lived through and described almost the entire war period, although most were less comprehensive in their experience and recording. Civilian accounts reflect the fact that most of Germany suffered the direct effects of war only during discrete parts of the 30 years, with central and southern Germany almost untouched until 1631. Consequently writers who make the conflict the focus of their personal accounts tend to describe fully the periods when it bore down upon them and to skim over the intervening relatively peaceful times, but they nevertheless offer a much broader perspective than the narrators of single episodes or very short periods. Hence an account covering years rather than days or weeks is generally preferable, although no precise time-limit can be specified. One further qualification is required; the text must be sufficiently developed to provide an adequate representation of experience rather than a mere list of events. The diary of one pastor notes local happenings during ten years of war from 1639 to 1648, but in four short pages from which, although some facts can be gleaned, no individual perception emerges.

Applying these loose criteria to the body of published personal writings from the period narrows the field considerably, while limiting attention to those written in German or English excludes a number of others. Thereafter it is a matter of judgement as to which are the most relevant of the sources. 66 are referred to in this book but some others may have been equally suitable or have added something to the study, which is by no means exhaustive although large enough to be representative.

It should be added that the sources themselves do not provide an even or comprehensive coverage of the war, either geographically or temporally. As the map at the end of this book shows (p. 201), examples are drawn from most parts of Germany, but with more coming from the main campaigning areas and through-routes for the armies in the centre and centre-south than from elsewhere. Similarly while there are accounts dealing with each main phase of the war there are more from the central period than from earlier or later, and individual long-running accounts also tend to devote more attention to this time. This reflects the way in which the war inflicted itself on the population, having a briefer and more localised impact during the earlier years but becoming more intense and widespread after the Swedish invasion of 1630. This more drastic experience perhaps prompted many authors to record, while the sparser coverage of the later years suggests a growing war-weariness and a sense that, terrible though it was, it was more of the same and thus less noteworthy.

Contemporaneous accounts

Before examining these eyewitness accounts in depth a look at their range and nature is appropriate, together with an introduction to some of the authors who will be most frequently quoted. This begins with accounts which were, or appear to have been, written substantially contemporaneously and which their authors did not later rework, apart perhaps from making a fair copy later in life. Evidence for the contemporaneous nature of the writing, which is clearer in some texts than in others, is mainly inferred, suggested by the diaristic nature of entries, relatively precise recording of dates and other factual or numerical information, phrases such as 'in this year 1632', and occasionally by clear lack of hindsight, such as the expression of hope that the first reports of the death of Gustavus Adolphus would prove false. Accounts of this type include a number of private diaries or chronicles maintained over extended periods, encompassing the full spectrum from the strongly author-centred 'what I did or saw today' diary to the impersonal but nevertheless eyewitness chronicle of events affecting a community.

The principal distinction between a contemporaneous record and an account written up later is that the former lacks the element of hindsight implicit in the latter, so that events and observations are noted according to the interest or importance they held for the author at the time rather than filtered and ordered by subsequent developments. Historians generally place greater value on contemporaneous records because of their lesser reliance on memory for the facts and the reduced likelihood that a later perspective influenced the author's selection and description of them. Even so caution is necessary, as 'contemporaneous' is a relative term. Few diarists consistently maintain up-to-date records, and while some entries may indeed refer to the events of the day others might have been written up weeks, months or even longer afterwards. In some cases, moreover, authors rewrote their texts later in life, raising the problem of whether the result is merely a fair copy, and thus still essentially contemporaneous, or whether it is a version reworked with the benefit of hindsight.

Peter Hagendorf, a long-serving professional soldier, kept a typical day-to-day diary for almost 25 years. Accounts of their experiences by German troopers, most of whom were illiterate, are rare, and this diary is unique in giving an extended description of the war as seen from the ranks. Watermarks establish that the manuscript was written up by the author in about 1647, with a continuation up to his discharge in 1649, but textual evidence indicates the content to be a transcript of an earlier contemporaneous diary. Pages are missing from front and back, so that the identity of the writer has been lost, but editorial research has established a possible name for him.

The diary commences in 1625 with Hagendorf *en route* to Italy, where he joined the Venetian army. He was then a young man, perhaps about 20 (making him about 45 by the time of his discharge) and he stayed two years in Italy, where he served two separate engagements as a soldier. Out of the army life was hard, as he found in Milan: 'Here we begged, because our money was gone.' He then returned to Germany, where after another spell of begging he joined the Pappenheim regiment, 'for I was in nothing but rags' (Ha.39, 43). Apart from a year of enforced service with the Swedes after being captured in 1633 he was to stay with this regiment, part of the Bavarian army, for 22 years, during which he marched as far as Neustettin (now in Poland) and deep into France, as well as criss-crossing central Germany repeatedly, covering over 25 000 kilometres on the march in his military career. For almost all of this time he was a non-commissioned officer, although he was promoted in November 1636 during the Imperialist campaign in France, to what he describes as 'leader' of a company, presumably the lowest officer rank in what was probably a depleted unit during a disastrous campaign. This proved to be temporary, as his company was captured at Rheinfelden in March 1638 and the soldiers were conscripted by the Swedes. The terms of the town's surrender set the officers free, Hagendorf among them, but after the loss of his men he apparently reverted to his former status. He made notes of his experiences throughout his war service, and he records items, sometimes important and sometimes trivial, as time permits and as the fancy takes him. The result is a collection of brief, often laconic observations which build up a striking picture of the requirements of military duty and of the parallel pursuit of a private life during a quarter of a century on campaign.

Hans Heberle, a shoemaker from a village outside Ulm, kept a long-term journal which was taken over by the experience of war. He claims to have been prompted to start recording his life and times by the remarkable comet of 1618, although he first compiled his work into book format, with title and introduction, in 1628, so that the earlier material may have been written or revised with a degree of hindsight. Thereafter his record is substantially contemporaneous, albeit with lapses which he wrote up later, and much of it is an account of the war, although he continued to make entries for the remainder of his long life, up to 1672.

Heberle learned to write at the parish school, which he attended up to the age of 13, and he was a keen reader of the pamphlet press, from which he drew information to use in his account – half diary, half chronicle – of the war years, often copying extracts from printed material into his personal record. He includes information on his private life, notably the births and early deaths of many children, as well as his personal experience of the war, which affected his area relatively little until 1630. Thereafter it became a through-route for continual troop movements, and as his village was small and exposed it was frequently raided for supplies or plundered for booty by passing forces, whereas the larger and better-defended city of Ulm was able to avoid the worst effects by shutting its gates on them. The villagers often took refuge there, and Heberle records fleeing to the city on no fewer than 30 occasions between 1630 and 1648, accompanied by his wife and children and such possessions as they could carry. He was called up for a couple of short periods in the Ulm militia, but otherwise his experience of war was mainly hunger, insecurity and loss of property; neither he nor his family were physically harmed sufficiently for him to record it, although a number of his relatives died of plague.

Other diarists give less personal detail and concentrate instead on particular aspects of their experiences. Dr Johann Heinrich von Pflummern, a lawyer from a Swabian noble family, held various official posts, including acting for the Bishop of Constance and as an emissary and negotiator for the city of Überlingen, of which he became mayor in 1644, holding the post for 26 years until the age of 85. He started his diary in 1633 and kept it for ten years, perhaps lapsing thereafter under the pressures of office. Almost half of his text concerns 1633 and 1634, and in this he describes mainly the military events in the area, setting out troop dispositions and minor actions in long-winded detail but reporting relatively little of his personal observations in and around Überlingen. He was out of the city on official business when it was besieged by the Swedes in May 1634, and his travels on its behalf in 1635 to 1637 took him away from the war zone to Linz, Regensburg and the Imperial court in Vienna, while much of the remainder of his diary deals with the endless negotiations over contributions and billeting in which he was involved in the later years.

Yet more impersonal are the works of a number of amateur chroniclers. The schoolmaster Gerlach, from Albertshausen, near Würzburg, covers the period from 1629 to 1650 in diaristic form but essentially impersonally, only rarely betraying any individual feelings or opinions. He records events affecting the area rather than relating his own experiences, and he seldom strays beyond his two main themes, the war itself and the consequent enforced local changes of religion. The Freiburg priest Thomas Mallinger ranges much more widely, chronicling minor local events over a long period, 1613 to 1660, and interpolating a variety of extraneous material into the earlier part of his text. He sharpens his focus strikingly when war first affected his area in 1632, his local chronicle thus becoming a de facto account of the war, which furnished material for his evident urge to record, previously perhaps little more than a pastime. Mallinger gives an account of the course of the conflict in south-west Germany and an eyewitness report of conditions in Freiburg, while himself remaining invisible in his text apart from occasional glimpses between the lines.

Adding notes to official registers was not unusual in the period, but in some cases these are extensive enough to form diaristic records in their own right. As with privately-kept diaries, the texts vary considerably in style and content, but a similar range of motivations may have prompted their authors to write, the principal difference being their implicit address to a wider posterity through an official rather than a private medium. A significant number of extant accounts are of this type, probably because of the greater chances of survival of the host documents in parish or town archives, although the inherent opportunity to record for posterity thus presented may have tempted many who might not otherwise have written. In contemporaneous records this often influences the nature of the resulting text, in that the keeper of a private diary has made a deliberate decision to write, although conscientiousness in the execution may vary, whereas notes in registers may be made on the spur of the moment, perhaps arising from a remarkable or traumatic incident. Some such writers made their notes in the next available space, randomly interspersed between births, deaths or other official entries, and sometimes in more than one register. Others demonstrated a more specific intent to record by setting aside pages for the purpose, although their writing was not necessarily more focused in practice. Indeed some of the more deliberate are also among the more eclectic, using their official registers to assemble a wide variety of material of personal interest, so that most accounts of this type have to be pieced together by extracting the relevant diaristic entries from either the official records or a range of other ephemera.

Martin Feilinger is typical of the long-term diarist using the medium of a church register. From 1605 he was the Lutheran pastor in a parish comprising three small villages in Hesse, and he kept a form of contemporaneous journal until shortly before his death from plague in 1635. It is clear that he did not set out specifically to make a record of the war but that this arose out of his wider diaristic writing, as his register is heavily annotated with a variety of non-official entries, many of which concern local or family matters, together with numerous Bible texts and other religious items, some in prose and others in verse form.

The additions to his parish register made by Johannes Schleyss, the Lutheran pastor at Gerstetten, near Ulm, comprise a more focused private chronicle which, like Mallinger's, converts itself into an account of the war under pressure of events. Covering the years from 1622 to 1634, shortly before his death, Schleyss's account is a continuous text in the back of his register, and may be a fair copy although evidently first written contemporaneously. Thus his diaristic entries have accurate dates, and he frequently concludes with comments indicating lack of knowledge of later times, such as 'what will come of it, time will tell', or suggesting that he was awaiting further information: 'I have not yet heard where to' (Sc.1. 85, 88). He adds a prayer to the first news of Gustavus Adolphus's death – 'Please God that the report is a fabrication!' – and on the departure of troublesome billeted soldiers he expresses the equally forlorn hope: 'God grant that no more come!' (Sc.1. 95, 2. 8).

Schleyss seems to have been motivated by no more than a desire to record, essentially for its own sake. He offers no explicit or implicit reason for writing, and although he had a large family they do not feature in the chronicle. Nor is his account overtly intended as a record of his own or his community's tribulations for the interest and instruction of future generations. Indeed the war is barely mentioned during the first six years, beyond the observation in 1622 that 'in this year the miserable war in the Palatinate was still going on' (Sc.1. 78). Instead Schleyss's account of this period is a typically unfocused amateur chronicle, comprising random entries on a range of local topics, the most frequent being prices and inflation but encompassing infanticide, murder, incest, accidental deaths, plague, hailstorms, lightning, the harvest and even the discovery of 'a snow-white stag' (Sc.1. 80). The character of the text changes abruptly at the beginning of 1628, as events provided the author with a new theme: 'Right at the beginning of this year a new and frightening catastrophe threatened us, as besides the burden of inflation a great danger of war appeared' (Sc.1. 82). For the following three years war-related matters are the principal but not the exclusive theme of Schleyss's chronicle. Prices, the harvest, lightning and accidental death still find a place among notes of local troop movements, billeting and contributions, as well as of recatholicisation in the area following the Edict of Restitution. A further change occurs in 1631, when Gustavus Adolphus's advance south brought active war to the region. Thereafter it dominates Schleyss's account, which also becomes longer, more detailed and wider ranging, increasingly recording what he heard of the war and politics in Swabia and southern Germany, as well as local events which he knew of directly. This progression indicates how, if the author has no more specific objective than merely to record, events rather than the writer tend to shape the text.

Partly contemporaneous accounts

A partly contemporaneous account is one which was written up at some later time by an author who used his own contemporaneous notes as an *aide-mémoire* and source of detailed information, but selected, supplemented and reinterpreted this material to produce a text which is also informed by a degree of hindsight. Written-up accounts are thus intrinsically different from contemporaneous records, which embody the perspective of the moment but lack the evaluation, relativisation and putting into a wider context which are the essential processes of converting a diary into a more structured narrative.

Some retrospective accounts also have contemporaneous continuations, usually because, having established the medium and brought events up to date, the author simply wrote on in diaristic fashion. Occasionally, however, the writing-up was undertaken specifically to form the basis of a continuing record of the war, suggesting that the author saw the conflict as a central event in his life and times. A case in point is Sebastian Bürster, a monk and in later years almoner at the large and wealthy monastery of Salem, near Überlingen, which he entered some time before 1610 and where he died in 1649. Like Mallinger, he seems to have kept a diary initially as a pastime, and his writing likewise became an account of the conflict as the dominant experience of the following years. Both rewrote their accounts later in life, but whereas Mallinger merely made a fair copy Bürster explicitly related his final text to the war, as he makes clear in his title and foreword of 1643:

> *Collectanea vel Collectitium*, a short collection, compilation and description of the most important points and things which took place round and about the monastery of Salem during the Swedish invasion, *ab anno* 1630, 1631 and stage by stage thereafter ... [dated] *anno* 1643, 22 July. (Bü.1)

Although this might suggest that the war provided his original impetus to record it seems more likely that he started his diary rather earlier, at the beginning of 1630, and independently of the war, which did not threaten the south-west until late in 1631. His introductory section is clearly retrospective but includes descriptions of events which he probably saw, including the 'passage of Ansbach and Brandenburg troops' in 1610 and other incidents up to 1627, ending with a clear lead into a new section: 'In what follows you will be astonished to learn how things happened, after it has been going on for so long' (Bü.6, 12). He continues on a new page with a description of the 1630 comet, which although rewritten and interpreted for the final manuscript suggests the starting point of his original record. This is followed by a diaristic account of the years 1630 and 1631, which is almost entirely concerned with the weather and the wine harvest, whereas the war features only as chronicle notes of more distant events until the monastery was first raided in 1632. The change in focus and tone is then abrupt, as Bürster announces: 'On 26 April the trouble really started around here' (Bü.20).

The existence of a previous contemporaneous record must be inferred from the text, and from the precise dates and details which Bürster provides. It is also implicit in his explanation for the lack of all the relevant details in his record:

> I did not suppose that this protracted and disastrous Swedish situation would drag on for so long; otherwise I would have applied myself more assiduously to noting everything in good time, describing it all in a more painstaking and orderly fashion, with place, year, month, day and hour, ... for (as it has been waiting for so long) I have not been able to recall everything as diligently, methodically and accurately as if fresh in the memory. (Bü.3)

Although he took pains to furnish his final text with a foreword to the 'dear reader', an index and marginal notes of key dates, he was nevertheless aware of weaknesses arising from this genesis, and he apologises for his omissions: 'For who could have described so many vile knaves, with all their evil tricks and wicked villainies. ... I would not have had time or opportunity, and nor could I have laid hands on enough pens, ink or paper' (Bü.1, 1–2).

Robert Monro, who both wrote and published his account during the war, started as a lieutenant in 1626, 'with the worthy Scots Regiment (called Mac-Keyes Regiment)', and ended as its colonel before it was effectively wiped out in 1634 (Mo. Title). After initially serving the king of Denmark this unit was engaged by Gustavus Adolphus for his invasion of Germany in 1630, forming part of the army under his own direct command until shortly before his death at Lützen. During this time Monro became personally acquainted with the king, observing and forming a very high opinion of his personality and methods of command. He was in Scotland recruiting fresh troops when disaster struck his regiment at Nördlingen, following which he remained in Britain and wrote up the notes he had made in the field into a book 'because I loved my Camerades', publishing it in 1637 'for my friends' and for 'the old and worthy Regiment; the memory whereof shall never be forgotten, but shall live in spite of time' (Mo.I. To the Reader, 2). Monro's character emerges clearly between the lines of his narrative. Proud of both his nationality and his religion, he attributes victory over the Catholic Imperialist forces at Breitenfeld largely to 'the invincible Scots, whose prayers to God were more effectual through Christ, then theirs through the intercession of Saints' (Mo.II. 68). Unlike many mercenaries Monro based his choice of side firmly on religious principle and opposition to 'those Catholique Potentates ... that would not onely overthrow our estates at home (if they could) but also would force us (if it lay in their powers) to make shipwracke of our consciences, by leading us unto Idolatry' (Mo.II. 75). Nevertheless he is capable of leavening his faith with more worldly matters, as when he describes his taste for 'the good Calvinists beere at Serbest, ... being the wholsomest for the body, and cleerest from all filth or barme, as their Religion is best for the soule, and cleerest from the dregs of superstition' (Mo. II. 47, 48).

Sydnam Poyntz was a different kind of man and a different kind of mercenary soldier. In about 1621, at the age of 16, he set off in search of adventure and fortune in the German wars, having decided that 'to bee bound an Apprentice that life I deemed little better then a dogs life and base'. 15 years later, after changing his religion and changing sides twice while rising to the rank of 'Sergeant Major of a Troop of 200 horse', and after marrying and losing two wives along the way, Poyntz returned to England much richer than when he left. There he was 'desired by many of my frends, to set downe in writing, what I had told them in familiar discourse, ... having formerly made to myself some particular notes in writing, of thinges of most importance which happened' (Po.45, 125, 45).

Poyntz went on to become a parliamentary general in the English Civil War, but his account of the Thirty Years War must be viewed with considerable reservations. Whereas the precise Monro gives a carefully chronological account, with details of dates, places and his own movements, Poyntz is often vague and sometimes wildly inaccurate. Despite having fought at Nördlingen he locates it in Westphalia, and his phonetic spelling of German names has required some editorial ingenuity to unravel, particularly for places less well known than Wollom, Drayson and Chritznocke (Ulm, Dresden and Kreuznach). Further doubts arise from his interpolated account of six years in Turkish captivity and his claim to have served a year in the galleys, allegedly at Belgrade. The editor of his manuscript notes that 'all students of seventeenth-century literature will recognise here a stock asset of the romancer. No story of adventure is complete without a "captivity among the Moors".' Poyntz describes how following his eventual escape he was converted to Catholicism by a 'poore English franciscan fryer', but later in life he is on record as vehemently denying ever having been anything but a staunch Protestant (Po.16, 54, 145). Immediately after this conversion he joined the army being raised by Johann Georg I of Saxony, one of Germany's staunchest Lutherans, although he later changed to the Imperialist side when he was unable to raise his ransom after being captured. Nevertheless Poyntz's personal reporting is useful, as are his comments and asides about aspects of military life. Some of the more horrific details, such as deflowering nuns or cutting off priests' genitals after the capture of Würzburg, may reflect the origin of the text as a soldier's tale, told 'in familiar discourse' to the credulous folk back home. If no more, Poyntz exemplifies one type of mercenary, the soldier of fortune with an easy conscience, as a counterpoint to the principled and serious Monro.

Accounts written up after the end of the war may reflect a different standpoint and perception of the experience. Such a perspective is evident in the chronicle of Gallus Zembroth, a wine-grower and frequently mayor of a village on Lake Constance, who in his title sets out the specific intention of recording the effects of the war on his community from 1632 until 1652. Although this suggests that he wrote up his account after the war it is also evident from the detail he gives that he must have been drawing on contemporaneous material, and it is possible that in composing his text he referred back to the municipal records to supplement his own notes and memory. Zembroth's chronicle deals almost exclusively with the effect of the war on the village, the principal exceptions being his frequent comments on the grape harvest and bad weather, and he is particularly concerned with the burden of official military extortions to pay for the war, from which the town seems to have suffered as much as from opportunist looting.

Colonel Augustin von Fritsch is quite specific that his memoir was written up in 1660, more than 40 years after the first events described, although it must be presumed that he kept some form of contemporaneous diary during his years of army service. Fritsch's military career offers both parallels and contrasts to those of the common soldier Hagendorf, and he served even longer in the Bavarian army, 31 years from 1618 to 1649, starting in the ranks as an 18-year-old musketeer. His experience of sieges, skirmishes, battles and endless marches was very similar to Hagendorf's, and they were often on the same campaign, but unlike the latter Fritsch climbed steadily up the military ladder. In the 1620s he worked his way through the non-commissioned ranks, gaining officer status in the early 1630s, and progressing to the rank of colonel by the later stages of the war. He was granted a patent of nobility in 1638 for his part in the storming of Heidelberg, and in the post-war years he became commandant of the fortress of Parkstein and the town of Weiden, where he died in 1662. Fritsch married towards the end of the war, seven children following by 1656, and references to them in his introduction suggest that, whatever his reasons for originally keeping a diary, his reworking of it in 1660 had his own posterity specifically in mind.

Retrospective but near-contemporaneous chronicles offer another perspective on the war, as a number were compiled by writers who supplemented research, common knowledge and hearsay with evident, even if not overtly claimed, personal observation. Examples are the wealthy merchant Jakob Wagner, who recorded events in Augsburg from 1612 to 1647, and Johann Jakob Walther, a successful artist with contacts at a number of German courts, who describes himself as 'a lover of history' and wrote a lengthy Strasbourg chronicle (Wl.9). Walther's manuscript, which is dated 1674, is probably his final fair copy of a work drafted over a number of years, describing the history of the city from its origins, although much more space is devoted to near-contemporary times. In keeping with his historiographical approach

Walther gives little personal information, but stylistic clues suggest that much of his account of the war years in Strasbourg is eyewitness, supplemented by research and the reports of others. From 1630 onwards there are also indicators that the original writing was substantially contemporaneous, including wishes for Gustavus Adolphus's success, while in 1647 he clearly writes without foreknowledge when he notes: 'There is a great deal of talk of blessed peace. May God grant it!' (Wl.39). Walther's account of these years is a typical local chronicle, albeit of a period in which war features largely in the events related. Thus he regularly records extreme weather, astronomical events and other perceived omens, comments on the harvest and the year's wine, and notes high prices or food shortages, as well as mentioning a wide variety of interesting or unusual happenings in the city. The picture he presents is thus not specifically of the war, which, particularly in the earlier years, appears in the context of the normal life of the city, but as time goes on the conflict increasingly dominates both that life and Walther's chronicle.

Non-contemporaneous accounts

The third category of texts comprises those apparently first written after the end of the events described, but which do not seem to have been based on earlier diaristic notes or other records. The evidence for this is essentially negative, the absence of factors suggesting underlying contemporaneous sources, together in most cases with a scarcity of precise information, particularly dates and numbers. Another frequent indicator is an anecdotal rather than a diaristic style, accounts sometimes being confined to possibly quite extended and colourful descriptions of relatively isolated incidents rather than giving a more complete narrative. Some authors offer little clue as to the time of writing while others either state or provide strong pointers to it, with a spread from quite shortly after the end of the period described to more than 30 years later.

Peter Thiele's account is an emotional reaction to the burdens of war and a bitter criticism of the heavy financial contributions demanded by the local militia, despite which they were unable to provide protection for the area. Thiele was one of the leading citizens of Beelitz, a small town near Potsdam, where he served as an official of the Brandenburg administration, regulating and taxing the brewing trade, as well as holding local office as a magistrate and deputy mayor. He also seems to have been the town clerk, as his account is another written into an official register, in this case the Beelitz town record. Thiele defines his scope as 'the war in the electorates of Brandenburg and Saxony, of which I deal with only a few years, from *anno* 1636 until 1641', but the nature of the text suggests that it was written from memory as a single exercise at the end of that period, rather than as a contemporaneous chronicle. Why he chose to begin in 1636 is not clear, although in an early paragraph he describes the 1635 peace of Prague, the effect of which in Brandenburg and Saxony was a change from the Swedish to the Imperialist side, a move not to Thiele's religious taste. His text becomes notably more detailed as it progresses towards the time of writing, with the largest part devoted to the events of 1640 and January 1641, and he ends his account of the latter month with the contemporaneous observation that 'what will follow upon this, *tempores dabit*' (Th.12, 25).

Accounts apparently written from memory during the war were often written relatively soon after the end of the events described, and some suggest more specific motives for writing than the mere wish to record. Vincent's book, *The Lamentations of Germany*, published in 1638, is a catalogue of horrors and atrocities clearly designed to shock with descriptions of the looting, rape, murder, famine, disease and cannibalism which were allegedly rife during the war, and the polemical intentions of the book are made clear by its subtitle: 'Wherein, As in a Glasse, we may behold her miserable condition, and reade the woefull effects of sinne. Composed by Dr Vincent Theol. an eye-witnesse thereof; and illustrated by Pictures, the more to affect the Reader.' Vincent appears to have ministered to bodies as well as to souls, mentioning his patients during the siege of Heidelberg and elsewhere, and in a few instances he supports his claim to be an eyewitness to atrocities with specific personal observation, as in his chapter on rape:

> The Sperenrentrish horse-men (as we came through Brunswick-lands) tooke by force a young maide ten yeeres old, and carried her into a wood to ravish her. The mother with up-reard hands, came running after our Coach, crying out to my Colonell, who was here a stranger without command, and could not relieve her: then saw wee the two horse-men come out of the wood, where they had left the poore child dead or alive I know not. (V.18)

Elsewhere his examples are less definitive: 'I have seene them beat out the braines of poore old decrepid women, as in sport, and commit other outrages of like nature' (V.30). In the main Vincent is either imprecise about what he saw personally, or more probably is relying on 'what I have had from sufficient testimonies', and the main interest in his book is that it is a compendium of the horrors associated with the Thirty Years War in the perceptions both of the time and of later centuries (V. To the Reader).

Among the accounts written after the war is one from an unusual perspective, that of a soldier's boy. Johann Georg Oberacker was born near Bruchsal (not far from Karlsruhe), where he returned after an adventurous childhood, working there as a miller for the remainder of his long life. At some stage he wrote a brief account of his youth, which from its structure appears designed to explain how he became a mill-owner, while a single comment suggests that this was intended for his family. Oberacker was a child during the last ten years of the war, and his account of this period is confined to three episodes, describing respectively how his family were killed by soldiers when he was five, how he became first a soldier's boy and then a piper in an Imperialist regiment, and how after four years he deserted to become a miller's apprentice. His style is anecdotal, including colourful details and direct speech to re-create the atmosphere of the moment, suggesting that his text is a written version of tales often told orally by the author. In this it has parallels to Anna Wolff's account, written in the 1660s but describing the siege and capture of her town, Schwabach, near Nuremberg, by Imperialist troops in 1632. Wolff, a young miller-woman at the time, avoided possible rape by hiding for five days in a dovecote, and later she hid the mayor and his wife from the occupying forces for several weeks. These experiences left their mark on her, as indicated by her impulse to record them in dramatic and emotional terms, with frequent religious references and appeals or thanks to God, some 30 years later.

Two other Englishmen also wrote memoirs describing their experiences during the Thirty Years War, although dealing more extensively with their later careers. Thomas Raymond, a younger son of minor English gentry, served for a little over a year, 1633 to 1634, as a soldier in Pakenham's regiment, campaigning in the Low Countries and on the German border near Maastricht. Although a gentleman, Raymond enlisted as a common soldier – 'in his company I traild a pike' – and he gives an account of his military experience from this standpoint (Ry.35). Sir James Turner's memoirs record his service with the Swedish army in Germany from 1632 to 1639, and afterwards in the wars at home, but he also published a substantial military treatise, *Pallas Armata*. In this he describes armies and the conduct of war as he had seen it in Germany, thus providing a more detached and professional but nevertheless eyewitness record of the conflict.

3
Military Perspectives

Military life

The armies that marched, fought and looted their way endlessly across Germany were mainly mercenaries. Gustavus Adolphus brought a core of Swedish and Finnish troops with him when he invaded, but even then his army was already a cosmopolitan one comprising individuals and regiments from many countries. Recruitment in Germany and enlistment of prisoners during campaigning compounded the original diversity, although some regiments did maintain a degree of national or linguistic homogeneity, but only a small proportion of the troops described for convenience by contemporaries and historians as Swedes would ever have seen Scandinavia. The Imperialist armies were little different, including not only troops from all parts of the Empire but many from outside it. Vincent sums this up in describing the notorious Croat horsemen: 'The tenth part of them are not of that Countrey: for they are a miscellany of all strange Nations, without God, without Religion, and have onely the outsides of men, and scarce that too' (V.29).

Recruitment had to be a continuous process. 'Where a War is of any long continuance, that Armies mouldring away, either new Regiments must be levied, or the old recruited', says Turner, describing how the recruiting officers 'invite by Trumpet and Drum all to take imployment, whom either the desire of honour, riches, booty, pay or wages may encourage' (T.166, 165). Sheer financial necessity was an influential recruiting sergeant, and Poyntz states plainly that 'my necessitie forced mee, my Money beeing growne short, to take the meanes of a private souldier' (Po.45). Raymond is no less frank about his own reasons for serving: 'I had noe great fancie to this kynde of life, but seeing no other way to make out a fortune, being a younger brother ... I buckled my selfe to the profession' (Ry.44).

Getting paid once enlisted was another matter, and a constant source of friction and discontent in the armies. Money was always scarce, and the wise commander knew how to turn an occasional issue of pay to advantage, almost as a reward rather than an entitlement, 'knowing well how hungry men could be contented with little, in time of neede', as Monro says of Gustavus Adolphus (Mo.II. 86). Those who joined up expecting to get regular pay were doomed to disappointment. Turner sardonically comments that the soldiers were called mercenaries, 'but if you will consider how their wages are paid, I suppose, you will rather think them Voluntaries, at least very generous, for doing the greatest part of their service for nothing'. Rates of pay in the emperor's army, he adds, were 'fair enough', but 'they got not three months Pay of twelve in a whole year' (T.198, 198–9). On more than one occasion armies effectively went on strike, and in the spring of 1633 Monro reports the Swedish army settling itself into camp for three months, 'resolving to enterprise no exploit or hostility against the Enemy, till such time as they should know, who should content them for their by-past service' (Mo.II. 178).

Turner takes a pessimistic view of the likely possessions of a common soldier: 'Suppose he hath a couple of Shirts, a pair of Stockins, and a pair of Shoos in his Knapsack, (and how many Souldiers have all these?)' (T.276). Vitzthum, a Saxon colonel, confirms this, noting the poor condition of the soldiers in one of the regiments: 'Hardly a man had a pair of shoes, so they went mostly barefoot, and there were many youths among them' (Vi.305). Hagendorf's finances followed the fluctuations of pay and military fortune; he was sometimes well off and at others almost destitute, once lamenting that 'this time I was completely finished, as I had no more than four taler left'. On occasions he had enough cash to buy a horse, although on his discharge he had to settle for a donkey, while another time 'I was forced to sell my horse, which was worth 24 gulden, as I was in need of money here' (Ha.93, 99).

The compensation for lack of pay was the opportunity for plunder, which was seen not as an abuse but as a recognised part of the system. Poyntz, the jocular soldier of fortune, comments that 'wee might bee our own carvers, for we had no other pay', while during his service with Mansfeld they had 'nothing from our Generall but what we got by pillage which as the Proverb is lightly come as lightly goes' (Po.127, 51). Hagendorf is matter-of-fact about plunder, noting when he did particularly well and wryly commenting after being seriously wounded at Magdeburg: 'That was my booty.' In Durlach he looted shirts: 'I was well off again' (Ha.47, 62). In Landshut he got '12 taler in cash, and plenty of clothes and linen', in Magdeburg his wife looted 'bedclothing … and a large pitcher holding four quarts of wine, as well as finding dresses and two silver belts', and at Le Câtelet in France she acquired 'a ball gown made of taffeta' (Ha.59, 47, 75). Plundering was also a standard part of battle and looting the enemy's baggage was common practice, although Monro sarcastically reports that at the battle of Breitenfeld supposed friends were as acquisitive as foes:

And all this night our brave Camerades, the Saxons were making use of their heeles in flying, thinking all was lost, they made booty of our waggons and goods, too good a recompence for Cullions that had left their Duke, betrayed their country and the good cause. (Mo.II. 67)

The fortunes of war sometimes intervened. Monro notes that Swedish booty at Neu-Brandenburg was the proceeds of previous looting by Imperialist troops, 'who though they gathered the whole money of the Country, yet they had not the wit to transport it away' (Mo.II. 15). Fritsch escaped from a lost battle in 1638 while his accumulated wealth fell prey to the enemy troops, but despite such setbacks the war provided scope for professional soldiers to gain promotion from the ranks and to enrich themselves, among them Wallenstein's principal murderer, Colonel Butler. Poyntz too knew how to take his chances, rising to the rank of captain in the Saxon army, 'but beeing taken Prisoner by the Imperialists I lost againe all that I had' (Po.125). Making the best of a bad job he changed sides, and finding favour with his captor, the selfsame Butler, he was able to rebuild his career and finances:

> But I beeing come to this height got to bee by Count Butlers favour Sergeant Major of a Troop of 200 horse but I was to raise them at my owne charge ... for I had then 3000 £ which I carried into the field with mee besides that I left at home with my Wife. ... And I made good use of my place for I could and did send home often tymes Mony to my Wife, who it seemes spent at home what I got abroad. (Po.125–6)

There was little difference in principle between allowing soldiers to find their own remuneration through booty in lieu of pay and the organised exploitation imposed on allied, neutral or enemy territory alike by the generals and colonels. Nevertheless the line was a fine one. Hagendorf's boy 'took a horse, a white one' in Durlach in 1634, and soon afterwards he 'led a fine cow out with him. It was sold for 11 taler at Wimpfen' (Ha.62, 63). In 1633 though, also in an Imperialist unit, a soldier was 'shot by the cavalry captain himself, because he had taken a citizen's horse' (Bü.29). Monro reports the disciplinary measures against unlicensed plundering which were taken by the Swedish army, as when men slipped away in 1631, 'and staying behinde did plunder, and oppresse the Boores, for remedy whereof, the Souldiers being complained on, accused and convicted, they were made, for punishment to suffer Gatlop, where they were well whip't for their insolency' (Mo.II. 47).

If pay, plunder and promotion were unreliable hopes rather than safe expectations, provision of food and accommodation was only a little better. In garrison the troops had sometimes to buy their own food, and at others they were billeted on hosts who had to provide for them. On the march there might be an issue of army bread, sutlers might have supplies for sale, or the troops might have to go foraging. Turner discusses rations with a healthy awareness of likely reality:

> The ordinary allowance for a Soldier in the field, is daily two pound of Bread, one pound of Flesh, or in lieu of it, one pound of Cheese, one pottle of Wine, or in lieu of it, two pottles of Beer. It is enough, crys the Soldiers, we desire no more, and it is enough in conscience. But this

allowance will not last very long, they must be contented to march sometimes one whole week, and scarce get two pound of Bread all the while,
and their Officers as little as they. (T.201)

Hagendorf regularly experienced both extremes: 'On Good Friday we had
bread and meat enough, but on holy Easter Sunday we couldn't get even a
mouthful of bread.' When times were good they seemed very good: 'Baden.
Here we lay in quarters, guzzling and boozing; it was wonderful.' He could
even afford to be fussy: 'In the land of the Cashubians ... we didn't want to
eat beef any more; we had to have goose, duck or chicken' (Ha.43, 42, 43). He
mentions hard times more often, noting once that 'bread was really scarce
in our camp this time', and adding soon afterwards: 'Here the bread and
meat were hung on the highest nail again because of the large number of
soldiers.' One Christmas he complains: 'Stayed put for 14 days; celebrated
Christmas with water from the Danube and didn't have a bite of bread'
(Ha.65–8, 69, 87). Hungry soldiers sought their own salvation: 'At this time
there was such a famine in the army that no horse in the stables was safe
from the soldiers. They would stab a horse in the chest with a knife and then
creep away, leaving it to bleed to death. Later they would eat it' (Ha.69–70).

Vincent encountered 'Italians and Spaniards, which had been at the skirmish at Nortlingen, ... so blacke and feeble through hunger, that had I not
given them part of my provision, I thinke they had rent mee in pieces, and
eaten mee' (V.36). Hunger did more damage than the enemy during the
Imperialist invasion of France in 1636. Fritsch was at Metz when the armies
confronted one another; there was no battle but both sides dug in for three
months, suffering greatly from famine 'right into the autumn, until it froze
bitterly hard and many thousand soldiers and horses perished and died.
When we couldn't hold on any longer because of hunger we marched back
out of Lorraine again' (F.150). Poyntz gives a graphic account of the French
retreat:

> All their Bravery which they showed at their comming was gonne, wee
> could see at their parting nether scarlet Coats nor feathers, but sneaked
> and stole away by little & by little from their Camp. And it seemes most
> of their brave horses were eaten or dead for few we could see at their
> departure nor heare so much neighing of horses as when they came.
> (Po.120–1)

Hagendorf often did well with billets and hosts: Johannes Strobel, a shop-
keeper, in Regensburg; Apollonia, a court clerk, in Braunau; Hans Brunner, a
brewer, in Ingolstadt. On one occasion he was billeted in a tavern and on
another with a wine-seller, good lodgings for a man who was fond of a
drink. He stayed a long time in some of them, four months in winter quarters in 1637, three months in 1638, five months in 1645, and from February

to September in 1647. Usually his wife was with him, and some of his children were born in these billets. On the other hand accommodation in camp
was rough and ready, as Raymond describes:

> Wee had at this league a full plenty of all provisions ... and soe longe as
> money lasted wee had a merry life. As for my selfe I only wanted a good
> bed and sheetes. Parts of an old tent, which I had provided my selfe of
> one for my bed, being stuffed with straw, and ther, my pillow layd upon
> boughs supported with 4 cruches 2 foote from the ground, lying in my
> wascoate and drawers and stocking, covered with my cloathes, my cloake
> being the coverlett, sleeping excellently well, and in this leagur pretty
> free from lice. (Ry.38)

On the march conditions could be much worse:

> These 3 dayes was a very hard march, for we were end of day very wet,
> and came soe and late to our quarters, lying 2 night *sub dis*, haveing only
> the panopie of heaven to cover us. ... I had nothing to keepe me from the
> cold wett ground but a little bundle of wett dryed flax, which by chance
> I litt on. And soe with my bootes full of water and wrapt up in my wett
> cloake, I lay as round as a hedgehogg, and at peep of day looked like a
> drowned ratt. (Ry.39–40)

Seventeenth-century armies were accompanied by a large train of relatives,
servants and providers of services of all kinds. Bürster reports General
Aldringer moving to relieve Constance in 1633 with 'some 30 000 soldiers,
but including the baggage train around 100 000 people' (Bü.17). Turner
describes the system acidly: 'The great number of Coaches, Waggons, Carts,
and Horses loaded with baggage, the needless numbers of Women and Boys
who follow Armies, renders a march, slow, uneasie and troublesome. And
therefore the Latins gave baggage the right name of *Impedimenta*, hinder-
ances' (T.274). He calculates that by Swedish standards a modest army of
5000 horse and 9000 foot would require 1800 wagons, not counting those
of the artillery but including 220 sutlers. In addition to wagoners, traders
and soldiers' families this train included personal servants, even the common soldier often employing someone, perhaps a boy, to look after his horse
or carry his booty. Turner notes that 'a Gudget or Boy was allowed to serve
two Soldiers, *inde* for 10 000 Souldiers, 5000 Gudgets, the very Vermine of an
Army' (T.275). He is more circumspect about women:

> As woman was created to be a helper to man, so women are great helpers
> in Armies to their husbands, especially those of the lower condition; ...
> they provide, buy and dress their husbands meat when their husbands
> are on duty, or newly come from it, they bring in fewel for fire, and wash

their linnens; ... especially they are useful in Camps and Leaguers, being permitted (which should not be refused them) to go some miles from the Camp to buy Victuals and other Necessaries. (T.277)

Monro's wife and family went with him to Germany, but unlike many senior officers he did not take them on active service. In 1631 he went to Stettin to visit them, but 'having stayed but one night, our march continued so farre in prosecuting our victories, that the enemy coming betwixt me and home, I was not suffered in three yeares time to returne, ... which was much to my prejudice' (Mo.II. 25). There were obvious risks for accompanying wives. Poyntz, on the winning side at Nördlingen, describes the pursuit of the defeated:

There wee got all their Canons and other field-pieces which were above fiftie in number and all their Amunition Wagons and Baggage-Wagons above fower thousand with all their Colours: and withall wee found such a number of Ladies and Commaunders Wives that I can not count them, and all of them taken Prisoners. (Po.113)

He adds sardonically that it was left to those still on the field to sing *Te Deum*, 'for those that followed the poursuite had more mynde of taking pray then of making prayer I thinke' (Po.114).

For the common soldier, family life meant marches, camps and billets, as it did for Hagendorf throughout his 20 years service with the Pappenheim regiment. After enlisting in April 1627 on his return from Italy he was married at Whitsun of the same year to the 'honourable and virtuous Anna Stadler, from Traunstein in Bavaria'. In six years of marriage Anna followed him up and down Germany and bore him four children, three of whom died in infancy, and the fourth little older, before she herself succumbed. 18 months later he married again: 'I celebrated the wedding at Pforzheim; it cost 45 gulden, to which her father contributed 10 gulden.' The latter was almost certainly a regimental comrade, and Hagendorf found his in-laws with him on campaign. In France the following year 'my wife's mother died of the plague. I buried her on the 30th of September in the year of 1636' (Ha.42, 64, 76–7). Two children of Hagendorf's second marriage died in infancy and a third at nine months, so that at the time of his discharge in 1649 only two were surviving, a son of six and a year-old daughter.

Family needs could be a major problem. During the spring of 1641 Hagendorf's wife was ill and unable to walk, 'so I led her on the horse. I came here like Joseph travelling into Egypt.' Eventually he had to leave her in Ingolstadt, selling the horse to pay for her care as duty called and he had to move on. Campaigning took him to Brunswick, Göttingen, Frankfurt, Cologne and Mannheim before he was reunited with his wife in Ingolstadt over a year later: 'She was hale and hearty again, but it cost a lot of money.'

Education of children was another problem for those – probably few among the ordinary soldiers – concerned about it. Hagendorf decided that four years of age was time for school, and when the regiment marched away in September 1647 'I left my son Melchert Christoff in Altheim with the school-master at St. Laurenz. I have to give him ten gulden a year plus clothes' (Ha.99, 108, 123). Wives and families also shared many of the risks on campaign, as he reports at Corbie in France:

> As we skirmished outside this fortress many stayed where they sat, both men and women. There was a cannon in there which we called the skirt-chaser, and one day early in the morning they shot all four legs off a man and his wife with it, tight up to the arse, in the hut next to my tent. (Ha.75–6)

'Staying where they sat' was a common euphemism for casualties, and Monro also ironically refers to encamped soldiers at the siege of Nuremberg getting 'life-rent-leases of their new built houses' (Mo.II. 134). At Magdeburg the wounded Hagendorf worried about his wife during her looting expedition:

> When I was bandaged up my wife went into the city, even though it was on fire everywhere, as she wanted to fetch a pillow for me to lie on and cloths for dressings, so I had the sick child lying by me too. Then the cry reached the camp that the houses were all collapsing on top of each other, so that many soldiers and women who were wanting to do a bit of looting were trapped inside them. As a result I was more worried about my wife, because of the sick child, than about my wounds. (Ha.47)

Shortly after his first wife died Hagendorf was captured and obliged to enlist with the Swedish army. He did not marry again until he rejoined his old regiment after Nördlingen in 1634, and during his period between marriages he twice records that he took a girl as part of his booty. After the Swedish capture of Landshut 'by storm of hand' the town was pillaged: 'Here I got a pretty lass as my plunder. ... When we moved on I sent her back to Landshut again' (Ha.59). Back in the Bavarian army later in the year he did the same at Pforzheim: 'I took a young girl out with me here too, but I let her go back in again because she had to carry linen out for me. I was often sorry about that because at that time I had no wife' (Ha.62–3).

During the winter the troops often spent months at a time billeted and without military employment, whereas the summer was a mixture of frantic activity and periods of idleness in camp. Sometimes the regiments simply marched from place to place without being called upon to fight; in the summer of 1629 Hagendorf records seven weeks during which his unit of 2000 men moved on every day, but after this hectic period they spent 20 weeks in one place. In the autumn of the following year they took part in the siege of Magdeburg, 'laid up the whole winter in the villages, until the spring of 1631', staying until 20 May, when the city was stormed (Ha.46). At other times the action came thick and fast. In one three-month period in 1641 they took part in eight sieges, six of them successful, although Göttingen and Wolfenbüttel defended themselves vigorously and the besiegers were forced to abandon their assaults.

During the interludes the soldiers and their families turned their hands to other things. A wise commander saw the dangers, and Gustavus Adolphus was a keen builder of defensive earthworks when in camp, which he did, Monro says, 'not onely to secure his Souldiers from the enemy, but also to keepe them from idlenesse. When they were not employed on service, they were kept by good discipline in awe and obedience' (Mo.II. 41–2). Civilian observers saw things differently. In Mallinger's view the Swedish soldiery too often spent their time in Freiburg engaging in petty theft: 'No-one was safe on the streets, whether by day or by night; they would take the hat from the head of one, tear the coat off the back of another, including the clergy. ... They snatched hats, headdresses, veils, coats and other articles from the women' (Ma.536). Their families seemed no better, occupying themselves in foraging at the citizenry's expense. During the first spring of Freiburg's occupation 'the soldiers' abominable wives' descended on gardens and fields to cut the produce 'as soon as a single green leaf peeped out' (Ma.537). To add insult to injury they sold what they did not need themselves in the Freiburg market.

Drinking stood high among the soldiers' preferred recreations. Even Fritsch mentions it in his rare personal comments, and in France he thought about his commander too, 'so from there I sent General of the Artillery von Reinach ... several barrels of wine, because the best in the whole of Alsace grew in that particular place'. He also records that immediately before attacking at the battle of Wimpfen 'our General Tilly ordered the issue of half a quart of wine to every soldier' (F.150, 109). Monro's perspective is that of a senior officer:

> This Regiment in nine yeeres time, under his Majesty of Denmarke, and in Dutch-land [Deutschland], had ever good lucke to get good quarters, where they did get much good wine, and great quantity of good beere, beginning first with Hamburg beere in Holsten, and after that in Denmarke they had plenty of Rustocke beere, and now at Barnoe, and thereafter they tasted the good Calvinists beere at Serbest, and our march continuing out of low Germany, towards the upper Circles of the Empire, as in Franconia, Swabland, Elsas and the Paltz, they were oft merry with the fruits and juice of the best berries that grew in those Circles, for to my knowledge, they never suffered either penury or want, I being the Leader, but oftimes I did complaine and grieve at their plenty, seeing they were better to be commanded, when they dranke water, then when they got too much beere or wine. (Mo.II. 47)

The pleasures of Bacchus did indeed bring problems. Monro admits to 'quarrelling and swaggering' under the influence of Barnoe beer, while Mallinger reports that guns had to be sent from Freiburg to Breisach without escort 'because most of the cavalrymen who had been detailed were full of wine, and none of them could or would ride along' (Mo.II. 46, Ma.556). The example often came from the top. The Saxon commander's drinking is a recurrent theme in Vitzthum's account: 'On the 9th the Lieutenant General swilled himself full of March beer in Templin, and until he had slept it off everything was left in suspense and everyone had to wait for orders.' Lunch parties were common, 'where there was very heavy drinking, so that not a living soul could waken Lieutenant General Baudissin'. The elector of Saxony was himself a notorious drinker and Vitzthum often reports his presence at lunch: 'On the 30th His Highness took his midday meal with the Lieutenant General and got very drunk, as did all the other officers' (Vi.359, 343, 373). Hagendorf too records some heroic drinking sprees. Following his return from Italy he begged enough money to buy shoes, 'but first I went into the inn. The wine was so good there that I forgot about the shoes. Bound the old ones up with willow.' On another occasion he spectacularly drank away a horse in Dinkelsbühl: 'Here I came across a cousin, a bellfounder called Adam Jeligan. Between us we spent one of the horses on booze and made ourselves very merry for three days on end. But the boy cried about the horse' (Ha.42, 56).

Everyday life in camp was too mundane to attract much comment from the diarists – thousands of small households struggling to create an element of normality in the peripatetic and uncertain lives of the soldiers and their families. The sutlers' market was an important centre both socially and commercially, Turner notes, and it was the main source of 'Wine, Beer, Tobaco, Vinegar, Oyl, Bread, Bacon, and other Provisions' (T.208). Raymond describes how 'every morneing there went fellowes about crying "Brandie, wyn, toback"'. He 'made choyce of the brandy which did me much kindnes', but his first experience of tobacco was less happy: 'I tryed but could by noe meanes like it, for it made me sick and ill all daye' (Ry.40). Turner adds that the military took measures to regulate trade, so that 'they permit not the Soldiers to wrong the Victualers and Sutlers, nor those to wrong the Soldiers, by taking greater Prices, or selling with less measures or weights than those appointed'. 'But the truth is', he adds, 'the Buyers are too often abused, and the Prices set too high by the collusion of the Provost-Marshal with Sutlers, and the Sutlers bribing the Judg-Marshal' (T.207–8).

Hagendorf hardly ever names his comrades, but the same three godparents appear for his children in 1643 and 1647: Melchert Bordt, the army surgeon, Christoff Isel, the provost marshal, and Benengel Didel, a sergeant, although by 1647 she (presumably) had become Benengel Hess, 'the captain's wife' (Ha.112, 126). Hagendorf does not explain Didel's military rank, *Feldwebelin*, but Turner describes how, in order to control the camp-followers, 'in some places they are put in Companies, and have one or more to command and over-see them, and these are called in Germany, Hureweibles, Rulers or Marshals of the Whores. I have seen them ride, keep Troop, rank and file very well, after that Captain of theirs who led them, and a Banner with them, which one of the Women carried' (T.277). Comradeship was also evident when the wounded Hagendorf was unable to go looting at Magdeburg with his more fortunate fellows: 'In the evening my comrades came round, and each of them gave me something, a taler or half a taler' (Ha.47). Mallinger describes the lighter side of army life among the Swedes once they had secured Freiburg and the surrounding villages: 'Meanwhile, as they met no resistance and felt themselves to be safe, they began to make merry, to wear fine clothes, to hold banquets and dances, and to have weddings, some 360 of them being married by priests and preachers' (Ma.537).

Animosities also arose in close-contact living. Mallinger reports discord at high level with fatal consequences when Ramstain, 'commandant at Freiburg', killed another officer in a duel, while Vitzthum himself killed Colonel Zähm, then commandant of Magdeburg, in an armed brawl arising from an argument (Ma.547). At a humbler level there were domestic crimes such as one described in the unknown soldier's diary: 'On the 10th of July a soldier's wife stabbed a corporal, who, so she claimed, tried to force her to sleep with him. She was held prisoner for several days but afterwards she was set free again' (Uk.174). Hagendorf reports that the tensions found other outlets too: 'On the 9th of September a soldier was burned in front of the camp, together with his horse, because he had committed bestiality with it' (Ha.106).

Despite the privations, for many recruits soldiering – if they survived – became a way of life. Vincent suggests that at its worst it may still have been better than the civilian alternative: 'Every one that is a man, betaketh himselfe to armes ... for hee that is not an actor with the rest, must needes be a sufferer among the miserable patients' (V.33). At its best there were compensations, as Monro found on the march from Würzburg to Frankfurt in 1631:

> This march, though in winter, was not so troublesome unto us, as their travelling is to them, who journey in forraine countries, for to see strange faces, where they must needs lay out monies for their entertainment, some of us on this march were well entertained, and did get money besides to spend at Francford. ... This march being profitable as it was pleasant to the eye, we see that Souldiers have not alwayes so hard a life, as the common opinion is. (Mo.II. 88, 89)

Campaigning and fighting

Although the ostensible purpose of soldiers is to fight, and there were soldiers enough in the Thirty Years War, there were relatively few full-scale battles. Tactics were cautious, as both princes and generals were reluctant to risk the consequences of a lost battle. They usually fought only if they could establish clear numerical superiority and a strong defensive position, or when cornered by an opponent. Consequently the war became one of attrition, a long-drawn-out struggle to control territory and resources and to deny them to the enemy. The size of the armies spiralled as occupied territory required the stationing of troops, and wider areas then had to be occupied to sustain the increased number of men. Gustavus Adolphus's campaigns of 1631–32 and the Imperialist resurgence of 1634 were exceptions to this pattern, with the most notable battles of the 30 years fought in this period. Monro and the unknown soldier diarist were at Breitenfeld, as was Hagendorf, who was also at Nördlingen, while Poyntz was at these and Lützen too. Fritsch was at Nördlingen and a number of other battles, although he arrived at Lützen with Pappenheim's artillery just as the fighting ended.

Monro describes the Swedish army, who had been campaigning all summer, joining up with their new and untried Saxon allies before Breitenfeld:

> The Duke with his followers did convey his Majestie to the sight of our Armie, which being called to their Armes, having lyen over-night on a parcell of plowd ground, they were so dusty, they looked out like Kitchinservants, with their uncleanely Rags, within which were hidden couragious hearts, being old experimented blades, which for the most part, had overcome by custome the toyle of warres; yet these Saxons gentry, in their bravery, did judge of us and ours, according to our out-sides; thinking but little of us; neverthelesse, we thought not the worse of our selves. (Mo.II. 62)

Once battle commenced the Saxons quickly broke and ran, Poyntz, as he readily admits, among them. Hagendorf was on the Imperialist right wing, which had the disheartening experience of putting the Saxons to flight and yet being defeated by the Swedish counter-attack from the left: 'It was the greatest good fortune when the night came about our ears, otherwise we would have had it too.' Wryly reflecting on their success at Magdeburg earlier that year he comments: 'But what we gobbled up in the Altmark we had to spew back out again outside Leipzig' (Ha.51).

Poyntz's account of the battle of Lützen is garbled and inaccurate, but he does include two personal incidents which have the ring of truth about them, even if his claim to have had three horses shot from under him invites scepticism:

> My last horse that was shot had almost killed mee for beeing shot in the guts, as I thinke, hee mounted on a suddaine such a height ... and fell upon mee and there lay groveling upon mee, that hee put mee out of my senses. I knew not how I was, but at length comming to myself, with much a doe got up, and found 2 or 3 brave horses stand fighting togeather. I tooke the best, but when I came to mount hym I was so

bruised & with the weight of my heavy Armour that I could not get my leg into the saddle that my horse run away with mee in that posture half in my saddle and half out. (Po.127)

The battle, despite the death of Gustavus Adolphus, was a stalemate, although the Swedes claimed victory because Wallenstein made a tactical retreat after night had fallen, as Poyntz describes:

> The night beeing farre in, both Armies retreated the space of one half English mile and refreshed themselves beeing wonderfull weary man and horse, so many of both as were left unkilled: wee were scarcely laid downe on the ground to rest and in dead sleep but comes a commaund from the Generall to all Coronells and Sergeant Majors to give in a Note how strong every Regiment was found to bee. ... I could give hym but account of 3 Officers of my Companie which lay there downe by my side. It seemes hee found most of his Companies as weake as myne, for presently that night the Army was commaunded to march away without sound of Drum or Trumpet. (Po.73, 126)

12 000 of the 25 000 strong Swedish army at Nördlingen were killed and a further 4000 captured (Parker, 1984, p. 141). Monro's regiment was reduced to a single company after the battle and Hagendorf was among the prisoners. Many of his comrades must have died in the slaughter, as he releases his anger and emotion in a burst of untranslatable but clearly vulgar invective quite unlike his normal laconic style: 'The Spanish did us great injury, for on that day the whole Swedish army, horse and foot, was smashed. The Spanish butchered everyone. Begging your pardon, oh *lutrian, begfutu, Madtza, hundtzfudt'* (Ha.62).

Sieges were a more common military activity and were conducted with a certain etiquette. A garrison was expected to put up stout resistance until it became clear that it would ultimately be overcome, whether because of the strength of the besieging force, its progress with undermining the defences or the lack of food and ammunition. If there was then no prospect of relief arriving the garrison could properly surrender and could negotiate often favourable terms for itself and perhaps for the town. This was a tricky decision for the commander. If he was later held to have surrendered too early he could be court-martialled and even executed for cowardice or treason. If he left it too late and the town was successfully stormed the opportunity to negotiate terms was lost, the garrison forfeited its right to quarter and could be put to the sword, and the town would usually be plundered and possibly sacked. Well aware of this, the citizenry would often press the commandant to surrender, adding to his problems. Monro quotes the case of Mainz:

> Our Cannon having from the Hessen side so spoyled the Burgers on the streets, and within their houses, finding their owne hurt, being stronger

than the Garrison, forced the Garrison to Accord, by that meanes preventing their owne ruine, and the losse of their goods, if the Towne had
beene taken by storme of hand. And therefore, for sparing of their Citie,
they promised his Majestie, for keeping good order, threescore thousand
Dollars. (Mo.II. 95)

The official treasury was not the only beneficiary. Fritsch records a businesslike transaction at a town he took but refrained from setting on fire:

Although the mayor and council would gladly have given me a sum of
money as a reward for saving the town from burning, ... since they didn't
have the means to hand in ready cash they gave me a note of hand drawn
up under the common seal of the town, promising to pay me a hundred
ducats within a term of one year at Strasbourg or wherever else I required.
(F.145–6)

Contemporary chronicles have many accounts of the fate of stormed
towns, their lurid nature overshadowing the much larger number of reports
of places duly surrendering or indeed successfully resisting siege. It is difficult
to separate the reality from partisan or sensationalist exaggeration, and in
recounting the horrors authors often adopt stereotyped forms of words, such
as Fritsch's frequent terse note: 'everyone in there killed' (F.108). Poyntz is
more explicit about the fate of a town in Moravia: 'Though wee were repulsed
the first tyme, yet the second tyme wee entred killing man, Woman and child:
the execution continued the space of two howers, the pillageing two dayes'
(Po.48). Monro states that at Donauwörth 'the enemy were pittifully cut downe
the most part of them in the fury. The Towne also was spoyled and quite plundered' (Mo.II. 114). Troops suffering casualties storming a position which might
honourably have surrendered were liable to be embittered, and sometimes the
personal enmities of a civil war intruded. Fritsch was in the forefront of the
assault when Rheinfelden was taken in 1633, and he and a captain eventually
cornered the commandant and the remnants of his garrison:

As we forced our way into the courtyard towards them, the commandant,
Lieutenant Colonel von Anlau, cried out to Captain Zinckh: '*Ach*, cousin
and brother Zinckh, give me and my soldiers quarter', to which he
replied: 'Cousin, you are a villain, serving against your emperor and your
fatherland.' With that, he gave him a thrust through the body with his
partisan, so that he sank to the ground, whereupon we cut them all
down, giving not a single one quarter, for our soldiers were in a great rage
because quite a lot of our men had been shot dead or crushed as we came
over the Rhine bridge. (F.137–8)

Direct assault often failed but a combination of undermining works and
hunger sometimes forced the defenders to concede, as Hagendorf notes: 'We

couldn't take this fortress at Helfenstein by gunfire, but we got up to it with approach trenches and saps, right into their fortifications. Then they made an accord. They also had nothing left to eat as they had eaten horses, dogs, cats, saddles, the lot' (Ha.79–80). Wagner mentions hides being cooked and eaten in blockaded Augsburg in 1634, and that 'the soldiers shot dogs and cats, so that little more was seen of these animals in the city' (Wa.56). Walther describes the survivors of one of the most protracted sieges, that of Breisach in 1638, when they reached Strasbourg after the surrender: 'It was an awful sight to see these poor, miserable, starving men, who looked more like ghosts and phantoms than living people. ... The whole city ran out to see these pathetic creatures' (Wl.35).

Accord terms varied considerably. At best the garrison might be allowed to march away with full military honours, perhaps taking a specified number of cannon and quantities of ammunition and supplies with them, while in less favourable circumstances they escaped with little more than their lives, the soldiers usually being forced to enlist with their captors while the officers might be held for ransom. Monro cites three cases during 1631. At Landsberg 'Colonell Hepburne being advanced towards the Skonce, tooke it in on accord, and the Souldiers were made to take service, and their Officers made prisoners'. The Imperialist garrison of a castle near Demmin were in a weak negotiating position, and 'fearing to be blowne up by a Mine, entred in treatie, and were content to take service under his Majestie, and to render their Colours' (Mo.II. 39, 18). On the other hand the garrison at Demmin itself secured good terms:

> Major Greeneland an English Cavalier then serving the Emperour, was sent out to make the accord with his Majesty, pledges delivered by both, the accord agreed on was subscribed; where it was concluded, the Governour should march out with flying Colours, and Armes, and with two peeces of Ordinance, with bag and baggage, and a convoy to the next Emperiall Garrison, providing the Governour should leave behinde him all cannon, being threescore peeces of Brasse, all store of Amunition and victuall, and all spare Armes, and to march forth precisely the next day by 12 of the clocke. (Mo.II. 19)

Armies were obliged to recruit continuously to make up losses, and after Breitenfeld Monro petitioned Gustavus Adolphus to let his regiment have all the 'Britaines and Irish' that were among the three thousand captives; he found only three, but soon afterwards at the surrender of the castle at Halle 'we did get 50 old Souldiers that tooke service under our Regiment' (Mo.II. 73). Such recruits were undependable. Hepburn enlisted nine companies of Italians, 'putting them in good Quarters till they were armed and clad againe. But their unthankfulnesse was such, that they stayed not, but disbandoned all, ... for having once got the warme ayre of the Summer, they were all gone before Winter' (Mo.II. 92). Vitzthum also illustrates the risk presented by such unreliable recruits: 'When the captured soldiers saw that our *armada* was approaching they said straight away: that is my troop; the other one is from my regiment. If the commandant won't make an accord we will break his neck ourselves' (Vi.334).

Surrender terms were not always honourably observed, and Fritsch was reluctantly involved in a breach of accord. In 1636 he besieged a force of French and German troops in a strongly-defended church, and with his colonel's approval agreed terms for their surrender. A more senior officer intervened, decreeing that 'we will keep no accord with them; they must all die'. As the defenders emerged the French and Germans were divided and ordered to lay down their weapons; 'At this the French sergeant shouted: "That is against the accord", whereupon Major General Schneder ordered that the sergeant should be hanged' (F.153). The unfortunate Frenchman was duly executed and the German lieutenant was shot. Fritsch was allowed to conscript the German soldiers but his objection to the killing of the French was overruled.

Hagendorf's change of sides to the Swedes resulted from a broken accord. In 1633 the Imperialists surrendered Straubing and marched away, but they were followed and recaptured: 'I thought that they would let us withdraw, as it said in the accord, but after five miles they ordered: "Dismount, hand over whatever you've got ...." We all had to enlist with them.' It is a comment on the general acceptance of changing sides to order that Hagendorf was immediately appointed to a position of responsibility 'as a sergeant in the Red Regiment' (Ha.54–5, 55).

Poyntz first joined the Spanish side when his money ran out in the Netherlands, but he was quickly captured and changed sides. He then served the Protestants, first under the Earl of Essex, later under Mansfeld and eventually in the Saxon army. Somewhere between Breitenfeld and Lützen he changed sides again, claiming to have been disillusioned by the elector of Saxony's treachery: 'When I found that hee was false to the Emperour, my heart was alwais from hym ... and would faine have got away from hym but I could not come of handsomely.' The more prosaic truth is that he was captured and held to ransom; unable to raise the money he wrote to the elector, asking him 'to pay my ransom or els I must starve in prison, or serve the Emperour (which is the custome on both sides in those German Warres) and I could never get any answeare from hym of my Letter' (Po.75, 75–6).

Hagendorf was a fortunate – or cautious – soldier, perhaps the secret of his survival for almost 25 years during which he only once mentions being wounded, at Magdeburg in 1631:

> On the 20th of May we attacked in earnest and took it by storm. I entered the city quite unhurt in the assault, but inside, at the Neustadt Gate, I was shot twice through the body. ... Afterwards I was taken back to the camp,

bound up, because I had one shot through the belly from the front and the second through both shoulders, so that the ball lodged in my shirt. The field surgeon tied my hands behind my back so that he could use a chisel. That's how I was brought back to my hut, half dead. (Ha.47)

Poyntz was wounded at the siege of Breda, 'where it was my fortune to escape with life, but to bee hurt on the right side with a pike', and at Lützen, where 'I hurt under my right side and in my thigh' (Po.46, 126). Fritsch was wounded in 1626 at the siege of Göttingen, 'shot in the knee and slashed across the hand'. In 1632 at Hildesheim he was hit three times by musket fire, 'so that the balls lodged in my head, in my leg, and above my eye, from which I ... suffered great pain'. This must have been less drastic than it sounds; the town surrendered three days later, and Fritsch was so quickly cured, 'through God's mercy', that he could leave ten days afterwards with his unit (F.115, 133, 133). In 1636 he was wounded again, hit in the eye with a stone and then shot in the arm during an attempt at storming Paderborn. Monro too was wounded three times, at Oldenburg in 1627, at the siege of Stralsund in 1628 and at Nuremberg in 1632.

The risks of battle are central to the soldier's profession, and Raymond describes coming to terms with them at his first taste of action: 'At my first comeing before the towne my courage began somewhat to faile me, and, being younge and never being on such an employment, wrought the more upon me. I remember I had an aurange tauny feather in my capp, and at first I thought that every great gun that was discharge towards our quarters had been aymed at it.' He soon became bolder: 'But within few dayes I tooke my selfe to be a very gallant fellow, and had noe more dread of danger then if I had been in a fayre' (Ry.38). For Raymond the dangers of battle were easier to bear than the privations on campaign, which he sums up in a sharp view of a soldier's life as seen from the ranks:

And truly, by what I have seene and felt, I cannott but thinck that the life of a private or comon soldier is the most miserable in the world; and that not soe much because his life is always in danger – that is little or nothing – but for the terrible miseries he endures in hunger and nakednes, in hard marches and bad quarters, 30 stivers being his pay for 8 days, of which they could not possibly subsist, but that they helpe themselves by forraging, stealing, furnishing wood in the feild to the officers, straw, some are coblers, taylers & c. (Ry.43)

4
Civilian Perceptions

If for the soldier the war was in the last analysis his livelihood, the civilian was ultimately the paymaster. The princes who employed the armies had neither the resources in their own territories to pay and maintain them, nor the machinery of the modern state needed to marshal such means as they had. Instead all parties fell back upon the expedient of making the citizenry of occupied territories, whether nominally friend or enemy, pay the cost of the campaigning. The opportunity of booty was a thinly disguised way of making the soldier responsible for finding a large part of his own pay, just as units in the field were made responsible for finding a significant proportion of their own food by foraging. This solved only part of the problem for the military authorities. The troops had to be given at least some pay and rations, and cash was necessary for other military supplies. These needs were met by contributions, a euphemism for the extortion of resources in cash or kind from civilians to support the armies. In practice the military themselves organised and managed this system, rather than the princes, ministers or court bureaucracies supposedly controlling them. Delegation was necessary, and raising contributions became a responsibility of every officer with an independent command. Methods varied correspondingly, ranging from relatively systematic imposition of taxation on communities to kidnapping prominent citizens and holding them to ransom. The eyewitnesses report many approaches.

Civilian accounts of these experiences tend to be variations on a common theme. The south-west, spared the war until 1632, felt its full impact in the following two years as the Swedes advanced to this furthest corner of Germany, contested control with their Imperialist opponents and then hastily withdrew northwards to regroup after Nördlingen. In their accounts, particularly of this period, Mallinger, Zembroth and Bürster, reporting respectively from Freiburg, an important city, Allensbach, a walled village, and Salem, a large monastery in the open countryside, describe experiences typical of other places and times as recorded by eyewitness diarists.

Freiburg experienced direct involvement in the fighting, as the city changed hands six times and was also once unsuccessfully besieged late in the war, but it seems to have escaped quite lightly. Mallinger records that the Swedish advance guard, which first reached the city on 26 December 1632, 'fired quite a number of cannon shots, but did little harm'. The main force arrived two days later and began to bombard the city in earnest, in course of which they 'lobbed in 25 incendiary shots, causing great damage', whereupon the citizens, lacking a garrison of regular troops, promptly surrendered. In October 1633 the Swedes made a tactical withdrawal from the city, taking a rather formal leave: '*Nocte hora nona* Colonel Cannosschki returned the keys of the city to the councillors, released them from their oaths, and expressed thanks for all kindnesses' (Ma.536, 536, 546).

When they returned in April 1634 the experience was worse. This time Freiburg was garrisoned and it resisted with more determination. Swedish gunfire commenced at five in the morning, making a breach in the walls by midday, and after further bombardment the city was successfully stormed late at night. Mallinger reports – presumably selectively – a single casualty from the bombardment, 'an adolescent girl of noble birth, Miss von Danckenschweil', but he notes many more as the Swedes entered the city: 'Everyone they found by the walls, young and old, citizens, farmers and soldiers, some 80 men, and most of the people in the Oberriet church, were tragically killed, plundered, and left naked where they lay' (Ma.555). The city was looted but Mallinger refers only to property being seized, mentioning no violence against the citizenry after the initial onslaught. In September 1634 the Swedes evacuated Freiburg for the second time, departing without a fight after a further round of looting.

Four years later Freiburg was retaken, this time by Bernard of Weimar's forces, who appeared before the city on 1 April 1638, attempting unsuccessfully to storm it on 3 April and three times on 9 April, by which time the defenders were ready to negotiate a surrender. Mallinger does not mention plundering or give details of damage, although he says with great precision that on 9 April 'between early morning and the approach of evening 327 heavy cannon-balls were fired into the city', adding that 'the commandant, Herr Joann. Christopherus von Ramstain, from the noble German family, was shot along with 12 other citizens, journeymen and students' (Ma.587). This time the occupation lasted over six years, until the Bavarian army besieged the city on 27 June 1644. After lengthy skirmishing outside the walls serious bombardment began, and when a breach was made on 27 July the defenders duly negotiated an accord and marched away, leaving the city to its liberators: 'On the 31st, *hora 9, Te deum laudamus* was sung, *solenniter und musicaliter in summo templo* … accompanied by both organs' (Ma.598).

Allensbach lies on a narrow peninsula of land forming the principal approach route to Constance, which was also an important city and the only one locally never taken by the Swedes, although they were active in the area from the middle of 1632 to the end of 1634, and then for a full ten years from 1638 to the end of the war. For almost all this time Hohentwiel, Radolfzell and other towns were in their hands, and for much of it they also held the fortress of Mainau, on the outskirts of Constance itself. Allensbach thus lay in disputed territory, a mere ten kilometres from the Imperialists in Constance and the Swedes in Radolfzell, subject to friendly occupation or enemy raids and exploited for contributions by both sides, but it seems to have suffered less than might be expected during 13 years in a war zone. Zembroth records two attacks which were made by the Swedes in 1633 specifically to enforce the payment of contributions; on the first occasion 32 cattle were driven off and two outlying houses and a mill were burned, while on the second the same fate befell 12 houses and the church tower. In 1634 the village was 'plundered through and through in the night' by a Swedish force, and ten years later Bavarian cavalry took hay from the village, 'as much as they could carry on their horses, ... but otherwise they did no damage', while in 1647 enemy cavalry took livestock and conscripted villagers temporarily to herd them (Z.571, 575). Allensbach was also plundered during an evacuation in 1633 and perhaps during another in 1647. On the other hand troops from Hohentwiel attempting to surprise Constance marched through Allensbach in 1642 without troubling it, and they also twice marched through in 1646 during an attack on Reichenau, Zembroth specifically noting that this was 'in fact without any harm being done' on the first occasion, and that on the second the troops had 'done nothing to anyone, apart from a little damage to two houses in Cappel' (Z.575, 576).

As mayor of Allensbach Zembroth frequently had direct responsibility for meeting the demands of the military. His chronicle begins in 1632 as the Swedes approached. Bavarian units moved in to defend the area and lost no time in imposing contributions:

> On the Saturday before Shrovetide representatives of the bishop's subjects everywhere within Empire territory were called to the castle in Meersburg. There a payment of 10000 florins was called for as a contribution for the Bavarian army.... This had to be delivered on three occasions, the first in eight days time, the second in four weeks and the third three weeks thereafter. (Z.568)

The imposition was shared out: 'For us it came to 160 florins. I collected in the first two payments but before the third fell due the enemy had moved close to us and no-one could give any more.' Meanwhile the village had to provide 20 men to a conscript levy, although this was soon disbanded without fighting, 'but each man was given 1½ florins by the municipality.' Defence works were constructed at nearby Stahringen using conscript labour, whose thirst the commune had to quench with substantial quantities of wine; they then had to provide 10 of the 50 militiamen sent to guard these works, and to supply each daily with 'a litre of wine and two [pounds] of bread' (Z.568).

Swedish and Württemberg troops occupied the neighbouring area that spring and Allensbach hastened to come to terms with their commandant,

> von Stainfels by name, to whom four men from here were sent to make an accord. We had to give him 175 Reichstaler straight away, within two days. ... There were six fine silver goblets in the town hall, which were put towards this, and the full balance was made up in cash by the citizens. (Z.569)

The commandant offered protection in return for contributions, but Zembroth was far from satisfied: 'This same Colonel Stainfels promised that he would secure us against burning, robbery and billeting, but he kept to this badly, if at all.' A few months later 'a strong company of French cavalry descended on us. They were here for five days, and we had to keep them, together with their horses, at great expense.' A regiment also moved into Radolfzell, 'to which we had to contribute 40 florins a month. ... That was paid for six months, making 240 florins' (Z.569).

Although 1632 had been expensive Allensbach had not come off too badly. Worse was to come. In the spring of 1633 Zembroth found himself caught between two fires, the Swedes ranging the countryside and the Imperialists still in control in Constance:

> They would not authorise or permit us to give any further help or to make any contributions to the enemy, either of money or of service, work or labour on fortifications. The enemy threatened us, in writing and by messenger, with military enforcement, which we reported to the authorities, his Princely Grace's councillors, and asked for their advice. But the colonel and officers at Constance ... were not prepared to allow us to satisfy the enemy, declaring that if we did the least thing they would carry out a sharper and stricter enforcement than the enemy would ever do. So we were in the greatest danger. (Z.569)

Faced with this stark choice Allensbach stopped payments to the Swedes, who promptly mounted retaliatory raids, forcing the citizens to evacuate the village, which was then plundered. After their return Zembroth comments mournfully that 'as we had nothing more, no-one sought much from us. They left us to live in misery' (Z.571). In the following years Allensbach was mainly burdened with billeting, although there was still the occasional raid, but Zembroth's most recurrent theme reflects the principal effect of the war on the villagers, the obligation to pay for it through contributions. Sometimes these were arbitrary, in the form of the rations and fodder required by passing troops billeted on them, but the extortion was often more systematic and the demands more precise. Typical was the lengthy siege of the fortress of Hohentwiel during 1635, 'to which blockade we had to give six bushels of grain, four kegs of wine and some money every month, and a tun of wine in the autumn'. In the main, contributions appear to have been calculated and shared out with some regard to the ability of the various villages to pay. In 1642 Allensbach was making contributions to three Imperialist garrisons, in Überlingen, Markdorf and Lindau respectively, their assessment in respect of the latter quite distant town being 30 florins per month. Because of damage done to the village in 1640, however, part of this burden was transferred to their better-protected neighbours; 'By comparison Wolmatingen, which had always been sheltered by the city of Constance, was in good shape, so that they had to relieve us of half of it' (Z.572, 574). Although the authorities in Constance attempted to forbid payments to the enemy this became increasingly unrealistic, and in fact the village made contributions to both sides for much of the time. By the latter years of the war a quite complex pattern had emerged:

> In this above-mentioned year of 47 we had to give [Hohent]wiel a monthly contribution of ten florins, together with three tuns of wine, ... four wagonloads of grain (which we exchanged with the villagers of Blumenfeld, on whose behalf we gave Mainau 16 quarters of corn, five quarters of rye and ten quarters of oats), ... and in the spring 2000 vine stakes (which Hans Schäpfl of Hausen made for us, for which we paid him 24 florins), while instead of hay and straw we regularly paid the captain of cavalry Hans Jerg Widerholt in cash, 86 florins and 6 batzen. The same year of 47 we supplied Constance with 2½ tuns of wine, many wagons of wood for watch fires, labourers for working parties and digging fortification works every day, and 100 hundredweight of hay. Likewise to Niclaus, Baron von Gramont, commandant of Zell, two florins service money every month, and 20 kegs of wine at the beginning of the year, as well as labourers and fortification workers at that time, and we had afterwards to pay out 16 batzen a week for the labour service. (Z.577)

This passage indicates many aspects of the workings of the contributions economy. Two villages traded off their respective obligations in order that each could deliver to the nearer garrison; a requirement to supply hay and straw was commuted for a cash payment; the necessary vine stakes were bought by the village from a manufacturer; garrisons required contributions in varying combinations of cash, kind and labour; the labourers, although forced as far as the military were concerned, were in fact paid for their work by the village. Underlying this is the fact that Allensbach's principal product was wine, which had to be sold in order to buy in most of the other specified contributions. Nor did the military necessarily drink all the wine supplied to them, some of which they in turn may have sold and converted into cash. It is thus apparent that rather than agricultural produce simply being seized on an arbitrary basis to meet the short-term needs of the troops a complex market economy was required and had to be sustained. This in turn suggests why Allensbach suffered less from raiding, robbery and violence than might at first sight have been expected; it was not in the interests of the military on either side to disrupt the production and trading economy on which they themselves depended for their long-term sustenance.

Contributions were also required from Salem after the Swedish arrival in 1632. Bürster notes: 'From this day on we had to send 400 army loaves, each of two [pounds], 15 bushels of oats, two oxen and a cart-load each of straw and hay to Ravensburg every day' (Bü.22). Mallinger says little about contributions, but in August 1633 he notes that 'they overburdened the unfortunate citizens, both rich and poor, as well as the clergy and the university, with soldiers, forcing them to give them so much as weekly upkeep and contributions that they could no longer see any salvation'. In 1639 he is more specific, recording three separate contributions required of the 'high bishopric of Basle', two of 150 and one of 300 Reichstaler. His evidence is incomplete and inconclusive but one can deduce from his limited comments that the burden imposed cannot generally have been intolerable, although he also mentions the effects of heavy extortions from the countryside to support the siege of Breisach in August 1633, 'which drove the poor people into such poverty, fear and need that they became ill through starvation and misery' (Ma.545, 589, 545). He outlines the procedure for requisitioning food in Freiburg at this time: 'They visited all the cellars and granaries. At first they wanted a third of the wine or grain, the second time they wanted half, and the third time they often took all the flour from the mills and all the bread from the bakeries' (Ma.545).

Towns were often prepared to pay a substantial initial cash sum to buy off plundering and damage, but repeated contributions over a prolonged period were another matter. The six silver goblets in Allensbach's town hall soon went and individuals became more circumspect about contributing. Mallinger describes how citizens of Freiburg who had managed to hide things from the Swedes were forced to disgorge them when their own side regained control temporarily in late 1633. The more sophisticated method of extortion used by the Imperialists was to arrest the 'masters of the guilds and many members of the council' of Freiburg, and to imprison them in the fortress of Breisach until they undertook to raise a large sum of money from the city; knowing their fellow-citizens' affairs better than the Swedes these worthies were able coax or coerce their hidden treasures and trinkets from them:

> Then they summoned one citizen after another into the market building, and required so much of them that they had to hand over everything which they had previously concealed and hidden away from the enemy

in order to have something to buy their food with in the future. One who came still had several silver goblets, which he paid over instead of cash, a second brought his wife's or daughter's silver belt and knife, while a third had sold something from his house or a young cow to help pay the money. (Ma.548)

Monks from Salem were twice held to ransom by the Swedes in 1632. On the first occasion:

They caught eight or nine of the monks, together with a number of horses and traps or coaches, into which they all had to get, and they took them with them to Ravensburg as prisoners. There they were to be held until such time as a ransom or protection money of 6000 taler was paid, which had to be promptly on the 28th, first thing in the morning. ... This 6000 taler was paid on the 28th of April, and the monks were set free again, although the time until the money arrived must have been long enough for them, as they were frequently threatened that if the ransom did not follow they would have to hang. (Bü.20–1, 21–2)

Bürster's second description vividly portrays the terror such a raid inspired as the Swedes surrounded the monastery:

Then laughter was scarce among us and all joy died, as we could see nothing but *memoria mortis*, so that many began to confess quickly to one another. ... After they had mustered and the gates had been opened to them they ordered all the clergy and lay brothers to gather together in one place. We went into the church, to the sacristy, all standing together, quaking with fear and expecting nothing other than blows and to be hacked down, but thank God we came out of it well. They wanted the prior or head of the monastery, but the rest had only to return to their places or cells and nothing was to happen to them. However the prior, at that time the *reverendissimus pater* Wilhelm Hülleson, had hidden himself away in the garden of the upper house, and as we were not prepared to betray him they took the cellar-master, then the *reverendissimum patrem* Thomas Hausser, *loco prioris, in aresto* with them to Ravensburg, so that he had to be ransomed again for 300 taler. (Bü.23–4)

The same methods were used in the smaller places too. After the Swedes had consolidated their first occupation of Freiburg Mallinger reports that raiding parties descended on the neighbouring villages: 'They not only drove off the cattle and horses, but wherever they caught a prosperous farmer or another honest man, they tied him up and took him with them. Then they put him in irons and threw him into jail until he had paid over 40 or 50, or even 100 taler' (Ma.538).

The armies' needs for food were even more pressing than their requirements for cash, and foraging raids supplemented levies of contributions in kind. The harvest was an easy target on Salem's extensive lands in 1632: 'On about the 20th of August Swedish and Biberach soldiers took away 200 quarters of grain from our farm at Saulgen.' In December, when that year's wine was ready, a well-prepared raid with appropriate security was made: 'The wine from our farm at Pfulendorff was carted off by the Württembergers in 20 wagons, and taken to Dudtlingen with a strong escort' (Bü.23, 25). Foraging was undertaken systematically and surpluses were often sold back to the civilians for cash. In the spring of 1634 the Mecklenburg cavalry were billeted in Freiburg:

> They sallied out every day, several companies strong, to seek out and plunder all the nearby valleys in the Black Forest. They not only drove off all the livestock – cows, oxen, calves, geese, horses – many hundred head, but they took all the grain and oats as well, many hundred quarters, not just as food for themselves and their horses but also large quantities to sell in the city. And as if this were not enough they also sent out gangs of their soldiers' boys all over the place with horses, wagons and carts to bring in all the fodder, hay and straw. (Ma.558)

Sometimes the raiders got little. By the summer of 1634 Allensbach had been picked almost clean: 'There was only a cow and two or three horses. They took them away, along with whatever else they could carry' (Z.571). Despite the raids the soldiers often went hungry, and mounted troops had to be sent out ever further from Freiburg to find supplies 'because the countryside everywhere ... had been plundered out, and the soldiers knew of nowhere with anything left to be had; likewise there was no food to be found in the towns' (Ma.564).

The population sometimes fought back against the plunderers. 150 Swedes raided Salem in 1633, creeping in at four in the morning, 'all with drawn swords and cocked pistols, and ... almost before anyone had noticed they injured three people with pistols and drove off some 30 horses and foals, but they left the oxen behind.' The raiders made the mistake of coming back for the cattle two hours later, by which time the monastery was ready 'and opened fire on them, driving them off' (Bü.32). A week later, expecting a further raid and encouraged by this success, the monastery gathered a considerable defence force:

> Straight away some 400 of our soldiers, well presented and well armed with muskets, as well as around 150 badly mounted Haylgenberg farmers with halberds, boar spears (of which they had many, as they had to hunt so much), badger-catching forks, clubs and cudgels, ... were gathered together here in Salem, mustered and drilled, with the intention of going out to meet them, greet them, attack them and defeat them. (Bü.33)

Perhaps fortunately for this makeshift militia the Swedes did not appear; instead 'they were discharged in the evening, and each man was given a loaf of bread and a good drink, so that they became merry and enthusiastically offered their services for the future' (Bü.33).

The area around Freiburg had divided loyalties, some villages being Habsburg hereditary lands and others belonging to the Margravate of Baden, which was then allied to the Swedes. Mallinger notes that these local rivalries added to the wider turmoil. Early in 1633, ostensibly to defend themselves against Swedish attack, farmers from the Habsburg villages banded together 'and began sallying out to rob people on the roads. They also attacked the Margravate villages, taking horses, cattle and other things from them' (Ma.537). The Margravate villagers duly retaliated against these hostile neighbours after the Swedes gained control of the area, and when the war turned against them again they helped their retreating Swedish allies to plunder Freiburg as they left:

> *Interim*, at exactly ten o'clock, the cavalry, helped by the soldiers, began to break in, the majority of them smashing into the dealers' shops on the Fishmarket, *item* the houses of the apothecaries, bakers, butchers and shoemakers, taking everything out and carrying off what each one found of use. The Margravate farmers and their wives, young and old, also helped in this, and loaded up what there was by way of household goods, bed linen and clothing, whatever each could drag or carry away. (Ma.575)

Predictably the Margravate villagers then found themselves on the receiving end again. Taking refuge in the forest, they left their villages unoccupied, so that 'both the Breisach and the Freiburg people, as well as some from other places, citizens and soldiers alike, ... began plundering all the villages .... This went on until they had searched through every district and settlement, and had taken from them whatever each thought of value to him' (Ma.578).

Freiburg experienced two Swedish occupations between 1632 and 1634, the first lasting, as Mallinger exactly records, 42 weeks and one day, from December 1632 to October 1633, and the second for 22 weeks and four days, from April to September 1634. He often complains about theft and damage caused by troops, although he says little specific of the first Swedish occupation in 1633 other than giving an initial account of a wave of break-ins, raids on wine cellars, petty theft from citizens on the streets and harassment of those on their way to church. As relieving Imperialist forces under the duke of Feria approached later in the year Mallinger echoes many other diarists in noting 'that they devastated and ate out the country much more than the enemy', before recording this same experience in Freiburg itself (Ma.547). That friend was as bad as foe was a common experience and opinion; Pflummer reports at this time that the citizens of Überlingen 'lamented *unâ voce* that the Imperialists have brought more desolation and ruin to this

land in the last ten days alone ... than the enemy did in almost a full year'
(Pf.25). In November 1633 the duke of Feria billeted his army in Freiburg.
Here the problem was that far more troops arrived than the city and its suburbs could accommodate; short of food and fuel, they stripped the district
of anything which could be eaten or burned:

> Often there were 10, 12 or even up to 20 people in a single house, to say
> nothing of the horses. Where there was any kind of outbuilding they put
> in 10, 20 or as many as 40 horses in one house or stable. In the suburbs
> outside and around the city all the houses, barns, stables, shelters and
> garden sheds were filled up and occupied by soldiers and horses, and as
> it was rather cold at the time they broke off all the woodwork in them,
> tore down the fences around the gardens, took hundreds of bundles of
> stakes out of the vines, hacked down many a fruitful tree, and threw
> everything on to the fire and burned it. (Ma.547)

They stayed until early January 1634, leaving behind a smaller garrison
which also caused problems: 'On the 14th and 15th there was so much
breaking in and stealing in Freiburg that no-one could keep a good enough
lookout, by day or by night' (Ma.548). This seems to have been an isolated
outbreak, however, for which 19 soldiers were arrested.

The Swedes were soon back, and as they took the city the garrison
retreated into the castle, from which refuge the Imperialist commandant
negotiated terms for safe conduct, 'and he himself, with all his officers, was
escorted to Breisach. The ordinary soldiers, of whom there were some 300,
were mostly forced to enlist' with their captors. The citizens were left to the
mercies of the Swedes: 'As soon as the cavalry entered the city, they rode or
ran here, there and everywhere, robbing anyone they found on the streets'
(Ma.556, 555). They broke into houses, and 'everything that was left by way
of household goods and bedding was taken out of the city on wagons and
carts by the Margravate farmers'. The Mecklenburg cavalry were billeted in
the city, leaving behind a trail of damage in their quarters, so that 'many
thousand gulden would not restore them as they were before, as every stove,
window, chair and bench, all panelling, doors and shutters were smashed
and broken off' (Ma.555, 559).

During this second occupation the Swedes again made a systematic survey
of food stocks in private hands in the city, requisitioning them stage by stage
until there was little left. Many citizens gave up the struggle to feed both their
unwelcome billeted guests and their families, and instead 'left house and
farm, and with wife and children made their way out of the city into destitu-
tion ... to seek their food elsewhere'. The occupying troops were unpaid and
not much better off: 'The soldiers began to suffer from food shortages and
hunger, and as they received no pay from anyone cavalry and foot-soldiers
alike were forced to rob and steal.' They not only broke into the houses to

take what food they could find; they also raided the bakers, the millers and the market. On market days soldiers lay in wait outside the city gates and stole the produce the peasants were bringing in, 'so that before long the market declined, and a great shortage developed in the city' (Ma.565). The difficulty appears to have been overcome relatively quickly, however, as Mallinger reports that by 2 September the city was able to send eight wagonloads of food to the garrisons at Rheinfelden and Neuenburg. When the Swedes left again on 17 September he summarises his complaints 'of such *bestiis*' who 'not only filled all the streets with filth and rubbish but also damaged the houses beyond all measure', and who ate the populace out of house and home as well as stealing whatever they could (Ma.574). His memory seems to have been short, as five months later he complains that friendly troops quartered in Freiburg 'caused great damage and inconvenience, the like of which no enemy had done before' (Ma.583). In his briefer account of the later war years Mallinger does not return to this theme, making no complaint during the six-year occupation from 1638 to 1644.

The smaller places also had experience of billeting. Soon after the war reached the area Allensbach was visited by 'a cavalry captain ... with a strong company of horsemen'. They stayed only four days but they ate well: 'Over and above what each citizen had to provide in his house, every day we gave them two beef cattle (while Wolmatingen and Kaltprun gave them one each), as well as eight quarters of oats from the church, which we had to pay for' (Z.568). Later in 1632 a similar force of French stayed for five days, but Zembroth does not report further billeting until 1639, when they had to accommodate 26 men of a Bavarian company in winter quarters. He itemises the costs according to the prescribed scale of provision by rank:

> A lieutenant, who got 80 florins in cash every month, hay for three horses, and wood for his housekeeping; a sergeant, 16 florins; a couple of corporals, 12 florins each; several lance-corporals, eight florins each; common soldiers, six florins per man. Even then we were still pestered by them and had to give them a good few quarts of wine every week. It all amounted to a cash sum of 270 florins every month, and this lasted for 13 weeks. (Z.572–3)

Imperialist troops billeted at Salem in February 1633 were thirsty and ungrateful guests: 'They drank wine like water ... and paid for nothing that was provided for them, but always wanted more; they celebrated Shrovetide and we fasted'. At the end of that September the duke of Feria's army arrived and 'billeted 4080 cavalry in the monastery itself, until the 5th of October' (Bü.28, 35). The conditions they left behind were not pleasant:

> Well, 4080 horses (and that was only the registered number) had been stabled here. Oh what misery and affliction, destruction and devastation

there was on all sides. ... The whole monastery looked like a sewer, a knacker's yard or a murderers' den. And it stank everywhere, so that one could scarcely live here any more. (Bü.36)

For the citizens of Freiburg billeting was a constant problem during the alternating Swedish and Imperialist occupations, but despite the pilfering soldiery they enjoyed at least a degree of security. The garrison provided protection from outside raids and the presence of military authorities in the city offered a modicum of protection from the garrison. The opposite was the case in the smaller places, in many of which billeting was an occasional imposition rather than a permanent state of affairs. Instead they had to live in constant fear of raids by soldiers from either side, or by guerilla bands from neighbouring but hostile villages. Zembroth describes the sense of insecurity in Allensbach during the Swedish siege of Überlingen in 1634: 'During this siege strong patrols from the enemy were a daily occurrence, so that we were never safe and had to move completely out of our houses. Even when the army was no longer there and we could move back the enemy garrison at Zell was always a worry to us'. (Z.571) They had good grounds for this concern, as in August 1633 a troop of horsemen from Radolfzell had descended on them at midnight:

They set the village on fire in five places, and 12 substantial houses were burned down, among them the parsonage, which stood right next to the church. From there the fire spread into the church tower, which had a beautiful high helm roof, and this was also burned, along with the clock and four good bells, which melted and fell to the ground. (Z.570)

Evacuations gave free rein to the plunderers. When Horn's army approached Salem in January 1634 'on that same day the whole of the lay brotherhood and all the clergy withdrew once again to Überlingen, in extremely cold weather'. During the following eight weeks the Swedes systematically looted the monastery, taking 'all the seed, grain, wine, cupboards, crates, tools, locks, iron, brass, lead, tin, the profane and all kinds of sacred things. ... In fact they cleared everything right out, so that not even a cat or a mouse could find anything more' (Bü.42, 43). The Swedes were evidently not as thorough as Bürster suggests, since they did indeed find more when another force arrived barely four months later. This time the monks decamped to Constance, leaving the Swedes to loot the church, taking 'everything made of brass or bronze, such as candlesticks, *epitaphia*, censers, gravestones [brasses?], and particularly the two great brass tablets *anti crates altaris summi* of both churches'. The bells in the main tower were too heavy for the plunderers to remove but they took those from the Lady Chapel, as well as 'the anvil from the smithy, saw blades, plane irons, locks from all the doors, cupboards, chests and troughs, *in summa* all the craftsmen's tools' (Bü.82, 83).

The citizenry of Freiburg must have had many unpleasant experiences of living with a garrison, whether nominally friend or foe, which was often unpaid and underfed, and therefore inclined to fend for itself at their expense. Nevertheless Mallinger's complaints have a rather petit-bourgeois tone: filth in the streets, rough soldiers' boys hacking down fruit and branches in the orchards, ladies being jostled on their way to Mass, a general lack of order and propriety. What he notably does not do is to complain, either in general terms or in specific incidents, of violence or atrocities. He reports break-ins and the equivalent of handbag snatching rather than troops beating, torturing or killing civilians while searching for hidden valuables, and although he waxes indignant about women coming from church being robbed of 'their headdresses, veils, hats, rosaries and prayerbooks', he makes no reference to them being robbed of their virtue (Ma.565). Matters only seem to have deteriorated further during specific periods of food shortage or overcrowding of large forces into the city, and Mallinger indicates that the military authorities were generally active in controlling the situation. The only killings of civilians he mentions (other than during the storming of the city) occurred elsewhere, including a passing carpenter murdered by two soldiers on a drinking spree near Rheinfelden. Justice was swift. The following day 'after the men had been quickly sought out, caught and imprisoned, and a military trial had been held for them *huius* here in Freiburg, the younger pleaded successfully for his life but the elder was executed by the sword on the Münsterplatz, *hora* 1 p.m.'. On another occasion a group of soldiers trying to break into a house in Freiburg were disturbed by the guard, whose captain was stabbed and wounded in the resulting scuffle. Most of the miscreants made off, but one 'was held by the aforementioned, placed under arrest, condemned to death that afternoon, and hanged, *hora* 4 a.m.'. An officer responsible for looting Jesuit property in September 1633 was likewise executed, the 19 soldiers arrested for robbery in January 1634 were court-martialled, and a supplies officer was arrested for his handling of food requisitioning in June 1634. Most of the other specific incidents Mallinger reports were commonplace and spread over a long period of time: a couple of duels between officers; a captain stabbed by a common soldier; one soldier executed for murdering another; a fire at an inn, 'which was started maliciously in a sack of straw by an Italian' (Ma.573, 565, 581). Clearly this is not an exhaustive record of all the military crime which occurred in Freiburg in those years, but the very fact that Mallinger mentions these incidents suggests that he saw them as noteworthy rather than everyday occurrences, strongly suggesting that more spectacular atrocities were not taking place.

Salem was raided many times between 1632 and 1634 but Bürster does not report any monks being killed or seriously injured, and although both he and Mallinger mention people being seized and held to ransom those taken were imprisoned and frightened with threats of hanging to extract money rather than subjected to exotic tortures. The most striking feature of Zembroth's account in this respect is the complete absence of mention of anyone from the village being physically harmed by soldiers, although he does record the murder of the mayor and two others in nearby Wollmatingen. He names the herdsman when cattle were driven off in 1633, he mentions the villagers forced to herd livestock for raiders in 1647 and he refers to others, including two named brothers, conscripted by opposite sides to work ships used to attack and defend Constance respectively in 1647, but he reports none of them as being killed or injured. In view of the other things, many of them relatively trivial, which he does remember and record it is hard to imagine that he has omitted many serious incidents of this nature which actually occurred, even if he chose to ignore minor or commonplace violence or may have been too discreet to refer to rape. Allensbach was of course better placed than most, with a ready refuge from danger across a few hundred yards of water; nevertheless the villagers had plenty of direct contact with troops but, like the citizens of Freiburg and the monks of Salem, they seem to have avoided the worst experiences.

5
Siege and Storm

Besieging towns, sometimes unsuccessfully and sometimes culminating in taking them by surrender or by storm, was much more common and typical of the military activity in the Thirty Years War than the relatively infrequent pitched battles. Many of the eyewitnesses report their experiences of such events, and in a number of cases a siege and storm is the central feature of the account.

Juliana Ernst, a nun from the convent of St Ursula in the Black Forest city of Villingen, describes the events leading up to the attack on the city by Württemberg troops, then allies of the Swedes, in 1632–33. Her account is one of the few extant records of their war experiences by women, but the manuscript is now lost, and its editor (from 1878) tells us infuriatingly little about it. Ernst's starting point was a chronicle written by two of her predecessors, entitled: 'A little record book of all kinds of things, begun *anno* 1594 and ended *anno* 1622' (Er.129). This was evidently a somewhat arbitrary chronicle of convent business matters, together with notes of unusual bad weather or other interesting occurrences, which Ernst continued from 1622 until an abrupt break in January 1633, although the manuscript also contains shorter entries up to 1731. The editor indicates that at first Ernst followed the style of the earlier chronicle, but he notes that her latter section, which he prints, is a more specific account of an episode in the war. This departure appears to have been quite deliberate, in that she opens with a summary of the Swedish incursion into Germany, and into the south in particular, before giving a detailed description of the period from October 1632 to January 1633 as it affected Villingen. Her account incorporates much specific information and precise dates, but was written up later, as she states that moats flooded before the attack remained 'full of water for two years', and she also observes that 'we had to suffer cruel hardship ... from the year of 32 until now in the year of 38' (Er.133, 132). Her final account may well have been copied up from contemporaneous notes, as is indicated by the pleas she inserts at particularly dangerous moments which suggest doubt about the outcome at the time of writing: 'O Mary, Queen of Heaven, help us, lest our enemies be gratified upon us' (Er.133).

Ernst opens by recording that in *'anno* 1631 there was great distress from the war, as the king from Sweden came over to Germany and occupied and despoiled the whole of Franconia'. She notes his propaganda claim that 'what he had taken for himself was only what had been entrusted to him because of our guilt for our sins', adding as a testimony to its effectiveness that 'many took him for God and blessed their children in the name of the Swede as they laid them down to sleep'. She also has a clear view of the underlying politics. Referring to the alliance with Sweden made by the duke of Württemberg, 'whose monasteries were taken from him four years ago in the year of 28 [*sic*] by our emperor', she notes that he 'and other Lutheran princes' invited Gustavus Adolphus into Germany 'and appealed to him for help so that they could get the monasteries back again' (Er.130). She then reports Swedish moves against Offenburg, Überlingen and Meersburg in 1632 before beginning her specifically local account.

The first approaches were diplomatic: *'Item* the 26th of May in the year of 32, the Württemberger gave a warning to our city, and to Rottweil, the first time with fine, smooth words, as though he wanted to be a good neighbour and our patron, and to help protect us from foreign princes and from attack.' The citizens were not deceived but opinion was divided: 'There was such anguish in the city. One faction were ready to defend themselves while the other said that they wanted to submit – what did it matter if we had to be Swedish for a while; it wouldn't last long.' On this occasion they were spared the necessity of choice: 'Through a special act of God's providence the king from Sweden summoned all his troops round and about urgently to Nuremberg and we were free of them again' (Er.131).

On 12 October the Württemberg army was back at Rottweil, which quickly surrendered: 'On the Thursday immediately following, at nine o'clock in the morning, a Württemberg dispatch rider arrived outside our city' (Er.131). Ernst was evidently well-informed, as she follows this precise information with an account of the demands and promises brought by the herald, and of the prevaricating reply of the mayor and council that they would first have to consult the city's overlord, the Austrian Archduke Leopold. An army quickly appeared outside Villingen: *'Ach!* What great fear and distress we were in; we packed up our few possessions and hid them where we could.' The Mother Superior instructed each nun to put together 'a bundle with bonnet, stick and personal necessities so that if the need arose we would have something to hand', while their confessor priest advised them to 'look around for worldly clothing so that we would not be recognised as nuns, as they have peculiarly and shamefully ill-treated the clergy wherever they have found or happened upon them'. Again, however, they escaped attack. Three days later, after plundering the outlying villages, the army moved on elsewhere, leaving a small force to watch the city: 'The whole citizenry and all of us were heartily well pleased.' The convent nevertheless suffered economically, securing only a small fraction of the tithes due from their lands: 'The steward at Biessingen also made everything of ours known, threshed it, stole it and carried it away to the enemy', Ernst comments bitterly, adding that 'he was a Lutheran steward' (Er.132).

On 7 November an Imperialist garrison of 520 men arrived, led by Colonel Escher, 'a well-practised and experienced cavalier', who promptly set about fortifying the city (Er.132). Ernst describes the process in surprisingly knowledgeable detail:

> Colonel Escher organised everything, appointing watches and instituting good military order. He had the loft doors in the roofs taken off, and he had big gabions woven, assembled and arranged on these doors in various places. He had them filled with earth and stones and had fortifications and batteries set up and built at intervals in the city, with the cannon and guns emplaced on them. He had a powder mill built in the city and gathered large supplies of powder, lead, iron, stones and lead bullets. ... He had the gates bastioned, leaving only the upper and lower gates open, and had the bridges raised elsewhere, as well as letting water into the inner moat. He made ordinances and instructed numbers of farmers as to what they should do. He turned citizens, young and old, into dragoons, organising them into troops and detailing them to their posts. Everyone knew what was required of him, day and night. (Er.133)

During this period the nuns busied themselves trying to hide their valuables, 'our farm lease documents, our sacred vessels and our silver plate, of which we had little left, as it had of necessity been used to provide bodily nourishment, ... and whatever was dear to each Mother or Sister and which they would not willingly lose' (Er.133). Unfortunately they concealed them in the cellar, and when the city moats were flooded so was their hiding-place:

> There was water in all the passages, and although the serving men waded in wearing boots there was so much water, and so deep, that the boots did not help them at all. So they waded in up to their armpits and brought us out what they could recover of the habits, furs and other stuff. (Er.133)

After reporting a number of skirmishes outside the city and the twice threatened recall of their garrison Ernst describes the deteriorating strategic situation. Breisach and Freiburg were besieged and the latter fell, leaving Villingen 'with few soldiers, surrounded on all sides and besieged by the enemy. God in his mercy help us; we are in great fear and danger. They say that they treat people so wantonly and shamefully, especially those in holy orders.' This fear increased on 29 November, 'when our city was called upon to capitulate by two trumpeters [threatening] fire, brimstone and great misery', this being the traditional summons to surrender before an attack. Ernst reports the nuns' state of mind: 'We were in great fright and fear, and we slept and ate little, all lying in the convent dormitory although no-one dared to sleep peacefully' (Er.134). Keeping up a war of nerves, the enemy offered Escher an accord, which he in turn put to a meeting of the citizenry: 'Every man is in great alarm and fear, while the authorities vacillate, waiting to see what the colonel will propose.' While Escher played for time, await-ing higher orders, the enemy sent two more trumpeters, an embassy and a letter mixing threats with promises of good treatment after a surrender. The town hesitated: 'Here we sit, caught between Scylla and Charybdis, with everyone anxious and distressed. Some people want us to defend ourselves and others are ready to surrender, while we pray, sing and call upon God.' As if the convent were not frightened enough already 'many of the soldiers talk of how they will treat the nuns'. Escher, however, 'did not let himself be panicked, nor was he afraid'. Reassuring the citizens, he rebuffed the offered accord, saying that if no other help was at hand 'he would hope and trust in God's mercy and in the Mother of God'. But yet again the threat was lifted: 'Truly God sent his instrument, and the army was ordered away into Swabia to defend it against Aldringer' (Er.135).

The respite was short, and the besiegers returned on 11 January 1633. The following morning one of the nuns died and was hastily buried, a reminder to all 'that tomorrow the grave could hold us'. By evening the outlying build-ings were on fire: 'It is a misery above all miseries. They have set light to the Outer Mill by our garden, and to the Hospital Mill and the nice inn. There was such a conflagration in front of our gate that they could see where and how we were in the convent.' At two in the morning of 13 January the enemy began to bombard the walls, soon making a breach. The convent came under heavy fire and Ernst reports several nuns having narrow escapes as they tried to shelter or to rescue cherished possessions. At seven in the morning their confessor came, 'wanting to hear our last confessions before death. Each one found a corner where she thought that no cannon ball would reach her and made her confession' (Er.136). Ernst had just been summoned from her shelter in a neighbouring building to make her own confession when her account abruptly breaks off.

The way in which Ernst presents her account is as striking as its content, and it is worth noting how she has turned her experiences during the attack on Villingen into a well-constructed and self-contained story. Using a pre-existing and rather random chronicle as her medium, she has completely changed its style to give a developed narrative account of a particular series of events. A significant feature of this is the way her narrative focus pro-gressively sharpens as the situation develops. Thus she begins with the gen-eral background of the war approaching the south-west – the story so far, as it were – before describing the moves of the invaders against other cities in the region. After this introduction the focus shifts to Villingen itself but remains at a political level, setting out the diplomatic approaches of the enemy and the divided opinion among the citizens collectively. On the occasion of the second approach, after the surrender of Rottweil, Ernst adopts a similar mode but intensifies the account of the negotiations with more detail of the demands of the enemy and the responses of the mayor. When troops actually appear outside the walls she sharpens her focus further, bringing in the reactions and feelings of the nuns as a body. The arrival of the Imperialist garrison provides a change of pace as Ernst relieves the tension of the main action with a description of the defensive measures put in hand by Colonel Escher, and of the nuns' own efforts to hide their valuables. The return to the main story is heralded by a further summary of the deteriorating wider situation as Freiburg falls to the Swedes, leading up to a fresh call on Villingen to surrender. Yet again Ernst intensifies the focus, providing more detail of the negotiations, much of it in approximate reported speech, and she first describes Escher's tactics and then his robust eventual response, in contrast to the indecisiveness of the city fathers. At the same time she emphasises the growing fears of the nuns as she builds up to the climax of the eventual assault. In this last phase she personalises her text, recounting the experiences of individual nuns as they have narrow escapes during the bombardment. This leads up to the final episode, the last confession before the expected storming of the city, where she introduces herself specifically into the story for the first time – at which point the surviving text dramatically breaks off.

This is not to say that Ernst deliberately or consciously structured her account into a developed narrative in this way. Her contemporaneous notes may well have become progressively fuller and more focused as the tension of the situation increased, and thereafter it may simply be a case of natural storytelling. Her writing itself is stylistically simple, unornamented, and unlike that of many of the priests, pastors and monks it contains no interpolated Latin phrases. Otherwise there is little in her text to mark it out as the work of a woman; indeed, apart from the added implicit fear of rape her account of the experiences and reactions of the nuns has clear parallels to Bürster's response to the capture of his monastery by Swedish troops. Ernst presumably completed her description of the attack on Villingen, as she wrote or copied it up some years later, but how the remainder of her manuscript was lost is not known, the editor adding only that she later became abbess of another convent.

Another account dealing with the capture of a town, also from a female perspective, is given by Anna Wolff, a miller's daughter from Schwabach, near Nuremberg, who ran what she describes as 'my mill' with her brother after the death of her parents. More than 30 years after the event she wrote an account of her experiences when the town was attacked and occupied by

Imperialist troops in the summer of 1632, noting that 'I and my sister-in-law Kratzerbettery are living yet, up to this year of 63' (Wo.108, 109). A section of the introduction appears to be missing, the first surviving paragraphs describing astronomical phenomena taken as omens, but the short text seems to be otherwise complete, suggesting that Wolff recorded only this one traumatic episode from her life and experiences of the war. She included this in her household book, which the editor says otherwise contained mostly notes of family events, devotional songs and Bible texts, together with a brief account of her own background: 'I, Anna Wolff, was born *anno* 1602, on St Catherine's day. My father was Ulrich Wolff, under-miller here at the Segmill, my mother's name was Barbara, and I was brought up by my parents, at school and at church, until the year of 23' (Wo.100).

Wolff's account is one of the first published by posterity, in 1791, and is interesting not only in itself but also as one of the few written by a woman, and even more strikingly by a woman who was neither a nun nor from the higher levels of society. She could write surprisingly competently, given the prevailing limited levels of education even among men in artisan families, and she makes a good story of the dramatic events she reports. She describes – possibly with some exaggeration – the relaxed view of the war in Schwabach before it touched the town directly for the first time: 'We had indeed heard tell of the war, but we had not thought that it would reach us in Schwabach in the year of 1632. On holy St John's day people were still living it up and leading the high life, just like Sodom and Gomorrah.' Some of the leading citizenry and clergy were not so naive, and 'our Reverend Dean and another pastor, Reverend Wollfart, and quite a number of other gentlemen fled to Nuremberg. They drove out with many wagons three hours before dawn, so that people didn't know, for they had received information that the soldiers were being sent here' (Wo.100, 101). The unexpected arrival of the attacking force, put by Wolff with the common exaggeration of the time at '80 000 men, ... cavalry and foot-soldiers', brings this part of her narrative to a climax: 'Hear, dear Christian; early on the Sunday after holy St Peter's day, in the middle of the sermon the horns began to blow furiously, so that everyone in the church ran out. When we looked outside we could see nothing but soldiers all round Schwabach' (Wo.103, 102–3). Wolff quotes a relevant biblical text: 'Thus it was as the kingly prophet David says in the 3rd Psalm: "Lord, how are they increased that trouble me! Many are they that rise up against me. But thou, O Lord, art a shield for me."' She likewise expresses her personal feelings in religious terms as the attack commenced: 'As in the 25th Psalm, "the troubles of my heart are enlarged: O bring thou me out of my distresses"' (Wo.103, 104).

The town defended itself well initially: 'The citizens put up a fight, shooting out and hitting many officers and colonels without suffering much injury themselves. This went on for seven hours' (Wo.104). Initial hopes of help from Gustavus Adolphus (then pinned down outside Nuremberg by

Wallenstein) soon faded, and under pressure of sustained artillery fire and attacks on the walls the citizenry began to despair:

> People were running hither and thither, not knowing where they should take refuge, so that again the cry was 'look upon mine affliction and my pain and forgive all my sins'. Hear, good soul; crowds of people fell on their knees in the streets and in the houses, raised up their hands and prayed. (Wo.104–5)

Recognising the inevitable, Schwabach sought to surrender on accord, but too late under the accepted rules of war at the time. Wolff reports the response of the besiegers: 'They were going to massacre us one and all, and they wouldn't spare even a child still in its mother's womb, because so many colonels and officers had lost their lives.' Eventually slightly better terms were obtained: 'They would simply plunder us and take what we had' (Wo.105, 106).

As the town prepared to surrender people looked for places to hide during the initial onslaught of the troops. Wolff and four other women found a refuge, where they stayed for five days:

> Hear, good soul; when the gate was to be opened the people were so afraid that they didn't know where to go. The majority fled into the two churches and locked themselves in; few stayed in the houses. I hid myself in a concealed dovecote in my mill, where the five of us could not stand up for five days, and while the bullets whistled back and forth truly God protected us. (Wo.106)

Possibly because of the conditions in this cramped shelter one of the women died eight days afterwards, and two more soon followed, leaving only Wolff and her sister-in-law as long-term survivors. Her account of the plundering is brief and not strictly eyewitness – she was in her hideout – but she records what she no doubt later learned, a common account of 'everything' being taken. She also gives a typical hearsay account of violence, in which she mentions no specific individuals: 'They persecuted the people. They tortured, whipped and beat the men, dragging them out into the camp and calling them rebels…. They dishonoured, tormented, pulled about and vilely mishandled the women they found.' Her mill was plundered, leaving 'not a grain of wheat, not a speck of flour. They cleaned out all the hoppers and silos, and took everything away' (Wo.107, 108). The soldiers did miss something, however, and Wolff attributes their lack of thoroughness to God's help: 'A chest full of flour was still left, right by the door. Many hundreds had gone past it, but not one had opened it. Thus one can see what God wished to save.' Officers and soldiers were billeted in the town, and after five days the mill was given a military guard so that it could be put to work to supply flour for the troops. Wolff could emerge: 'Then I also came down from my dovecote with my companions, after great hardship, but the Good Lord had preserved our honour' (Wo.108, 109).

Wolff's description of the two-month occupation which followed centres on the prevalent hunger among the citizenry as the troops ate all the available food: 'Hear, good Christian soul; what misery and distress there was, what hunger and grief, what fear and need. Many, many hundreds died of starvation, emaciated and not getting another bite of bread before their end.' Oddly, she indicates that the troops did not take all the meat: 'we had enough meat, a pound for a kreuzer, but no salt, no fat, no bread' (Wo.111). Later an epidemic affected citizens and soldiers alike, many dying of the plague, despite which military operations and skirmishing around the town continued. The troops created further panic among the inhabitants by threatening that 'when they broke camp and marched off, then they would scorch and burn everything', but in the event they did not do so, moving on once they had exhausted the town's capacity to supply them (Wo.117).

Wolff is careful to stress her own good works during the occupation, and although she draws no direct comparison her description of others escaping is nevertheless pointed: 'We still had four pastors, but one of those also deserted his flock. He dressed himself in mill-hand's clothes and got out with the soldiers.' She refers back to the flour the soldiers overlooked in the first round of plundering: 'We divided the chest of flour that was left to us among the poor people, who hadn't had a bite of bread in eight days. I went into the mill myself to beg flour to make gruel for the small children, just boiled in water.' Despite the supposed watch on it she also raided a large barrel of beer in the mill cellar: 'I dared to go there every day and draw a jugful, which I distributed among the sick and those in childbed, so that they thanked me profusely and prayed that God would preserve me' (Wo.110, 112, 112–13).

Wolff also gives an account of her part in rescuing the mayor, who the Imperialists held responsible for organising and prolonging the defence of the town, and hence for the deaths of many of the attackers: 'Afterwards they threatened that if they caught him they would cut him in four and hang him out over the walls because so many officers had been shot' (Wo.113). Wolff hid him: 'So we kept him, Herr Triller, with his wife, in a closet in the mill for 11 weeks. No-one knew about it except me, my brother and my maid, and no-one visited him except me, which I did twice every day.' She emphasises the risk she took: 'Later they beat it around the town, making announcements with three rolls on the drums that they were going to search from house to house, and wherever they found him and whoever was protecting him, they would be hanged one with the other.' Wolff also took steps to put the Imperialists off the scent: 'Then he (Mayor Triller) advised me to say to people that the farmers bringing supplies for the army had taken him to Regensburg in a barrel and that he had been seen there. Word of this went round the whole town so that nobody enquired further about him' (Wo.114).

After the troops left Wolff reports better times, at least for a while, although her comment has a somewhat ironic ring: 'Afterwards our Good Lord granted us a cheap year, as we could reap even though we hadn't sown. There was so much grass and grain growing in the streets that one could scarcely see the cobbles.' The town even had the opportunity to make good some of its losses by buying at bargain prices from other soldiers: 'When troops marched by they brought their booty here, and one could buy a cow for a taler or even for a gulden, a sheep for a kopfstück, and a bushel of corn for three gulden. Then people thought that everything was all right again and they took to marrying, men, women and young folk – every week there were three or four weddings.' Wolff was among those who married, although it would appear from her oblique reference that her husband became a casualty of the war soon afterwards: 'I myself married that same summer, on St Sebald's day, but we lived together for only four weeks before a great army of soldiers arrived. Then it was soon a case of "the wedded state is a woeful state".' She is equally brief about the troubles which followed: 'And so it continued from this time on, from 1632 until the year of 48. The cry was always "give peace in our time, O Lord, for great affliction is upon us"' (Wo.120).

The most notorious event of the war was the storming of Magdeburg by Tilly's army in May 1631, and the disastrous fire which followed, causing the destruction of the city and the death of most of its population. A number of eyewitnesses report their experiences. Jürgen Ackermann, a captain in Pappenheim's regiment, notes that as they prepared for the final assault 'the general had good Rhenish wine issued to all the soldiers and officers, which gave them great courage' (A.14). He gives a brief but graphic description of the attack:

> There was such a thunder and crack of muskets, incendiary mortars and great cannon that no-one could either see or hear, and many supporting troops followed us, so that the whole rampart was filled, covered and black with soldiers and storm ladders. Eventually, after several hundred men had fallen, we broke in over the defences, putting the remainder to flight to the precinct gate and into Lackermacher Street. In assaults of this kind our soldiers brought some four hundred storm ladders over the earthworks and up to the walls. (A.14)

No sooner were the attackers inside the city than they fell to looting, putting aside their cumbersome pikes, 'all the better to scout through the houses'. Too soon, as the defenders were far from giving up, 'but fought desperately and unceasingly in all parts of the city, together with their cavalry, so that we lost our strength' (A.14, 15). Meanwhile following troops had made a breach in the walls, bringing relief just in time:

> The fighting in the streets, some of which were obstructed with chains, had so exhausted our nine attacks, each by 3000 men, that we could

scarcely gasp. But now when our cavalry came advancing through Lackermacher Street with the sounding of trumpets and kettledrums the enemy began to weaken. We drove their cavalry as far as the new market-place and the citizenry out of the Bridge Gate, while the administrator and all the remaining soldiers were captured. (A.15)

Ackermann attributes the destruction of Magdeburg by fire to orders from the general adjutant 'to set fire to a few houses ... with the intention of diverting the citizens from their weapons to fire-fighting' (A.14–15). At the time the day was fine and the houses burned 'for a good hour or more, as bright as a beacon', but 'not a single citizen relinquished his weapons to put them out'. Soon after the conquest was complete 'a strong storm-wind blew up and the city caught fire in every quarter, so that there was no hope as it was quite beyond saving' (A.15).

Nevertheless the troops, Ackermann included, quickly took to looting. He describes how he entered 'a vaulted, stone-built house' on the old market square, and seizing an axe from a soldier 'broke the hinge of the inner door wide open'. This could have cost him his life as the owner was waiting inside with levelled gun, but his shot missed Ackermann, hitting a man beside him instead. The householder then fled upstairs, slamming an iron door behind him and leaving the soldiers to ransack the lower floor. Finding a servant, they offered him mercy provided that he showed them where valuables were to be found: 'He said yes, he knew of good booty, whereupon he led us into a chamber, helped to move a bedstead, and there was a vault, out of which we hauled an iron chest' (A.16). This proved to be a costly and troublesome acquisition. As they carried it out of the house the owner above shot down a second soldier, while the lock resisted all attempts to burst it open. Eventually they hacked a hole in the chest with the axe: 'Then we groped through the hole, one after another, as one does in a lucky dip. ... Among other things I got some good silver and gold dishes and a pretty gold chain with a valuable jewel.' After making a hasty exit from the city Ackermann looked back: 'There I saw the whole city of Magdeburg, apart from the cathedral, monastery and new market, lying in embers and ashes. It had lasted only three to three-and-a-half hours, in which I could perceive God's almighty power and punishment' (A.16–17, 17).

Simon Prinz, a prominent citizen of Magdeburg, acted as a gun captain during the siege 'because I had previously learned the art of gunnery'. He gives only a brief report of the fighting but fully describes his lucky escape afterwards. In company with a group of comrades, two of whom were killed *en route*, he made his way towards his home, 'but first we had to give a soldier everything we had with us'. Surrounded by more soldiers he had nothing left to give, but one agreed to escort him home against a promise of booty on arrival. Both he and his guardian were disappointed; the house had already been plundered when they reached it, but despite threats Prinz experienced nothing worse than a poke in the ribs with a musket before the soldiers moved on elsewhere. Seizing his opportunity he quickly hid himself under the straw in the attic; 'There I found a moment to make my prayer to God, which I couldn't do earlier because of the terrible circumstances' (Pn.23, 24, 25).

Meanwhile Prinz's wife had also made her way home, 'but as she crossed Broad Street they ripped the fur off her back, thinking that she had sewn money into it'. Neither she nor their four children came to any more harm, and seeing a group of officers passing she sought help from them: 'They promised her that her husband would have quarter, as true as they were honest men, but they also wanted a reward; she must surely still have something hidden away which she would have to give them' (Pn.24, 26). At this Prinz emerged and was indeed able to pay his protectors, 'because I had some things buried in an iron chest in the cellar – silver and gold goblets, bracelets and rings, together with a variety of other good things – which I was keeping for a rainy day'. As the fire approached Prinz begged one of the officers, a lieutenant-colonel, to take him and his family with him out of the city, which the latter agreed to do although driving a hard bargain: '"You can all come along with me, but outside you must give me more money. I will let you go wherever you want, but what will I get for it?" I promised him 100 taler' (Pn.26, 27).

Holding on to the colonel's horse for protection the whole family made their way through the city to the Sudenburg Gate. There the watch refused to allow them through 'but the lieutenant-colonel spoke to the sentries in a foreign language' and persuaded them to let Prinz and his son pass, while his wife and daughters were permitted to stay in a house by the gate 'where there were also a number of women from the nobility, as well as Tilly himself, and a guard had been posted' (Pn.27, 28). It was an anxious parting, the wife fearful for her husband's safety 'as she saw so many dead bodies lying all around, right before her eyes'. Even the colonel's protection only prevailed with some difficulty: 'As we went out the musketeers were all blind drunk. They had big gilt goblets in their hands and all kinds of other things, and they shouted out "cut down the rebellious scoundrel", but the lieutenant-colonel protected me well' (Pn.28). Eventually they reached the Imperialist camp and Prinz was invited to join the officers for dinner, a trying experience in the circumstances, with the added irony that he saw his own property gracing the table. The colonel 'began drinking to Tilly's health out of my goblet and I couldn't refuse to toast him too. There I was, just like an owl among the crows' (Pn.29).

Otto von Guericke, who later achieved enduring fame for his scientific experiments, was the city engineer and a member of the council at Magdeburg during the siege. He reports that plundering after the successful assault lasted little more than two hours, although in this time 'many thousand innocent men, women and children were abominably murdered or wretchedly executed in all kinds of ways, amid apprehensive screams and hideous shrieks, something which cannot be adequately described with words or sufficiently lamented with tears'. Then the wind caught hold of the diversionary fires (for which Guericke supports Ackermann's explanation) 'so that by ten o'clock in the morning everything was on fire, and by ten o'clock at night the whole city, complete with its beautiful town hall and all the churches and monasteries, had been reduced to ashes and heaps of stone' (G.83). There was one major exception, the refuge of most of the survivors: 'In the cathedral there were some 4000 people, who had retreated there and hidden themselves away. And although at the beginning some Imperialist soldiers got in and killed a number of people, as well as allegedly raping two women, guards were soon posted on the doors and further violence was prevented' (G.86). These were the fortunate minority. Guericke describes the aftermath:

The number of those who were killed or died in the city – for not only the sword but also the fire swallowed up many people – cannot be accurately known. Soon after this appalling conflagration General Tilly had the corpses of those who had been burned or killed in other ways loaded from the streets, ramparts and elsewhere on to wagons and put into the waters of the Elbe, but for almost a full year afterwards many dead bodies were found – five, six, eight, ten or more at a time – in the ruined cellars where they had been overcome and had suffocated. Furthermore those who lay in the streets had been so consumed by the fire and shattered by the falling buildings that the pieces often had to be loaded up with pitchforks, with the result that no-one will be able to give the real number. By and large, however, it is thought that of the order of 20000 people, adults and children, had to end their lives or suffered bodily injuries in such grim circumstances. This includes the two suburbs, and those of the Imperialist soldiers who died and were burned, for not only did many fall at various points in the assault but a good number were also late in leaving, spending too long searching houses or cellars or otherwise getting lost. The dead bodies which were put into the Elbe outside, in front of the Water Gate, were unable or unwilling to drift quickly away because at that point there is a whirlpool or eddy. Thus many floated about there for a long time, some with their heads out of the water and others with their hands outstretched as if to heaven, making a gruesome spectacle for onlookers. There was much prattle about this, folk saying that it was exactly as though these dead people were still praying, singing and crying out to heaven for vengeance. (G.86–7)

6
Faith and Experience

Religion and superstition

The war is often interpreted as being at least in part one of religion, but whatever the significance of religion in the politics of the princes it does not emerge from the testimony of these eyewitnesses as the central issue for most of the ordinary people, pastors and priests apart. Whether nominally Protestant or Catholic the armies were as religiously as they were ethnically cosmopolitan, embracing men of all religions or none so long as they would serve. In the many accounts of soldiers from defeated units being enlisted by their captors there are no suggestions of a religious test being applied. Monro was as keen to have the potentially Catholic Irish as the English and Scots. Hagendorf served equally conscientiously with the Protestant Swedish and the Catholic Bavarian armies. Poyntz changed both sides and religion but did not specifically match the two, enlisting with Protestant Saxony soon after his own conversion to Catholicism. Just as natives of Sweden were a relatively small minority among the troops referred to in convenient short-hand as Swedes, so the religious labels applied to the armies reflected more the political allegiances of their princes than the personal beliefs of soldiers or commanders.

For Protestant pastors the religious aspect of the war had a direct and personal significance, as the Imperialist military success of the late 1620s provided the opportunity for militant recatholicisation. When the disputed territory of Kitzingen was awarded to Catholic Würzburg rather than Protestant Ansbach in January 1629 the bishop lost no time in asserting his religious as well as his secular authority. Dietwar, a Lutheran pastor, was deprived of his living and given 14 days to leave. Laymen had a choice: 'A new inquisition was then held in Kitzingen and it was decreed that anyone who did not want to turn Papist must leave the town within 14 days'. Some 'worshipped the Antichrist Baal' while others 'preferred to wend their way into misery' (Di.64, 65). Lutheran texts went on the bonfire: 'They took away all the Protestant books from the houses and burned a huge pile of them in the open market-place in Kitzingen.' Then after Gustavus Adolphus's victory at Breitenfeld in 1631 the newly-appointed Catholic priests fled, 'with their housekeepers', as Dietwar sardonically notes. He was duly reappointed pastor in his old parish, and as the Protestant military successes continued 'those from Hoheim who had turned Papist all reconverted of their own free will, except Jörg Hirtz, who was buried at Kitzingen on the 14th of November and remained a malicious blasphemer and denier of the truth' (Di.64, 72, 79). The Imperialists returned after the change in fortunes at Nördlingen in 1634 and Dietwar was again expelled, surviving for the next three years as best he could with the help of gifts from his co-religionists before being appointed to a living in still-Lutheran Ansbach territory nearby. Kitzingen remained in Catholic hands and he reports that repeated efforts were made to suppress Lutheran worship. In 1636 people were forbidden to travel elsewhere to hear Lutheran sermons and in 1637 those who did were fined a Reichstaler every time. These measures were evidently unsuccessful, as in 1641 they had to be repeated: 'At Kitzingen the Protestant inhabitants were forbidden by public decree to attend sermons in Protestant places' (Di.108).

The schoolmaster Gerlach, a Lutheran from a village outside Kitzingen, also records these changes in religious control and the reactions of the population. In October 1631 'as the Catholic priest was away, the Baden folk in Üngershausen dared to have church bells rung and the Gospel read and sung'. In May 1635, after the second recatholicisation, a priest attempted to preach in the village of Fuchstadt 'but he was chased away by the farmers', and when in June 'he announced from the pulpit that the visitation of Mary would be celebrated the farmers complained about it and refused to perform any more labour service on the church land, but the festival was held nevertheless' (Ge.9, 17, 18). Gerlach also notes anti-Protestant sentiment, mentioning that the estate steward 'seized many Lutheran books and heated the stoves in the castle at Rottenbauer with them', while in October 1639 'the Catholic millers in Essfeld, Hetzfeld, Darstadt and Gassdorf were forbidden to grind for Lutherans and the Hetzfeld bakers were not allowed to sell bread to Lutherans any more' (Ge.16, 27).

Although Kitzingen was a special case because of its disputed ownership it was by no means unique, and two other pastor diarists, Büttner and Henrici, were likewise expelled from and reappointed to their livings in parishes in Baden and Hesse respectively. Mallinger's experience provides a contrast. Soon after occupying Freiburg the Swedes made provision for their own religious practices: 'On the 4th of January [1633] a preacher went up into the pulpit in the Augustinian monastery for the first time and gave a sermon. After that the senior officers sought a church in which they could hold their Lutheran *exercitium* for themselves and the soldiers under their command.' Mallinger notes regretfully that these Lutheran preachers 'reached so far into the hearts not only of their co-religionists, but also of many supposed

Catholics' (Ma.536). In June the margrave of Baden arrived in Freiburg, calling an assembly of the citizens and asking

> whether they would hold to their old and long-established Catholic religion or whether they would accept their liberation. But the calm resolution and response of the pious and zealous Catholic citizens was *unanimiter* that they wanted to live and die by their old, well-founded religion. Because of this constancy nothing more was asked of them. (Ma.541)

The long and short of this understandably partisan account is that after making a ritual gesture towards converting them the Swedes and their allies left the Catholics of Freiburg to their religion. This seems generally to have been the case, although the Naumburg chronicler Zader, himself a Protestant, does note mistaken religious zeal among Gustavus Adolphus's Finnish troops: 'At that time the Cloister Gate, or School Gate, which was close by Naumburg, was virtually razed to the ground by the Finns, who took it for a Roman Catholic monastery' (Za.28). The monks of Salem, although frequently raided and plundered, were targeted more for material than religious reasons, and violations of churches reported by Bürster likewise had more to do with looting than religious opposition. Even so there were incidents, as when Swedes plundered a village in 1633,

> injuring no more than three people but catching a priest at the altar during Mass, *post consecrationem*. They threw *sacram hostiam* away, tipped over the chalice, which they smashed up and took with them, and held the priest captive, but after a ransom of ten taler was paid they set him free again and moved on. (Bü.28)

In Protestant areas measures against Catholics were sometimes taken on security grounds, as in Strasbourg, which survived the war without occupation but lived in fear of betrayal by a Catholic fifth column. Walther describes Catholic cloisters with access to the walls being compulsorily evacuated in 1633, and Catholics in the city were also disarmed:

> *Dato* it was proclaimed and read out to the sound of trumpets that all farmers and people from elsewhere, as well as those belonging here, who were of the Papist religion were immediately to surrender all their hand-weapons and firearms at the Tailors' Hall, under penalty of corporal or capital punishment; which they did. (Wl.28)

Wagner reports similar measures in Augsburg after it admitted the Swedes in 1632. Initially the city's leading Lutherans were more circumspect, suggesting that 'to begin with the Roman Catholics should not all be displaced and excluded, one with another, from authority and *officiis*, but that at least some of them might be tolerated and stay on'. This met with a sharp response from Gustavus Adolphus: 'It wouldn't do to entrust the sheep to the wolf again' (Wa.10). Catholics were accordingly dismissed and a few days later 'all the Papists here were also disarmed by the Swedes'. In January 1633 'all towers in the Papist churches and cloisters were closed off so that they could no longer look out and give signs of various kinds to the enemy' (Wa.18, 29). Many of the monks were expelled from the city, and those who remained were suspect. Wagner reports that he himself, accompanied by workmen, went to a monastery and 'had the suspicious exits, particularly those from the cloister into the Maierhof, barred and even walled up', while a convent also came under scrutiny and was raided, 'when many weapons were found in the tower referred to' (Wa.43).

Sometimes the religious outlooks of the authors show through, and these are naturally more prominent in the accounts of monks, priests and pastors. The laymen range from Zembroth, who barely mentions religion in his brief and to-the-point chronicle entries, through others who make conventional religious references from time to time, to those such as Heberle and Preis who constantly insert pious expressions at moments of notable tribulation or relief. Among the soldiers Poyntz wears his religion lightly whereas Monro comes across as a rather opinionated and self-righteous Calvinist. Nevertheless outspokenly partisan comments are infrequent in these accounts, religious loyalties usually being implicit rather than explicit, or indicated merely in passing; Gerlach is one of many to refer to Catholic clerics as 'Papist jack-priests', while the Munich chorister Hellgemayr calls the Swedes 'the heretics' (Ge.13, Hl.202). There are exceptions. The pastor Schleyss is strongly partisan, regarding the armies raised by the Protestant German princes as God's own and praying: 'God grant his soldiers luck and victory!' He repeats the wish before Lützen, later adding an epitaph for Gustavus Adolphus: 'May the Almighty God in his goodness raise up another hero for the succour of his oppressed Christendom! Amen' (Sc.1. 86, 95). Walther echoes this, describing the king as 'this beloved hero' who 'poured out his kingly blood for religion, for German freedom, and for our good' (Wl.27). Schleyss displays his prejudices in referring to Protestant subjects as 'poor, defenceless and abandoned people' when they were forced to acquiesce in the recatholicisation of monastic lands, whereas he notes with satisfaction the removal of Catholics from office in Augsburg: 'Here God, the righteous justice, has passed judgement and gladdened the worthy Protestant citizenry' (Sc.1. 85, 93).

Hagendorf's occasional comments shed light on the religious views of a common soldier, albeit one more intelligent and educated than the average. He was conventionally religious rather than particularly pious, but the deaths of his children are always marked with a benediction and on his wife's safe return from the flames of Magdeburg he expresses his relief: 'Truly God protected her' (Ha.47). He is even more emphatic about his own escape from the carnage at Nördlingen:

> On this occasion the Almighty kept a special watch over me, so that I will owe great thanks to the Good Lord for as long as I live, as I had not so much as a finger injured. Apart from me not a single one of all those who came back to the regiment was unhurt. (Ha.62)

In between such traumatic events he makes little mention of religion and he was certainly not partisan in a religious sense in his military duties. The enemy were simply the opponents of the army in which he was for the time being serving, possibly his former comrades after his enforced changes of side, and he betrays no personal, political or religious animosity.

Hagendorf illustrates the coexistence of faith, scepticism and superstition. In Arras during the French campaign he visited the Chapel of the Holy Light to see a miraculous candle given by the Virgin Mary in the Middle Ages: 'It has, so they say, already been burning for three hundred years and the same candle hasn't burned out yet. I will leave it there; anyone who wants to can believe it, but I don't' (Ha.78). Elsewhere he refers matter-of-factly to 'Heuberg, where the evil spirits gather', and he records unquestioningly the experience of a group of gambling soldiers:

> On one occasion there was such a cursing and swearing at the gaming area. Then when one of the players bent down after a dice, for they were playing on a table and it had fallen off, he saw someone with a cloven hoof standing by the board. This figure began: 'O Lord Jesus, what kind of gamblers have we got at this table!' Then he suddenly disappeared, leaving a foul stench behind him. (Ha.88, 95)

Hagendorf also reports burnings for witchcraft: 'There is good dark beer in Lippstadt, but also evil people. I saw seven of them burned. Among them was a pretty young girl of 18, but even so she was burned' (Ha.46).

Clergymen too sometimes hovered on the boundary between faith and superstition. Bürster tells of soldiers looting the monastery church being awed by a picture of the Virgin apparently crying, and of a sacrilegious looter dogged by bad luck: 'One of them had also stolen a priest's Mass robe, but soon afterwards, on the second or third day following, he lost his coat and two horses. He admitted frankly that from that hour onwards he had had neither good fortune nor a lucky star' (Bü.45). Among the Protestant pastors Dietwar carefully records a variety of omens after the recatholicisation of Kitzingen in 1629, noting that the first woman to go to confession was struck by lightning, the officer who came to burn the Lutheran prayer-books fell ill, knockings were heard in the night at Hoheim, and an 'ugly owl' sat on the altar during *Ave Maria* (Di.58). Spiegel notes another ominous owl: 'Through almost the whole of this winter a big owl or eagle-owl sat up in the church tower every night, rejoicing and gloating horribly, doubtless over the terrible misfortune, ruin and destruction of this town and country, according to God's threat in Isaiah 13, v. 21 *et* 22' (Sp.33). Plebanus believed that storm winds foreshadowed new catastrophes of war: 'battles, skirmishes, robbing, plundering, burning', adding that 'I too was not infrequently afflicted with losses' (Pl.280).

Laymen such as Heberle, Walther and Wagner also refer frequently to omens, while many of the diarists saw the comets of 1618 and 1630 as portents of the war as a whole or of the sufferings of their particular area. Even the widely travelled and highly educated lawyer Pflummer was credulous. He repeats a tale told by a Catholic priest who was captured in a Swedish raid under cover of fog. He found that many of his captors were also Catholics, including their lieutenant, who boasted that the fog was not natural but had been conjured up by one of his troop. He invited the man, a Finn, to demonstrate:

> To please the priest the man agreed, whereupon he positioned himself on a particular spot. First he uttered a number of incomprehensible magic words and then he stretched out his hands and shook them. It was as though an ash fell from them, which spread out bit by bit, and like a fog covered first the magician and then the entire *compagnia*, so that they became quite invisible. (Pf.63)

After reporting further supernatural powers attributed to the Finn Pflummer adds his own comment: 'And since there are doubtless more such magicians to be found with the Swedish *armada*, one may well conclude that some of their victories are attributable more to this devilish *praestigiis* than to their courage *et verae virtuti*' (Pf.63).

Plague, famine and depopulation

War, plague and famine were commonly linked in the perception of the time, and often seen as punishments from God. The Strausberg town clerk Schuster held this view of the war, describing it as 'our Lord God's punishment, which afflicts Germany on account of her sins and vices, which have become rife far and wide in these times' (Sh.16). The pastor Minck was equally clear: 'In between, and alongside the scourge of war, God sent the pestilence here after us' (Mi.254). Another town clerk, Raph, completed the trilogy: 'Thereafter followed the third scourge of the just and angry God, namely the coal-black bitter hunger' (Ra.198).

It is not surprising that the diarists saw a link between plague and war, although this is questionable epidemiologically. The consequences where plague did strike are beyond doubt, and these accounts show that individuals were much more likely to lose relatives and that communities suffered far more deaths from epidemics than from either famine or the direct effects of war. Central southern Germany suffered particularly badly in 1634 and 1635, when Heberle lost his stepmother, a brother, four sisters and three children among the 'many thousand people' whose deaths he attributes to hunger, war and 'the terrible sickness, the pestilence' (He.161, 152). In Hesse Cervinus lost his entire family: 'My beloved wife Dorothea, with six dear children, and "Pitzi" Margarete, who looked after them, departed this life into God's peace within a few days.' He himself was near death but recovered, 'perhaps to endure more misfortune than has already occurred', as he bitterly comments (C.91). He assesses deaths locally at over half the population, noting 334 burials during the month of August 1635 in the small town of Grünberg, 27 at a single ceremony. At Bietigheim Raph reports that 'over 585 people died' out of a population quoted as 1800 in 1634, 'among them 60 married couples, and quite a number of whole families and households' (Ra.191, 196). Lang, from Isny, names some 30 individuals, mostly 'close friends of mine' but including his sister and his son, who died in the plague epidemic of 1635, of which he says: 'Since July this year there have been so many deaths that the like of it has never been heard in human memory' (La.29). Minck is similarly specific, listing by name the 25 survivors of the 'over 300 souls' living in Biberau before the epidemic, and noting that four of those died of hunger soon afterwards (Mi.256). He gives a horrific account of rotting bodies lying unburied before eventually being collected and consigned to mass graves. Writers who give few numbers and little detail about the war can be quite precise about plague deaths; Feilinger notes 22 in the village of Elm in an outbreak in June 1631 and another 26 in October of the same year.

Towns were more prone to epidemics than the countryside, and the effect of disease on a city such as Strasbourg, which escaped the worst effects of the war itself, is striking. Walther reports that during an outbreak in 1633 'within 20 weeks 4392 people died in this city' (Wl.30). Murr reports the onset of plague in Nuremberg in October 1634 and notes that by January 1635 there had been twice as many cases as in the 'great death' of 1585 (Mu.83). Infection spread even faster when cities were crowded with refugees. Pflummer makes the point in reporting an outbreak of 'Hungarian fever' in Überlingen in 1634, from which many people died, 'but for the most part only farm folk from elsewhere, or poor citizens, because of their slovenly way of living or lack of cleanliness in their housekeeping'. He links this to overcrowding arising from the war 'on account of the overwhelming numbers of country people, with their horses and cattle, who have taken refuge in the city' (Pf.138). Vincent, although also seeing such infections as divine punishment, adds a medical man's practical comment:

> Besieged in the Castle of Heydelberg, I visited every day divers sicke of the Plague, and like diseases. But in neither of these two great Plagues in

London, nor in any other, that I have beene in, did I ever finde the cause so virulent, the symptoms so incorrigible, the disease so incurable. ... The divine hand and finger of God was more conspicuous in this, than in any other visitation I had seene, though I doubt not but our foode with the aire might also helpe to impoyson our bodies extraordinarily. (V.57–8)

That hunger was frequently a consequence of war is evident from the eyewitness accounts. Armies did not produce but had to be fed, and when they passed through an area sutlers and troops descended on the farms and markets. Heberle reports from Ulm: 'They have bought up all the available bread, meat and beer, as well as grain and other things, so that it has all become very dear' (He.212). What they could not buy they requisitioned or stole. Often food was cleared from an area or simply destroyed in the fields to deny it to the enemy, but well-organised raids were also made at harvest time to supply the armies' needs. Minck describes Imperialist troops descending on the corn already cut and sheaved in the fields, threshing it, taking their own requirements and 'selling what they didn't need themselves in the cities on the Rhine and Main. They made such a good job of it that within a few days no grain was to be had in the region' (Mi.257). Hagendorf was more than once employed on such work, prompting an ironic comment: 'Here we stopped over to harvest, but it wasn't for the farmers' benefit' (Ha.100). Preis describes the scale of such operations:

At that time a strong force of Swedes came, 4000 on horses and on foot, with a large number of wagons, and they threshed all the grain in the fields around our village ... and took it to their camp. They also took the hay from our village, as well as the cabbages in the gardens, the apples and the pears, the whole lot. They left us not the least thing. (Pr.120–1)

The war also affected agricultural production in other ways. Cervinus reports how repeated and prolonged flights from the countryside to the protection of walled towns prevented sowing for the next harvest. Minck laments land running wild for lack of husbandry and 'so overgrown with firs that one would take it for woods rather than fields' (Mi.261). Heberle notes the same effect and identifies a reason: 'Because things had gone so badly here and as there were virtually no horses or cattle the fields too were left wild and uncultivated' (He.167). Raph reports that in Bietigheim men yoked themselves to the plough, and Preis did much the same despite still having some draught animals: 'We couldn't bring any livestock into the village because of the soldiers, ... so I yoked myself to the harrow, together with my farm-hand and the boy, and harrowed the four acres of land' (Pr.123).

Nevertheless most local famines probably arose from natural causes. According to Raph's account drought, not war, caused crop failures at

Bietigheim in 1626, leading some people to live on 'grass, thistle heads and greenery of that kind', and others to beg, while 'those who were ashamed to do that died of hunger' (Ra.188). High prices, food shortages and hunger were common experiences for troops and civilians alike during the war but episodes of full-scale famine were exceptional, as indicated by the shocked descriptions given by the diarists. The plague epidemic of 1635 in central southern Germany was followed by such a famine, possibly at least in part as a consequence, and Heberle, Minck and Raph all provide graphic accounts of how anything and everything was eaten, 'for hunger is a good cook' (He.161). At Bietigheim Raph attributes 365 deaths 'for the most part' to hunger in the following three years (Ra.199). Plebanus describes conditions in his area in 1636:

In recent days people without care and attention have died of hunger, one here in the Dam Mill, three at Weissbach, and one at Neuwhofen. There are also quite a number of particularly poor abandoned children round here, who look more like corpses than living people, although their parents had been very rich, with cattle, money and farms. These children call on me every day, at my parlour door, and content themselves with a small slice [of bread] or an apple. They also ask for the apple or pear peelings lying under the stove. (Pl.276)

Terrible though these reports are, they resemble other descriptions of famine not directly linked to war, for example in late seventeenth-century France (Williams, 1970, pp. 191–2). That the effects were localised and did not extend to everyone is indicated by Minck, who notes that 'if at that time I had not had money from my *patrimonio* [church endowment] at Giessen, and had been obliged to live solely from [the emoluments of] this post, then I would have had to suffer from hunger like others' (Mi.260). Even so the effects of famine were aggravated by war, particularly the dangers from raiding troops. Plebanus records how, after much of their population had fled as soldiers moved into the area, some villages were inhabited only by the sick or those caring for them, many of whom fell victim to starvation, and he gives gruesome accounts of unburied bodies partly eaten by hungry dogs. He describes a visit to the village of Endlichhofen, 'in which there wasn't a living person, just two big dogs in front of Michelengen's house'. He went in,

but apprehensively, for right in the front of the house I found a person whose shirt had been pulled right down to the feet, and whose neck, shoulders and arms, as well as the *pudenda* or genitals, had been eaten away. As the head was not to be found I couldn't tell whether it had been a man or a woman. In the parlour ... there were several more legs and bones of children. (Pl.259)

The substance of Vincent's description of rural depopulation matches other accounts despite the air of exaggeration: 'From Basil to Strasburg, from Strasburg to Heydelberg, from thence to Marpurg, I scarce saw a man in the Fields, or Villages' (V.34). Soon after Nördlingen Minck reports inhabitants fleeing villages, adding that 'Reinheim and Zwingenberg stood quite empty and deserted for two years' (Mi.253). Raph notes the decline in the population of Bietigheim, the number of citizens (heads of households) falling to 40 in 1638 against 350 in 1634 owing to deaths or emigration, which he attributes to the burden of military extortions. Plebanus records the decline in population at Miehlen by 1636: 'And there are just 20 married couples, quite a few of whom are now frail. *Anno* 1618, *anno sc. ingressus mei ad Millenses* [the second year after my arrival at Miehlen], there were 115 people occupying homes in the village, and a few years before it was 130 strong' (Pl.258). Spiegel complains of the effect of depopulation on his congregations, reporting from Eltersdorf in 1636 that 'because I didn't meet or find even three people at home here I couldn't do anything'. A month later he did hold a service there, but 'I had no more than four old people, two men and two women, and a boy. May God increase the congregation and defend them from further despoliation of the country' (Sp.52). In March 1637 he gathered seven people in Bruck, although three were children, but in October 1638 he had to abandon a service in Eltersdorf 'because no more than two men were available, and no-one who could sing'. By January 1639 he notes: 'To Bruck at New Year. From then on no services could be held because there was nobody left at home, and nor did anybody want to go home because of the soldiers' (Sp.65, 66). Spiegel also lists, house by house, the dwellings in Eltersdorf and their condition in May 1642, indicating that only 7 of 64 were occupied by a total of 27 people: 4 couples, 2 widows, 1 widower and their households.

Signs of the times

Many of the authors include anecdotes, asides or self-revealing comments which illustrate the effect of the war on attitudes and social behaviour. Prices are a case in point. Many of the earlier writers include descriptions of the inflation of the early 1620s which bring to mind the lasting impression that inflation made three hundred years later in Germany. Freund comments sharply on the devaluation of money at this time 'on account of the accursed goings-on with the coinage'. Departing from his generally unemotive style he refers to the 'betrayers of the currency', 'cutpurse swine' and 'children of Baal' who 'have talked princes and lords into setting up a whole lot of private mints in the country' (Fr.29). Walther's account in particular foreshadows the 1920s:

> On top of this misery came another misfortune, namely that all the sound coinage disappeared from the country and the money began to climb high, so that the Reichstaler was already worth 2 gulden 18 kreuzer ... and

went higher by the day. ... And although almost everyone had money enough one couldn't get anything for it. People were taking bread from the bakers still hot out of the oven. (Wl.15, 17)

The way writers describe their own experiences indicates their attitudes and expectations. The pastor Beck gives the measure of his poverty in the mid-1630s: 'I often had to eat my food without fat and without salt ... and for three whole years I drank water' (Be.84). From Hesse Ludolph adds another clerical perspective: 'In such times we held baptisms and church fairs without meat soups, roasts or boiled meats. We had to learn to eat green cabbage, dried pears, pea soup without fat – yes, I said without fat!' He is particularly vehement about his own predicament: 'Well over a year has gone by in which I, the pastor of a parish, have not been able – in a whole year – to have a dish of meat on my table'. Need changed values: 'People have sold a house or a barn for a quarter or a bushel of corn or the like. When it's a matter of saving his skin a man will give whatever he has for his life' (Lu.53). Walther makes the same point: 'In the country many people died of hunger who had 50, 60 or even up to 100 acres. An acre would be given for a loaf of bread' (Wl.32). These examples should not be taken too literally but they are indicative, as is the implied change in the social order, which Ludolph makes explicit: 'Those who were otherwise the richest and highest-ranking in Reichensachsen have become the poorest. They have carried loads of wood or a little corn over the fields for payment or for themselves, barefoot or only in stockings, and without shoes, as they had none, to earn their bread' (Lu.53). The same occurred in the man-made famine of a siege, in this case Wagner's Augsburg: 'The rich have just as little by way of provisions and to eat as the poor, and in this equality has almost been reached, while in such a famine Christian love comes to an end' (Wa.58).

Several authors reflect social attitudes in noting that the burdens of war were not evenly shared, the better off often making a hasty getaway and leaving the lower orders to the mercy of advancing troops. Hellgemayr describes events as the Swedes approached Munich in 1632:

There was such a fright and fear here in Munich that everyone fled. Most of the great lords and the rich took all their best things away with them; rich and poor went, in coaches, on horseback or on foot. It was a great misery. In the name of God and all the holy saints I stayed here with my wife and beloved children, waiting at home in my poverty for God's help. ... On this day the nuns also fled and almost all the clergy – the deans, canons, parish priests and their assistants – all ran away. (Hl.204–5)

Wolff gives a similar report from Schwabach, as does the nun Junius from Bamberg, the latter making clear the hostility such flights aroused amongst the citizenry. She reports that the hierarchy were quick to leave when danger threatened:

> The prince [bishop] was sitting at dinner when this cry arose, so he quickly had everything taken from the table, hurriedly got into his coach, and was driven off to Forchheim. The provost and other cathedral officers, as well as the mayor and many other leading citizens, also made off hastily to Forchheim. (J.21–2)

This turned out to be a false alarm and a spectacle which was several times repeated, causing the populace to barrack the prince-bishop on another occasion:

> When he drove out the wicked people shouted: 'He's getting out again now and leaving us in the lurch; may this and that [the devil, the hangman] take you; may you fall and break every bone in your body', and they wished many other terrible things on him. (J.27)

While most writers complain about plundering by soldiers only a few recognise the inherent complicity of civilians in the system. The principal beneficiaries of the plundering were often not the soldiers but the citizens of neighbouring towns, who bought up the stolen goods for a fraction of their value from looters mainly interested in cash, either as a more portable form of booty or as the price of the next meal. Hellgemayr describes the Swedish occupation of Munich:

> At this time much robbing and plundering took place, particularly in the countryside, and all kinds of things were brought in here. There was no scarcity of buyers, and in the mornings when the Swedes brought in a number of loaded wagons everything was sold out in a few hours, so then they went back out to get more booty. ... Thus you could get a horse or a cow for ten kreuzer, or for up to a gulden or a taler you could buy a really magnificent beast, if you could get fodder for it and if they didn't steal it back from you again. (Hl.209)

He also notes that after the Swedish withdrawal many of the purchasers were quick to turn a profit: 'Many of those here who had bought horses, cows or other things from the Swedes, for example a horse or a cow for 10, 20 or 30 kreuzer, afterwards sold them again for as many gulden, which was a great shame' (Hl.210). Wagner reports a similar trade in Augsburg:

> Even though bringing stolen goods into the city to sell was strictly forbidden many times, it could nevertheless not be prevented because the colonels and senior officers had an interest in it, and indeed those from

here who helped introduce the prohibition bought such loot themselves. Thus it came about that a horse could be bought for a gulden and a cow for 30 kreuzer or a kopfstück, while tin, copper, linen and all kinds of movable goods were likewise given away for a song. It was pitiable to see whole herds of cattle, big and small, large numbers of horses, numerous wagons loaded with copper, tin, bedding, clothes, linen and all kinds of other things which had been plundered from the countryside or other towns offered for sale on every street and square in the city, where they were sold for miserable little sums of money. And this went on for weeks on end. (Wa.31)

Ironically soldiers themselves were sometimes the victims, and Walther indicates the eventual fate of many. After the defeat of Goetz's Bavarian army at Wittenweier in 1638 the dead were buried and looted by peasants, who 'found so much stuff that many did well out of it. For weeks afterwards people were bringing all sorts of weapons and other plunder here to sell, which became popularly known as Goetz's housewares' (Wl.34). When the losers were soldiers or strangers the usual victim class had no compunction about gaining a little benefit, as at Albertshausen when 'on the 24th of June the cavalry who were quartered here sold hat strings, gold braid and other things cheaply, which they had taken from Nördlingen merchants on the Hetzfeld bridge' (Ge.31). On the other hand Thiele, from Beelitz, near Berlin, complains that plunderers sold booty taken from his town in neighbouring Treuenbrietzen, commenting sarcastically that 'when they were asked afterwards if they were prepared to give them up again they were all holy folk in the town of Brietzen, and they denied everything. But my wife recognised her own bonnet and took it from a Brietzen woman' (Th.15). Some writers report more direct complicity. Thus when Dressel's monastery was raided by Weimar troops the humbler servants helped the plunderers: 'Certain specific items such as silver jewellery ... were disclosed by the monastery's vassals, namely the son of Thomas the gardener and the lake overseer's boy, who was brought up and has fed for years off monastery alms, and various other scoundrels' (Dr.27. 379). The pastor Renner angrily claims that one of his parishioners gave details of his alleged wealth to Imperialist troops, as a result of which he was captured and held to ransom. He adds a venomous note to the record of the funeral of the wife of the man, Caspar Nagel, 'the slanderer who so shamefully informed on me to the Imperialists, making out that I had 6000 Reichstaler deposited on interest in Nuremberg, 300 bushels of grain stored in the same city, and that I ate off silver dishes. As a result I was held to ransom for 400 Reichstaler' (Re.30).

A few anecdotes contribute something of the feel of the times. Celebrations normally taken for granted carried a risk, as in Feilinger's report of the experience of a wedding group: 'While this groom was having his bride escorted from Haybach, on the way back they encountered some cavalry, who robbed the festive procession of their money and clothes, as well as taking three horses out of their harness' (Fe. 241). Spiegel likewise mentions a party raided by soldiers: 'At Gremsdorf they came across the guests at a wedding breakfast, who all ran away, whereupon the cavalrymen ate the lot' (Sp.66). Gerlach laconically indicates that a christening fared no better: 'Croats in Albertshausen for winter quarters. Behaved badly. Broke into a christening; ate, drank, and desecrated everything' (Ge.30). Zader reports how Imperialist troops treated Naumburg's womenfolk in 1633: 'Their soldiers took more than 140 servant girls as wives, but when they had gone a few leagues from here they stripped the whores and chased them away' (Za.28–9). More poignantly, Spiegel adds a later marginal note to a register entry of a wedding: 'They parted from each other, he to the war and she off somewhere else, and since dead' (Sp.32). Gerlach tells a sad story of the misdeeds and misfortunes arising from an illicit affair between people whose lives had been disrupted by war; 'She had a husband, who was at the war; he had no wife':

On the 16th of May soldiers searched the cellars of Fuchstadt for buried money, but they found a buried child which had been interred by Salveter and his maid the previous Christmas. He was a customs official and councillor. On Friday the 19th of May he was taken from Eibelstadt and she from Winterhausen to Ochsenfurt, where they were imprisoned. ... On the Monday after Repentance Day they were both beheaded at Ochsenfurt. (Ge.24)

7
Counting the Cost

Money is a recurrent theme in accounts of the war. Some of the military men record the value of their plunder and the civilians often put a price on their losses, whether it be the value of items taken by soldiers or the amount of cash they were obliged to hand over, the sums levied as contributions or their expenses for troops billeted on them. In many cases the figures are quite precise, and for some of the writers the opportunity to quote a cash value appears to be a way of authenticating the account, a hard number which can be seized almost with relief, while for others money seems central to their perception of the burdens of war. The figures they give are complicated by the varied units of money and abbreviations they use, and cannot readily be converted into modern equivalents, but the significance the authors themselves attached to them is clear.

A number of the diarists kept careful financial records, an example being the baker Strampfer, who concludes his account with the final reckoning that '*summa*, all my contributions to the war from *anno* 1634 until 1650 cost me 2895 rx. 8$^1/_2$ k.' (S.36). Earlier he describes his record-keeping and calculations:

> When I made an estimate of the costs after the departure of these troops I found that to my certain knowledge I had given the soldiers 417 Reichstaler in cash alone. I am also sure that the food and drink they had cost as much again, as I had to feed 18 people for several weeks, real soldier riff-raff. Such expenses could mount up to 1000 rx. (S.33)

Strampfer adds pious thanks that things were not worse: 'Although I was stretched to the limit by this unbearable and all too heavy garrisoning... with God's help I have lived to see the end of it. May God mercifully protect us further from the like' (S.33).

The pastor Freund also kept a record of his losses in raids. On the first occasion, in September 1631, he notes: 'In this plundering I suffered losses in money, silverware, linen and household goods of 97 R. 15 g. at the lowest reckoning, including my cassock, ruff and hood, which were stolen out of the church' (Fr.33). In October and November 1632 he calculated his costs 'in cattle, household goods, beer, bread and oats as at least 147 R. 3 g.', while he assessed the two raids in 1633 'at 131 R. in cash, plus two horses' (Fr.34, 35). For 1634 he is less explicit, noting one raid in October 'in which I lost all of the few cattle and little provisions I had', and another in which he was 'plundered down to the ground by the enemy' (Fr.36–7, 37). He is more specific about the effects of a fire started by looters in 1637: 'Besides my parsonage, both my barns and all the remaining supplies I had on hand were destroyed, including 42 bushels of fallow-corn, other grain and a supply of wheat in storerooms, as well as more than 24 bushels of winter barley on my [fields at] New Gate Lane. My best featherbeds were also burned in the church' (Fr.41). Underlying these statements were detailed calculations; the manuscript includes an itemised account of Freund's losses from raids and the costs of billeting he had to bear during 1631 to 1634, items such as:

> Taken from my sons: one hat; one old coat; a dress coat made of London cloth; one new pair of trousers; all estimated at the least at … 8R.
> A woman's good bonnet … 2 R.
> After the holidays, as the Swedish artillery from Zwickau passed through here: provisions for two gun-captains with three horses and six people for one night; reckoned at … 2 R. 6 g. (Fr.69, 69, 71)

Freund summarises his costs for the four years from 1631 to 1634 at 700 Reichstaler, and in the three years from 1634 onwards at 'well over 4000 R.' (Fr.41). Implicit in this is that he (and many others, to judge from similar indications in their texts) was able to hide a great deal from the raiders on each occasion, undermining earlier claims of being plundered down to the ground. These no doubt reflect his own perception at the time that he had been completely stripped of his possessions, rather than being deliberately misleading or exaggeration for effect. Thus on 15 February 1637 he asserts that the village was completely cleaned out by the Imperialists 'and not so much as a bit of bread was left us, still less any butter, cheese or other food, nor any livestock, large or small, clothes or other goods … . Anything of use or that was worth anything was seized.' Nevertheless he notes that in a further raid on 6 May 'everything that we had got together again had to go'. Even then the villagers still had cash or the means to obtain it, as later in the same month he records the amounts they paid for a military guard (Fr.40).

Many of the writers had experiences of being robbed and they often give considerable detail of what was taken, sometimes with valuations. Lang reports that his wife was held up on a journey from Ulm to Biberach: 'On the way, by Achstetten or Laupheim, she encountered several horsemen, and the rings on her fingers, her belt, cutlery and two ducats were taken from her, and his horse, pistol and a coat of my wife's from the secretary, all of which is worth 80 Reichstaler' (La.26–7). Büttner was 'caught and robbed by an Imperialist patrol and lost 12 fl. in cash, a new hat and a knife and fork inlaid with silver' (Bt.144). Sautter describes how after two soldiers had taken his money a third searched him and 'found a cutlery set on me, knife, fork and spoon, which might have been worth 7 or 8 R., my rosary and my gloves, and he took them all. Finally he ripped my jacket off me, cut off the neckband, which was also worth at least 8 R., and took it with him' (Sa.695). In the same vein Dobel records that Swedish riders 'took a pair of boots and two shirts from me' (Do.113). Renner was caught by four Croats, 'to whom I had to give a pair of knitted stockings, two loaves of white bread, my purse along with my seal, my children's coral necklaces and 12 fl. in cash, as I wanted to save my life'. He adds that it could have been worse: 'At that time many pastors from the Margravate were shot or cut down, so I thank my God for the preservation of my life' (Re.21).

Salva guardia, paying for the stationing of some soldiers to prevent looting by others, was a well-established form of exploitation. Freund notes the sums which were squeezed out of his villagers: 'On the 10th of May 1 Thl. from each house, on the 13th of May 1 R. again, on the 19th of May 12 g., on the 27th of May another 2 g., and eventually on the 30th of May 4 g. from every house, just as before.' The soldiers extorted so much in contributions and upkeep that 'as the outcome showed, these sentries were more concerned about other things than about our protection' (Fr.40). Schleyss also recorded what it cost him: 'For exemption of the parsonage [from billeting] and for a military guard to prevent danger to myself and my family I had to give the lieutenant six beautiful shirts made of pure cambric, which had cost over six Reichstaler.' He adds doubtfully: 'Whether we will actually get the military protection I don't yet know' (Sc.1. 83). Wendell's village had to pay Spanish troops in 1647: 'We have to give two cavalrymen two Reichstaler every week so that they stay here by us as protection; otherwise they wouldn't leave Winterburg' (We.38). Contacts and wealth helped, as the ex-officer Ackermann found when Swedish and French troops marched through his village in 1641: 'The whole of Croppenstedt was plundered and nothing except the church and my farm was spared, as I had begged the general for a *salva guardia* until the army had gone. He left me his steward and four mounted soldiers to protect my house. I gave a rose noble to the former and also something to the riders' (A.47). However even the best connected could not always buy exemption, and Ackermann suffered at the hands of the Imperialists in 1644: 'On the 25th of July we were completely plundered out by the Gallas foragers and I was stabbed through the left arm. I stayed almost alone and guarded the fire station, town hall and brewhouse, along with the church, as well as I could. ... This time I too suffered great losses' (A.53–4).

Protection money was also levied on a larger scale as the price for sparing a town or city greater damage, or for not pillaging or burning it after capture as allowed by an ancient law of war (*Brandschatzung*). Götzenius reports that

Colonel Deveroux – one of Wallenstein's murderers – was billeted in Friedberg in 1639, and 'on his departure he demanded 40 000 gulden, received 2000 Reichstaler, and took away all the cattle' (Gö.148–9). Gustavus Adolphus imposed a 300 000 taler *Brandschatzung* on Munich in 1632, for which the civic authorities collected in all the available cash and precious metal, Hellgemayr commenting bitterly that 'the lower orders and the poor were required to give better than the rich' (Hl.208).

Many individuals were held to ransom, yet another device for extracting money from the population, with clerics particularly but by no means exclusively at risk. In Hueber's case the whole complement of his cloister was involved:

> During the Swedish siege all of us from the monastery were in the castle except the Reverend Father and two priests, who stayed in Ingolstadt. After the castle was taken we had to give a Swedish general, Major General Rüthwein, a ransom of 400 Reichstaler for our release, and we had to leave behind all that had been taken into the castle. The monastery, as we well recall, had been totally despoiled in the 14 days. (Hu.20)

Sautter, having first been robbed in his church while celebrating Mass, was forced to ride off with the patrol of soldiers, until he finally agreed to the corporal's demand for a 60 taler ransom and arranged for some of his tenant farmers to bring the money: 'There on the horses I counted the cash out into his hat.' The corporal was satisfied and rode off, keeping his word by leaving Sautter three horses and a small escort home. The escort promptly stole the horses: '"Don't you hear, you ranting thief, dismount! You promise a great deal but you don't deliver." … So we parted from one another, they towards Rottenacker, and I, badly beaten, tired and weary, *per pedes* home' (Sa.698, 699). In the same year the pastor Renner was abducted by Imperialist troops, who descended on his village:

> They took away all the cattle, plundered the village, and dragged me, a critically ill man, out of bed, giving me such blows that I was running with blood, and then took me with them to Höchstadt. There they put me and my son Hans Jorg into a secure prison for six weeks, until eventually I gave them 400 Reichstaler as a ransom and I was set free again. (Re.29)

He could only raise part of the money immediately, so that his son 'had to sit there in my place for two more weeks … until I sent on the remaining 130 Reichstaler' (Re.30).

The lawyer Johann Georg Maul, a navigation and tax official for the elector of Brandenburg in Naumburg, makes the cost of war the main theme of his account, obsessively cataloguing the impositions and expropriations which brought about his financial decline from considerable wealth to near penury. Although an extreme case he illustrates both the kind of things which happened to many people and the way in which they may have perceived the experience. His summary of expenses arising from the first of many billetings is typical:

> This was a certain Sergeant von Beulewitz from the Altenburg cuirassier regiment, with three privates, a boy and five horses. He himself, together with his guests, ate his way through 17 taler 12 groschen in 11 weeks, as the sergeant received 1¹/₂ taler a week for his food, plus 38 taler for the three privates and the boy, at 3¹/₂ taler a week. There was also 115 taler 12 groschen for 22 barrels of beer, which the aforementioned boozed away with his guests every night, when they became so rowdy that a prince lodging in Hennig Kamm's house had several times to ask for quiet. I had at that time to give 15 taler 18 groschen to the commissariat. 10 taler for a horse which the major took from me as a mount for his fool, who was called Pointynose. 15 taler for 5 kegs of wine, 41 taler 6 Gr. for 55 bushels of oats at 18 Gr., 9 taler 12 Gr. for 12 bushels of store oats, 13 taler paid to the commissariat, 5 taler for hay and straw for the guests, of whom he always had a great number but never counted the cost of the meals. 280 taler 12 groschen for the first billeting. (Ml.5–6)

As well as having to provide billets, Maul too was robbed several times. He records '3 taler 12 Gr. for a pair of boots for a Corporal Klipsen, who was going to shoot me' (Ml.12). He had to give five taler to another corporal 'when he held up my wife and me with drawn sword at twelve o'clock one night in my parlour, where I was lying sick at the time, wanting to have the same amount from us as we had given the Swedes'. Another time 'soldiers opened a big chest during the night and stole 23 items of household linen worth 15 Gr. each from my wife, who had inherited them from her mother, … not to mention stripping off two bedcovers and taking them, which I can also quite readily value at 16 taler 18 Gr.' (Ml.8, 9). A common trick of the time to hide valuables proved ineffectual: 'Moreover I had to cut out and hand over a gold chain which I had given to my wife and which she had sewn into her dress.' She also lost two heavy gold bracelets, and Maul complains that 'I had to look on while my wife herself fastened her bracelets around a cavalry captain's wrists, and I did not dare to look angry about it' (Ml.8, 7).

Maul records billetings, sometimes several, in virtually every year from 1631 to 1645, over which period his fortune was gradually eroded. By 1638 he was forced to sell things to raise ready cash: 'Because of this appalling and tyrannical enforcement [of contributions] I have repeatedly had to sell things to Joachim Heideck, the goldsmith: 67 half-ounces of silver, from my hunting knife which my dear father-in-law gave me, a sword inlaid with silver and a silver belt, all for 8 Gr. a half-ounce.' Later in the same year he notes: 'I have had to sell the two gilded goblets which I received from the elector's hands' (Ml.10). Clearly some of the citizens were not so hard hit, in that the goldsmiths could still buy, no doubt profitably. Maul confirms this the following year, when he had to sell a heavy gold chain of his wife's, this time to Christoph Voigt: the chain weighed 35 units, for which Maul got one taler per unit, 'and although it was accepted at the Town Hall at $1\frac{1}{2}$ taler he still gave me nothing more for it, so that he made and I lost 17 taler 12 Gr. in this way' (Ml.11).

Maul's declining wealth is reflected in the growing difficulty the military had in extorting contributions from him. In 1635 a cavalry captain demanded 300 taler, 'failing which he was going to take me with him as a prisoner'. As Maul did not pay 'he had me guarded for two long days by ten troopers, who waited in my study, cursing and blaspheming amid a thick cloud of tobacco smoke, until I imploringly promised that because of my lack of cash I would pay 200 taler in jewellery' (Ml.7). In 1638 he fell behind with a weekly contribution of 7 taler, in consequence of which 'I and my family were several times attacked without warning, and I was so much tormented and tortured, especially during the holy festival time, that it would have moved a stone in the ground to pity'. By 1640 it was, he says, evident even to the soldiers that he had little left to give: 'On the 30th three troopers sent to enforce payment stayed the night at my house and I had to give them 3 taler 15 Gr. worth of wine and beer, but since they saw for themselves that I had no money they agreed to leave, taking a handkerchief each which my wife gave them, worth a taler, and some bread' (Ml.9, 13).

Maul complains bitterly about the town administration and its part in arranging billeting and contributions, particularly as he felt that those he regarded as the rich were better treated than himself:

> Now may God forgive the conscienceless tax-gatherers; how will they fare on the Day of Judgement! These unjust and unscrupulous collectors made the assessments only on the basis of favouritism and their own inclinations, while those rich people who should have been keeping an eye on them said absolutely nothing on account of their own interests. Hence there was neither love nor pity to be had from them towards me and my wife, so that they tortured the blood from our hearts and the marrow from our bones with enforcers, and they took their earthly possessions away from our poor children. (Ml.11)

Andreas Schuster, the town clerk from Strausberg, near Berlin, gives a wider perspective on the burdens borne by the community as a whole, the outlook of the municipal official showing through in his repeated and often precise references to the cost of contributions. In August 1627 a large Imperialist army passed by and officers were billeted in the town overnight: 'In accordance with the specified scale a senior official had to give them 35 thl. for wine, 12 thl. to the quartermaster, 8 thl. to the secretary, 10 thl. 18 gr. for confectionery and spices and 6 thl. 12 gr. to the table-dresser and the laundress.' In the earlier phase of the war billeting by friendly forces was – in theory – paid for, and the citizens submitted claims for their costs to the military, particularly during longer periods such as winter-quartering. At the end of the nineteenth century many such claims, including some of Schuster's own, were still to be found in the town archives. 'When it came to settlement at the end of each month, however, and each citizen submitted his bills, in some cases nothing and in others barely a third was allowed them, so that it was all water down the drain even though it had cost many people a great deal' (Sh.22, 27). Despite such experiences the municipality continued to reckon precise expenses and to seek guarantees for their payment, not very successfully, as Schuster sadly observes in November 1628, when a body of Imperialist troops under Arnim were billeted: 'On the orders of the said Bernd von Arnim the citizens submitted their claim for 109 thl. to the officers, which this von Arnim signed, promising in writing to pay the 109 thl., but until now nothing has come of it.' Worse still, the troops had consumed a great deal of beer with neither payment nor security: '94 barrels of beer went to the commissary but the citizens were left unpaid – in money, at 4 thl. per barrel – 376 thl.' (Sh.32–3).

Although Schuster reports a number of relatively minor cases of robbery and intimidation the main burden on the town was the legalised extortion of contributions, and particularly feeding or billeting passing troops. 500 of Mansfeld's cavalry descended in July 1626, although having had warning 'the people hurried to bury or hide their belongings and household goods in whatever place each of them knew'. The troops demanded food, drink and fodder 'with violent words and blows', but then rode on, leaving Schuster to comment that 'they did not inflict much damage on this town, God be praised, other than what they were able to wolf and swill down' (Sh.13, 14). In November of the same year another 450 arrived, 'so that the citizens were eaten out of house and home, for many had six, eight, ten or more to feed'. The latter were friendly troops, although, like other writers, Schuster notes that 'the enemy could scarcely have been nastier or done worse' (Sh.20, 19). The following year saw repeated visitations by hungry troops, and in November a company took up winter quarters in the town. 'Every soldier ... had to be supplied daily with two pounds of bread, two pounds of meat, and two quarts of beer for his upkeep' (Sh.26–7). Military commissary arrangements should have met this need, but predictably these failed and 'it fell upon the unfortunate citizenry, who had to give over what they had, under great duress and compulsion. Nor did the soldiers bother about the regulations as to what and how much they should be given each day, but instead they scoffed and quaffed as much as they could get.' Schuster reports the effect of these burdens on the citizens and the town:

> The consequence of this was that many of the citizens ran away, left their things standing and just went. Many fell ill and died from their great

sufferings and grief, until eventually no more than 96 out of 222 citizens [heads of households] remained in their homes. (Sh.27)

The town took what steps it could to defend itself. Unlike the neighbouring villages it had the benefit of walls, and Schuster describes how they successfully excluded the main body of Mansfeld's passing army in 1626:

> Finally the farmers also brought their livestock and belongings into the town. Then the citizens pulled down the bridge in front of the Müncheberg Gate, the Wrietzen Gate was fixed firmly closed, and a ditch was dug in front of it. Wagons and very large pieces of timber were set up inside the Wrietzen Gate to bar it, as was also done at the front gate. At night-time the citizenry, who had to be on watch and in readiness with their guns and muskets day and night, were summoned to sentry duty by a drum, ladders having been placed so that they could see out over the walls. At the Landberg Gate a scaffolding with a wooden platform had been set up and equipped with a pile of stones to be used as weapons in case of need, and this was also provided with protection and a guard. ... Everybody in the city had to have a 14-day holiday on account of Mansfeld's army, and as no-one did any work because of the alarm the rye harvest was held up. (Sh.15, 16)

The walls could be used against friend as well as foe, and some months afterwards the town refused to admit a Brandenburg lieutenant and his men, sent to collect a contribution payment of 800 taler. A fortnight later a stronger force under a more resourceful officer arrived. After hiding his men in a wood and loading their muskets on to a wagon,

> the lieutenant and two or three men drove up, pretending to be traders wanting to travel to Frankfurt. Once they were into the gateway and the gate could not be barred in front of the wagon and horses he gave a signal with a musket to those stationed behind, who immediately came running as fast as they could into the town. (Sh.18)

The lieutenant said bluntly that if the townsfolk did not pay up his orders were to treat them as rebellious, even hostile. They had previously claimed that it was impossible 'to collect together such a high sum of money so quickly, as the citizenry had already been sucked dry and there was nothing but poverty here'; now they gathered in 533 taler in four days so that 'this ruffianly mob wouldn't hang around our necks for long' (Sh.17–18, 18).

Sometimes the burdens were self-imposed but none the less onerous. Strasbourg successfully avoided direct military involvement in the war, but at a price, that of maintaining its own militia and undertaking an ambitious and almost continuous programme of improvements to its fortifications.

Walther records that taxes were repeatedly levied in the city to that end, and 'over and above this the citizenry were urged and exhorted to pay a voluntary supplementary tax for the purchase of all kinds of materials for the intended new fortification works' (Wl.29). When the war was over Walther, an enthusiast for the Protestant cause, discovered that there was also a price to be paid 'to the crown of Sweden for the faithful service which they had performed for the benefit of the evangelical community, ... namely five million Reichstaler'. Strasbourg's share of this 'frighteningly large sum' was 90 000 gulden, 'which had to be divided out in proportion to each person's assets'.

> For a lot of people this aroused misery almost as great as the joy, in that many an honest man did not have as much of his property in cash as he was required at once to pay. Moreover it was rather inequitably divided, an ordinary craftsman with heavy household costs and many children being assessed at 50 gulden, to be paid straight away. The servants, farmhands and maids also had to contribute, and each had to pay a gulden or two according to their respective wages, or their masters had to pay it for them. For that reason there was nothing but wailing and lamentation to be heard in many quarters, and for us this peace was expensively over-salted. (Wl.41)

Of course there were those who profited from the war. Lang describes one of his military supply contracts:

> I had to get hold of everything necessary for the upkeep of the soldiers at my own risk, and if the price of food went up or down I lost or gained from it. ... Our Lord God sent good fortune, in that all grain, meat and wine became cheaper and, thank God, readily available, so I came out well, eternal praise be to the All Highest. I must admit, though, that of all the commissions I never did better than from the provisioning of the troops while I had 100 fl. daily from each company. And because everything for the contract was to be had inexpensively I made an honest profit, as ten companies or a regiment often cost no more than 500 taler, against which I received 1000 fl. (La.18)

Even so he had his problems, and getting paid was not always so easy. He describes how pursuit of a long-standing claim for supplies to the Imperialist armies took him first to Vienna and then to Bratislava in 1637. Eventually he received confirmation of the debt and a warrant for payment of '2662 fl. 24 kr.' after part of his claim had been struck out, although 'the remaining items were all approved as I could produce proper receipts for everything' (La.33). Nevertheless it was not until July 1638 that Lang was able to present his warrant to the paymaster-general in Augsburg: 'I was given the answer that the warrant was valid but that there was no money available.' Finally he was offered a settlement of 675 florins in cash, plus 14 horses and three vehicles:

> So I took it, in God's name, and gave him a full receipt. However I could not get more than 1038 fl. in cash for the horses, and I estimate the wagon, carriage and coach at 142 fl., so that in total I received 1900 fl. The unpaid balance is 762 fl. 24 kr., not counting my subsistence in Vienna and Augsburg, which cost a pretty penny. (La.35)

Some of the soldiers, usually the more senior, also did well, although Monro remarks on 'having seene many make bootie, who had never the happinesse to enjoy it long', and others experienced the changing fortunes of war (Mo.I. 32). Hagendorf, who was sometimes flush and sometimes near destitute, was twice captured, losing all that he had acquired, and he was also twice robbed. The first time was shortly before the battle of Nördlingen, when his baggage was taken from his boy: 'It was stolen during the night when we wanted to attack, as we all had to stand by in readiness, with my leave permit and everything I had. So all my booty was gone again' (Ha.59). On the second occasion he was set upon by locals:

> Here I got a bit drunk in the evening, and in the morning I was lagging a stone's throw behind the regiment because of a headache. Three peasants who were hiding in the hedge boldly struck out at me, and they took my coat, knapsack and the lot. All of a sudden they jumped off me, through God's protection, just as though someone was chasing them, although there wasn't a single man there in the rear. Thus I got back to the regiment, beaten and without coat or pack, but they only laughed at me. (Ha.103)

Fritsch, in this case not as prudent as fellow officers who had sent their booty to safety before going on campaign, lost much of his possessions at the battle of Wittenweier in 1638, but he was more fortunate than Hagendorf or Poyntz, in that when he was captured at Wolfenbüttel in 1641 he was not only promptly exchanged but also handsomely rewarded: 'On the fifth day I was set free through Field Marshall General Count Wahl, and then I had an audience with His Highness the Duke, who gave me 200 ducats, and 300 fl. was also given to me from our treasury' (F.182). Poyntz too twice lost everything when he was captured, as well as having to abandon much of what he had in the hasty night-time withdrawal after Lützen:

> The march was so suddaine, that every one that had baggage horse and Wagons were glad to leave his baggage behind hym, for our horses were all strayd and run away beeing played upon continually by the Swevish

Canon though they stood a Mile of. ... I lost most of my wealth, and could bring no more away then I and my 3 weary Officers could carry. (Po.126)

Poyntz also gained two rich wives in Germany, the first of whom died in childbed after less than two years of marriage. The second fared even worse, tragically demonstrating that the cost of war in personal terms could fall upon civilian and soldier families alike:

Having bene almost a whole yeare in Warres, I set up my rest of going home, and mee thought a private life after these wandring wearisome marches did relish sweetly in my thoughts and so after a long march I came nere home, where I heare the true tryall of fortunes mutability, which was that my Wife was killed & my child, my house burned and my goods all pillaged: My Tenants and Neighbours all served in the same sauce, the whole Village beeing burned; nether horse, Cowe, sheep nor Corne left to feed a Mouse. ... This was donne by a party of french that came out of Italy going homewards. (Po.127–8)

8
Three Nuns' Accounts

Many writers report experiences during the Thirty Years War which were in principle similar, although the details differed. Previous chapters have looked at the war through a synthesis of these common factors, but a balanced view also requires closer examination of some specific cases. The accounts of Ernst, Wolff, Ackermann, Prinz, Maul and Schuster have already been reviewed, and the next two chapters consider in more detail the experiences of three nuns and their convents, and the personal histories of two priests. This also provides the opportunity to look not only at *what* they wrote, but also at *how* and *why* they wrote, topics which will be developed further through consideration of individual texts in Chapters 10 to 13.

Few of the available personal accounts of the Thirty Years War were written by women, and of the five referred to in this book all but one were written by nuns, who were more likely to be literate than most women of the time, while the chances of survival of their manuscripts in convent archives were also much greater than for the private papers of a laywoman.

Maria Magdalena Haidenbucher, abbess of the convent of Frauenwörth, kept a diary throughout her period of office, which covered the full 30 years of the war, but this is mainly concerned with the convent. Admissions and deaths form the largest category of items noted, together with visitations, tax payments, building works, exceptional weather and the like. There is relatively little specifically about the war as the convent largely escaped its effects, other than taxation, because of its location on an island in the far south-east of Germany. Haidenbucher's approach is businesslike and she makes entries only when there is something of significance to record, so that the coverage of some years comprises only a few paragraphs. Nevertheless she does provide a view of the war, which several times threatened the area, while her convent was often a refuge for nuns displaced from their own cloisters by danger from the armies.

Clara Staiger was an Augustinian nun at Mariastein, just outside the Bavarian city of Eichstätt. She entered the convent at the age of 11, formally becoming a novice a few months before her sixteenth birthday, and she was elected prioress in June 1632, aged 43, shortly after the Swedish invasion had brought the war to Bavaria. Upon taking office she started to write a 'record and description of when I, Sister Clara Staiger, was born and entered the convent, and the principal things which happened and took place each year' (St.43). This begins with a summary of her earlier life and brief mention of a few events of the 1620s, followed by a fuller account of the last few months before her predecessor's death, but she then maintained a substantially contemporaneous diary for most of the rest of her life. This timing means that it effectively became an account of the war almost from the outset, and for the early years it is very full, with entries sometimes daily and rarely with gaps of more than a week. Later her coverage becomes sparser, with periods missing in the 1640s, probably due to ill health, and the diary ends in the autumn of 1651, some five years before her death. Almost half of her text relates to the three-year period from mid-1632 to mid-1635, and this is the most comprehensive and interesting section, both personally in that it covers her earlier years of office, and with reference to the war during its first and most significant phase in the region.

Maria Anna Junius wrote an account of the war as it affected Bamberg and its surroundings between 1632 and 1634. She entered the convent in 1622 on the same day that her sister was married, and the two events were celebrated jointly, causing the guests to remark that 'such a thing had never happened to them in their lives before, to be invited by one father on one day to the weddings of two of his daughters, the one a heavenly bride and the other a worldly one'. 11 years later, in April 1633, she started to write her account, 'a short record of what has transpired and taken place since the year of 1622, when I, Sister Maria Anna Junius, entered the Convent of the Holy Sepulchre, which I have set down as briefly as possible' (J.10, 7). She is specific about her intention to provide a description of the sufferings of the convent during the war for the information and benefit of future generations of nuns, setting this out in her introduction, which is quoted in Chapter 15.

Junius was the daughter of a leading citizen of Bamberg, a member of the council for 20 years and from time to time mayor before he was accused of witchcraft and executed in 1628. She opens her account with a short summary of the period from 1622 to 1633, in which she refers guardedly to witchcraft, linking it to the inflation and coinage debasement of the early 1620s, 'for I think none other than that the Evil One scattered the money abroad at that time so that many people would get caught up in this accursed witchcraft, as one later saw' (J.8). She gives a brief account of witchhunting in Bamberg from 1627 onwards, noting that 'several hundred people were tried and burned, among them many attractive and well-to-do young men and women'. She comments that 'whether it was all rightly done is known to God alone', adding that 'these burnings continued until the year of 1631' (J.13). Unlike Haidenbucher and Staiger, Junius did not maintain her record as an ongoing contemporaneous diary but brought it to a clear conclusion in September 1634, following the withdrawal of the Swedes from Bamberg after their defeat at Nördlingen. Her concluding prayer suggests that she saw this as the end of the war, at least locally: 'To God Almighty be the honour, praise and thanks, as he has again helped us to surmount a storm. May he grant and confer his heavenly peace upon us once more, but his supreme will, and not mine, be done in all things' (J.223). There was indeed relative peace in the area for a time afterwards, but when war returned Junius did not, so far as we know, continue her recording.

Haidenbucher and Staiger give much longer views, encompassing the whole of the war from the first incursion of the Swedes into Bavaria until 1648, whereas Junius confines herself to three eventful years, but all of them – Junius to a lesser extent – shift back and forth between the war and the everyday, reflecting the ebb and flow of the conflict and its impact on individuals and areas. The three accounts are further differentiated by variations both in actual experience and in intention in writing. The war is less central to Haidenbucher's text because her convent largely escaped its direct effects, whereas Junius was not so fortunate and consciously set out to describe the war as it affected her own cloister. Conversely Staiger's text is essentially a personal and convent diary, prompted by her election as prioress rather than by the approach of war, which is a dominant theme in her writing only because it was for much of the time the dominant factor in the convent's life.

Staiger's style is quite plain, although she does introduce occasional flashes of colour or sharp comment which illuminate both the subject matter and her own personality. She was evidently a competent writer, but unlike most of the male clerical authors she employs very few Latin phrases, even though she notes that one of the conditions made in accepting a new novice in 1635 was 'that in the meantime she … should learn Latin and singing' (St.165). Her entries are quite full and indeed she sometimes becomes long-winded in recording details of conversations. She also includes many lists: of damage to the convent in 1633, of alms and gifts of food received by the nuns during a flight to Ingolstadt in the same year, or of gifts and gratuities she in her turn distributed, for example after the nuns took refuge in another convent – 'List of what I paid out and gave to people when leaving St Walburg's' – ranging from 'two double ducats to Her Grace', to '30 kreuzer for the gatekeeper' and 'six kreuzer to the head maid' (St.110–11). These indicate that Staiger's text, although in essence a private diary, still had a semi-public function as part of the records of the convent.

Although Junius writes at length – and she too tends to be long-winded in recounting many episodes in considerable detail – her style is simple, with little colour or imagery other than that evidently derived and repeated from her sources. She is usually precise with dates for her entries, suggesting that for the earlier retrospective part of her account she was able to refer to diary or calendar notes, while the later section was clearly written contemporaneously, a point confirmed by such notes as 'our vineyard overseer said today' (J.138). There is a distinct difference between these sections, the former being a more focused account of what actually happened, selected and ordered with the benefit of hindsight, whereas the latter is diaristic, anecdotal and concerned with the rumours, fears and conditions of the day. Although a shift of emphasis rather than a sharp distinction, the earlier part is more centred on the war as it affected Bamberg and the nuns themselves, events elsewhere usually only being reported if they represented an approaching threat to Bamberg, whereas later Junius ranges more widely in recording what she had heard. Likewise the first part tends to deal with events and say little of conditions, barely mentioning the experiences of the citizenry and peasants, whereas the latter section contains frequent descriptions of their tribulations as well as a few glimpses of surviving normality.

Staiger indicates various sources of news about wider events. Thus she mentions letters from Jesuits in Neuburg, reports brought back to the convent by farmers making deliveries further afield, and a report from a cousin who 'told me how it all went while the king and queen from Sweden were in Neuburg these last weeks'. She also mentions rumours, as of Lützen: 'The saying these last 14 days is that the Swedish king, along with many thousand others, has been killed in a battle near Leipzig.' Some of these rumours were clearly wrong, as was an account of the battle of Nördlingen: 'Duke Weinmayr [Bernard of Weimar] was shot there and it is said that he is certainly dead' (St.63, 73, 149). Staiger was evidently aware of such unreliability, commenting on reports that the Imperialists had taken Augsburg in September 1633: 'It would be good if it were true, but there have been such lies throughout this time of war that we can't believe it.' Nevertheless she unquestioningly repeats reports of cannibalism in March 1635: 'On Saturday the 31st a messenger came from Swabia, telling of such great hunger in that land that a woman had eaten five children, while another woman had dug up her dead husband and two others from their graves.' Her report of the murder of Wallenstein has many of the circumstantial details which appear in contemporary chronicles and pamphlets, suggesting that she had seen such accounts, although her final comment on the generalissimo and his associates is clearly her own: 'All of them received their just deserts' (St.100, 174, 129).

Junius also incorporates hearsay reports of events elsewhere into her account, and her recorded or implied sources indicate not only how news travelled over the convent wall but also how it often reached the more general public of the time. Thus she notes: 'I heard from the Swedes themselves'; 'a soldier's wife told us'; 'a sutler here said so himself' (J.200, 202, 203). Other sources include the lieutenant of the convent's military guard, a Scottish quartermaster, 'a *Bürgermeister* from Nuremberg' (literally the mayor but perhaps one of the councillors) and 'a young boy ... who had to carry a pack to Forchheim for the soldiers' (J.202, 195). Such sources probably contributed the black humour in the report that 'this was the biggest gun in Forchheim, and it was called the dancer because it had made the Swedes dance so much at that time', or the image she employs in noting that the battle of Lützen 'went on from early morning until nightfall, for night was the arbiter'. Some of her wider information was probably drawn from the contemporary press, either directly or second-hand, including her note of Gustavus Adolphus's narrow escape at Ingolstadt, which was widely reported and is mentioned by a number of other diarists: 'Then they immediately opened heavy fire on the king and his soldiers, and they shot the king's horse from under him' (J.116, 101, 72). A long report she gives of a speech Gustavus Adolphus made to his officers complaining about plundering is clearly copied from a pamphlet, and Wagner includes the same text almost word for word in his Augsburg chronicle.

In her account of incidents she observed personally Junius often employs a dramatic style and near-verbatim reported speech, as in her description of the convent receiving warning of a rumoured Swedish approach:

> Early on Monday the 7th of February, just as our service was over, some-one came running hard into our cloister, and as we looked out Mayor Keim came hurrying across the courtyard, all in a sweat. He told us that the enemy was nearby and would certainly be here with us that night, so what did we want to do? We answered that we wanted to stay in our convent and to live and die here. To that the mayor replied: 'In the name of God I entrust myself and the citizenry to your reverent prayers', and with these words he ran post haste across the courtyard and out again. (J.104)

Sometimes she seems to be carried away by the drama of the occasion. When the Swedes first took Bamberg the nuns waited anxiously in their convent:

> Just as we were in the greatest fear and terror a Jesuit came to us, saying: 'Good virgins, it is true, the enemy is here; stay in your convent; no harm will come to you but we [Jesuits] will be shown no mercy. ... I must make my escape quickly. Many hundred thousand good nights, dear virgins, I must be away, they are chasing after me. My name is Dominicus. Stay in your convent; stay in your convent; no harm will come to you but I must be off.' This pious man's comfort fortified us a little. (J.32)

Haidenbucher scarcely mentions the war before 1632, at which time her convent became a refuge for nuns forced out elsewhere by the approach of Swedish troops, many staying until October 1634 before returning home. She gives only limited, generalised and hearsay accounts of the war based on reports from these refugees and others, having no eyewitness experience of her own. Her comment in 1632 proved to be valid for the whole war: 'Never did a single Swedish soldier reach our beloved house of God, although we and all our dear Sisters suffered much anxiety and fear. To God be everlasting praise, honour and thanks' (Hd.61. 421). The other two convents were less fortunate, although their apprehensions proved worse than their experiences, and they often exhibited this same anxiety and fear, which is a recurrent theme in the accounts.

In December 1633 the war came close enough to cause great trepidation in Frauenwörth. Haidenbucher reports troops, supposedly allies, in winter quarters not far away:

> Many places have been plundered by the Spanish and Imperialist troops, and we were greatly afraid that something might also happen to our beloved house of God. We gathered together our sacred vessels, convent deeds and rent rolls, and sent them to Kopfstain for safe keeping until such time as our Good Lord sends peace in accordance with his heavenly will. (Hd.61. 428)

After Nördlingen the war rarely impinged on the convent or on Haidenbucher's diary until the last years. In 1646 she noted the renewed approach of enemy armies, ascribing the war to God's punishment: 'Because God the Almighty, according to his heavenly will and our deserts, laid a richly deserved punishment upon our dear fatherland, the enemy power marched in against the Christian church once more' (Hd.66. 503). Again the convent's direct experience was confined to taking in refugee nuns from elsewhere, as well as the 85-year-old Bavarian chancellor and his retinue. In June 1648 the danger came very close:

> We could hear the big guns from here, and everyone believed that the whole of Bavaria would be ruined. The prelates and members of all the cloisters fled – Herrenchiemsee, Seeon and Baumburg. We too were advised to flee to a safe place with our dear Sisters. God alone knows the dread and fear we experienced at that time. (Hd.66. 507)

Most of the nuns were evacuated for six to eight weeks but Haidenbucher and a few others stayed behind:

> With a small number of Sisters and women we ventured to stay on as long as we could, with the help of God; I, Maria Magdalena Haidenbucher, in my 71st year and the 41st of my rule. ... We did indeed stay, but never other than in the greatest fear. (Hd.66. 508)

Junius's convent had good cause for anxiety. Bamberg changed hands several times in the three years she records, usually without prolonged fighting, but there were constant reports of approaching hostile armies or rumours of imminent raids on the convent, although in the event it was never attacked in this period. Her description of the first advance of the Swedes is typical: 'When we heard of this, we felt indescribable anxiety and apprehension. We were ready to take flight at any minute and we had worldly clothes which had been brought from the city, but we didn't know where we should go.' Their situation was especially precarious as the convent lay just outside rather than within the walls, but it was not until six weeks later that the Swedes attacked the city in earnest; 'At this time we scarcely slept at night because of our great fear' (J.15, 24). When Bamberg fell the nuns expected the worst:

> People had told us … that they would not spare a single person, but would kill everyone and set fire to the city. *Ach*, what terror and fear of death we experienced at that time. … We were expecting death at any hour or moment, which truly we did not fear as much as something else. (J.33)

They took comfort in their religion: 'We surrendered ourselves to the will of God, relying completely on the help and compassion of our beloved bride-groom Jesus, and we stayed strong, courageous and constant in our cloister' (J.33).

Staiger describes her nuns' fears in even direr circumstances. As the Swedes approached Eichstätt in April 1633 they fled into the city: '*Ach*, God, what anguish, misery and need we felt; it was very hard to leave the convent' (St.80). After the Swedes arrived the city quickly surrendered but the nuns took refuge in the castle with the garrison, which held out during a two-week artillery battle. The nuns were understandably afraid: 'We prayed almost the whole day and night, and once at night, when it was said that the enemy was about to make an assault, we made our confessions in great terror. … We had to endure the well-deserved punishment of God in great fear of death' (St.82, 83). Their anxiety increased when an accord was made on terms which included provisions 'that nothing was to happen to the clergy, and that the garrison were to withdraw with all their equipment'. The nuns were not reassured: 'It is impossible to describe what anxiety and need this accord aroused in us, for every one was afraid for her life and honour' (St.83).

Both Junius and Staiger describe the fears when enemy soldiers entered their convents. When the Swedes first took Bamberg the nuns desperately sent a let-ter to their commander asking for protection. Junius relates what followed:

> It was already gone seven o'clock. Several Sisters were in the chancel, and when they looked out they saw a number of soldiers coming towards our convent. They thought it was the enemy, so they ran down as fast as they could, crying: '*Ach, ach*, dear Sisters, the enemy is coming and approach-ing our convent. *Ach*, let us go into the parlour together and beg for mercy when they arrive, or else die together, just as God wishes.' We were in such great misery, but then another Sister came, saying: 'Take comfort,

dear Sisters, the farm-hand who took our letter there is coming with the soldiers; they must be our military guard.' ... *Ach*, who was happier than us, for it was as though we had been dead and were alive again. (J.35–6)

In August 1633 soldiers broke into Staiger's convent but they proved to be more interested in food, drink and livestock than in looting, rape or murder:

At twelve o'clock at night Swedish soldiers broke into the farmyard through the upper gate, and with fierce threats and weapons in their hands they immediately demanded horses and cattle. Our seven dear Sisters who had ventured into the convent on account of worldly duties and much work – washing, baking, mowing and cutting in the garden – ran to the bells in great fear and rang the alarm, then up into the courtyard, where they hid themselves. They caught Sister Dorothea Lemm in the cloisters, and with their weapons drawn they demanded cattle, food and drink, but in response to her terrified answer, trembling and pleas they let her go without harming her. They went straight into the stables and took away four horses and nine cows. 30 cavalrymen from the court chased after them, but in vain, as they could not find or recover a single animal. (St.96–7)

The Swedish authorities made efforts to help, and after soldiers stole horses from labourers harvesting the convent fields a few weeks later a guard was sent, although Staiger comments pointedly on their thirst:

Five Swedish sentries were sent from the court to make sure that this time nothing else happened to the convent. They immediately drove the other soldiers out of the kitchen garden and protected our men, escorting them back and forth. We straight away bought them meat and beer – of which they drank 40 quarts by Sunday morning. (St.101)

This Swedish approach to maintaining order, irrespective of the religious difference although within the limits of the practicable, had been demonstrated earlier, when the castle at Eichstätt surrendered on accord with the nuns inside. In the event they came to no harm and they were given a guard in their lodgings on the personal order of Bernard of Weimar. Ten days later they returned to their convent, leaving the city with a military escort and with the support of Swedish officers' wives who had befriended them, although they had to face jeering soldiers as they went: 'Even among the guards there was drumming and whistling, and many scornful comments and much laughter came our way, but they were quickly and firmly stopped by our companions' (St.90).

The most remarkable feature of the experiences of the nuns in Junius's convent was the protection they received from successive Swedish commanders in Bamberg, who responded to their pleas on every occasion, providing them with a military guard on arrival and maintaining it until the last stages of withdrawal to protect the convent from stragglers and looters. Senior officers showed themselves friendly in other ways, visiting the convent, sometimes with their wives, first as sightseers but later as benefactors, some giving the nuns money and even a cow. During the first Swedish occupation the nuns were astonished: 'Colonels often visited us too ... and then they made conversation with us for long periods. They behaved so amicably, politely, modestly and innocently towards us that we couldn't wonder at it enough.' Bernard of Weimar himself came to the convent twice, Junius recording that 'he asked us if we would sing Compline, as he would like to hear our singing'. Initially the nuns were suspicious, 'for we thought all the time, *ach*, God, who knows whether your hearts really are as your mouths say' (J.44, 125, 45). Later they came to rely on help from these sources, and at the time of a later Swedish withdrawal from Bamberg Junius refers to one colonel, 'who has done much good to us', and to two others, 'who have done so much good to us and the whole city' (J.123, 131).

Apart from constant anxieties about possible attacks the nuns seem to have fared relatively well in a combat zone, keeping themselves and indeed many of the poor fed while the war swung backwards and forwards around them. Junius makes no mention of plundering or of contributions being demanded from the convent, and they even managed to fend off fortification works which would have impinged on their property. They may have been specially favoured, as she notes that both the Jesuits and the Carmelites were plundered, and at one stage she reports: 'At that time a watch was kept on all the monasteries. Wherever there was a door, there stood a sentry, so that no-one could go either in or out, also at another convent, but on us there was no watch whatever.' The Swedes made no attempt to interfere with their religious observances: 'They also allowed us to carry on holding our services as usual, as on many occasions the colonels who visited us sang Vespers and Compline with us.' In this period they never fled from the convent, instead firmly maintaining their wish to stay despite contrary advice, although 'the Swedes themselves were amazed that we, all women, stayed living here in such danger' (J.121, 119, 187). Junius sums up the nuns' experiences in her concluding passage:

> Although people spoke much evil of us I can bear witness before God that not the slightest thing happened to a single Sister from our convent contrary to the preservation of her virgin status. Although the Swedes came and went daily here they behaved at all times in a modest and respectful manner towards us. For if from time to time they approached like furious lions or bears, as soon as they had seen and talked to us they all became as meek and gentle as lambs. (J.222)

Staiger's convent found no such protectors and the nuns experienced hard times. Their convent too lay outside the walls but here it had to be evacuated when enemy forces threatened, obliging them to seek refuge in the city and to find lodgings wherever they could. Eichstätt also changed hands several times, and from December 1633 to September 1634 Staiger and many of her nuns moved to Ingolstadt, during which time their convent was burned. They returned to it after Nördlingen, although only a small part was usable, and further flights followed in the 1640s.

When soldiers were in the area the nuns shared the general experience; the convent farm was raided, horses were stolen, food and firewood were scarce and difficult to get. Prospects often looked bleak: 'There was still continual war and soldiers throughout the diocese, and we had little to comfort us that the coming spring would be better than the last.' In the summer of 1634 the nuns had to plead for bread in Ingolstadt: 'We begged, both in writing and by word of mouth, from His Princely Grace's chamberlain and other good friends, until we managed to get four large and two small loaves. May God reward them for it now and hereafter, and continue to preserve us' (St.76, 139). Although they survived Staiger reports a common experience of refugees, that their hosts were sometimes less than willing to help: 'We received much charity, ... God be praised, but more from the Neuburgers and outsiders than from the Ingolstadters, to whom strangers were of no consequence. They did not even try to appreciate our misery, let alone succeed.' After the Swedish withdrawal conditions eased for a time and food became more readily available. The respite was short-lived and on 30 March 1635 Staiger complains: 'We could get no more grain or money ... so that we had a miserable fast, as we had already exhausted our own grain' (St.142, 174).

It was a time of contrasts, as barely two months earlier Staiger was enjoying some festive dinners, such as one at the end of January:

> On Sunday the 28th the lord prelate dined with us in the guest house, in response to our frequent invitations. We had five quarts of wine brought from the city, at 18 kreuzer a quart, with five batzen worth of white bread, and we gave him: 1. a soup with sliced beet; 2. a lamb roast; 3. boiled meat; 4. siskin [a small wild bird]; 5. a partridge; 6. cabbage, bacon and liver sausage; 7. roast pork and grilled sausage; 8. a steamed wild duck; 9. rose hips boiled with sugar; 10. for dessert, apples and cheese. His Grace was in fine good humour. (St.168)

On 7 and 9 February Staiger reports two more dinners. At the first she and four senior nuns dined with four priests: 'We all sat at a large round table in honourable contentment. Master Raphel gave the wine and His Grace gave the food, entertaining us well.' Two days later it was a similar story: 'In the afternoon His Grace Father Hans Heinrich and Father Wunibaldt called in on us and sent for wine. We baked farmhouse cakes to go with it and we made merry together' (St.170). At this time the nuns were lodging in a monastery and Staiger cryptically reports that comment arose and action followed: 'Saturday the 3rd of March. After Holy Mass the lord prelate prohibited us from using the entrance through the cloisters because of wicked talk. ... On account of these evil suspicions he excluded men, which could cost us much company at meals' (St.172–3).

In 1633 the nuns were twice caught up in the fighting as the Swedes took Eichstätt, first in May and again in December. The Imperialists had retaken the city in between, in October, and Staiger's report of this perhaps justifies fears of a Catholic fifth column in other cities at this time: 'At one o'clock in the morning there was a great crowd in the city as the Imperialist army arrived from Ingolstadt. ... They were let in by the Jesuits, as there was no Swedish guard on the gates' (St.102). During the siege in May the nuns, from their refuge in the city, had watched their convent outside the walls being plundered; later they were able to inspect the damage:

> When we arrived in the courtyard of the convent we saw nothing but mess, with hay, straw, feathers and broken things strewn everywhere. ... In the priory, domestic quarters and infirmary the feathers came up over our knees. The cells and other rooms were turned completely upside down, with chests and cupboards chopped up, while the two dormitories were full of broken pictures, undressed Christ-child figures and other stuff. ... The refectory was smeared with filth and they had used the little chest of drawers as a chamber pot. All the copper vessels had been broken out from the kitchen, the bakehouse, the wash-house and the brewhouse. The new graves had been dug up, leaving one deceased Sister with her right hand raised. ... We found the altars in the church and the cloisters broken open and the holy relics scattered about. Not a single alarm clock or table clock was left and they had removed all the ropes from the bells and the clock. It is impossible to describe what a miserable state and a mess every part of the convent was in. (St.86–8)

Staiger's account of the Swedish assault on the city in December 1633 is cut short where pages are missing from the manuscript, but her description of the surprise attack begins dramatically:

> On the morning of 6th December, as day broke, all of a sudden we heard shooting and shouts in the street that the enemy was breaking in at the gates. With a loud ringing on the gate bell a priest shouted to us that we should get back to St Walburg's as fast as we could. The sub-prioress and another Sister ran off in fright straight away and arrived unhurt at the cloister, but I and the majority who fled with and after me ran into the raging enemy. With guns and drawn weapons in their hands they ran and rode towards us, demanding our money or our lives, and they set ... (St.111)

Staiger and some of the nuns got away but others were left behind. Soldiers caught and sought to rob some of these 'but God quickly sent a colonel, who was billeted there, and they cried to him for help, which he promised them and indeed provided' (St.125). Three hid on the city walls with the help of a relative of Staiger's:

> My cousin's sister Anna Maria pulled our dear housekeeper, Sister Paula, with Sister Charitas and Sister Veronica, up on to the city walls on a long ladder. There they sat a whole night and two days in the bitter cold and almost froze, as they had lost their headdresses, veils and bonnets in the great crush around the gate. Eventually the soldiers who were patrolling around the city walls caught and searched them. They too demanded their money or their lives but otherwise did nothing to them, and in the end, in response to their pleas, they took them into a warm room belonging to the chantry Sisters, who they also searched and miserably tormented. (St.125)

On this occasion the Swedes stayed only seven days before withdrawing, setting fire to the city as they left. Some of the nuns were still there:

> They were very afraid as they saw all parts burning, while anyone who escaped was to be cut down and they knew of nowhere they could flee to. Eventually my cousin rigged up a device with tablecloths, ropes and poles, and let himself down over the city walls on to a high tree, where he stationed himself. Then he pulled them out one after another, hanging on to the rope with their feet set on the ladder and at risk to life and limb, until he had brought down 11 of my Sisters and five from Mariaburg. (St.126)

Junius and Staiger both note the effects of war on the wider population, and their observation of events and conditions correspond to those of other diarists. Junius comments on the disparity between officers and soldiers in gains from booty and contributions: 'The colonels got a great deal of money here but the poor soldiers had to suffer hunger.' She reports plundering, although only briefly, adding a reflection on the citizenry's own behaviour: 'Their houses out there were also smashed up and dug through so that practically nothing remained hidden, for what the soldiers didn't find themselves was betrayed by their evil neighbours' (J.190, 111). Her description of booty being sold is familiar:

> Everything that the people buried or bricked up was found and the soldiers put it up for sale in the city, so that the poor folk had to buy their own possessions back again. ... Moreover when people who had bought things had only gone a little way other soldiers took them from them again, so that many items were sold three or four times. ... The unfortunate people even had to drive their own cattle in for the soldiers, who then sold them, a fine

ox for three taler and a cow for two taler or a taler and a half. On one occasion they wanted to sell us 12 sheep for a taler, but we were not willing to
buy them. (J.116–17)

Later in her account Junius frequently reports hunger among both population
and soldiery, supporting her more general descriptions with the personal
experience of one of the convent's workers:

He and his children had no other food to eat but bran bread, which they
poured hot water over now and again so that they would at least have
something warm. They had neither fat nor salt, for in many villages there
was not a single cow, and as soon as they bought anything again the soldiers took it from them once more. He told us how his little daughter had
said to him: 'Really, Daddy, when I've eaten the bran bread I'm going to die
so that I can go to heaven, where I won't have to eat any more of it.' At the
time this child was bright and healthy but on the next day she suddenly
died, as this good man told us, crying bitterly. *Ach*, God, what suffering,
misery and lamentation we hear about from these poor people. (J.138)

Junius says almost nothing about how the nuns themselves were affected
but she does note that at the worst time they were still able to give alms to
the poor and the hungry from the city:

We let no-one go away completely empty-handed but gave them at least
a loaf of bread. I can say in truth that it would not have been possible for
the little bit of grain we had in our lofts to suffice, had not our Lord God
blessed this on account of the poor people. (J.189)

Forced out of her convent for much of the time during 1632 to 1635, Staiger
provides a number of observations and insights into the wider experience of
war. Thus as the Swedes advanced into Bavaria in late 1632 she notes: 'Many
times there has been such a pathetic flight of people, children and livestock
from the villages and suburbs that it can't be described.' In August 1634
Imperialist armies moved through the area towards Nördlingen, clearing the
area of food as they went 'so that no-one could get any meat, wine, beer, bread
or other food. Many would have given a Reichstaler or even his horse for a loaf
of bread, if anyone would have accepted it'. While the troops took from the
land the dealers purchased in the city: 'The sutlers have bought up everything
which people brought in on the river or on the roads, in order to provision the
soldiers, so that there is very little beer, wine or other things to be had' (St.49,
145, 149). Food was already scarce, 'which on many a day has brought tears
into my eyes', and Staiger describes how soldiers profiteered with stolen bread:

There was such a crush in the castle when it was known that there was a
bit of bread to be bought that it was as though it were being given away,

but the soldiers climbed up on the people and threw them out of the way. They attacked those who had already bought, took the bread from them, and ran off down or outside the gate with it, selling it to those who could not come into the city for double or treble the price. (St.139)

All three convents experienced economic pressures. Although Frauenwörth was less directly affected during the war period Haidenbucher regularly refers to tax and contribution levies, orders for horses to be supplied to the elector in Munich, and the occasional more surprising demand on a convent: 'On the 26th of August [1646] an electoral command again arrived, demanding pistols, powder, powder horns, guns and the things that go with them, but as we were not provided with such items we had to buy them all' (Hd.66. 502). Although she does not even mention the ending of the war she does record a heavy post-war tax which the convent was unable to pay because of lost revenues 'from our feudal tenants, who had been ruined by the soldiers, friend and foe alike, so that our beloved house of God suffered losses of 2943 florins' (Hd.66. 509). Junius also records a drastic fall in the convent's income from tithes and rents, first in November 1632: 'This year we wanted to get something for us to live on from our feudal tenants, but they were scarcely able to give a third part of their dues' (J.100). A year later the situation was worse:

Where our tenants would otherwise have brought us 30, 40 or 50 bushels of corn, this year they brought three or four bushels. ... It is to be wondered how we are going to be able to bring 30 people through the winter with what they have provided and the little that we still have to thresh, quite apart from what we give out every day. (J.164–5)

Staiger reports the effect on the harvest of 1632, and on the convent's income: 'For lack of horses they have had to leave the precious grain lying in the fields in many places, or else they didn't dare bring it in because of the soldiers. They couldn't manure, till or sow the fields, and they couldn't pay the rent money or tithes.' Another entry of Staiger's is a comment on the times. The convent officers sent to collect a nun's inheritance left to her by her parents brought back only a few pieces of silverware and a small sum in cash: 'Their beloved daughter and member of our convent, Sister Febronia, knew of and had expected much more, but the other heirs hid it and blamed the Swedish soldiers who had plundered them' (St.66, 61).

After the Swedish defeat at Nördlingen people started to rebuild their lives and homes. For those who could afford to buy, the poverty of others made supplies cheap. The nuns obtained enough money to make a start on repairing the convent buildings, and Staiger reports:

In those weeks I bought many kinds of household goods, copper and iron vessels, picks, shovels, wash tubs, window panes, stove tiles, carts, chains, ropes and other things, which people pleadingly gave up and sold for next to nothing or for a bit of bread. Those who had previously lived well and used to have plenty to eat carried everything out of their own houses, and poor folk likewise out of other people's, breaking out the stoves and windows and selling them for bread and bran, as they didn't have enough to eat. (St.167–8)

The daily life of the convent figures strongly in Staiger's diary, with many routine matters being regularly noted and religious observances carefully recorded. Housekeeping and supplies are constant concerns, naturally enough during periods of war-induced hardship but also in easier times, where details of the daily menu are recorded intermittently for no apparent reason beyond providing material for an entry. Staiger gives less information about the nuns' daily work, although she does note the less routine tasks when they occur, such as making candles or soap, while another aspect of life in a nunnery of the time emerges in recurrent references to blood-letting and purging the bowels. She notes new admissions to the order and describes illnesses and deaths, often in detail, including a sequence of six in the period October to December 1634.

In contrast Junius gives little space to everyday matters in her account of the war, but her occasional digressions do offer some insight into the times. Thus reports of religious festivals being held, albeit in straitened circumstances, indicate the efforts of both priests and population to maintain a degree of normality despite the effects of war:

Monday the 25th [of April 1633] was St Mark's day, which in our church is a great festival and a day of indulgence [remission of punishment due for sins]. Usually the three villages of Hallstadt, Memelsdorf and Güssbach made a pilgrimage to our convent with their banners, but this year nothing took place as all three villages have been plundered, ruined and partly burned down. Nevertheless the three parish priests came to us and said that even though they could not come to our House of God in procession as usual they still wanted to perform their obligations, to hold the office of Holy Mass and give a sermon in accordance with the old custom. We were truly glad to see this, for on that day our church was so full that the people could not all get in. Schoolchildren also made a pilgrimage to us, and they sang so beautifully. (J.136–7)

In her account of the war Staiger maintains a religious view, often referring to it as a punishment from God. She links war, famine and plague, seeking intercession and pleading that 'through the prayers of the Holy Virgin Walburgis, God may be moved to protect us further and turn the well-deserved punishments of war, rising prices and the terrible sickness away from us' (St.77–8). Although she is philosophical – '*Pacientia*; the Lord has given, and the Lord has taken away. Blessed be the name of the Lord' – she is nevertheless partisan from both a political and a religious standpoint: 'On Monday the 12th of September the Imperialist troops regained Neuburg, taking it by storm. May God bestow yet more mercies and good fortune, so that our beloved Germany may once again be cleansed of heretics' (St.67, 99). This does not prevent her from seeing the faults on her own side, and she is frequently pointed in her criticism of the behaviour of Imperialist troops: 'They plundered more than the Swedish themselves ... and stayed only until there was no more wine or beer available.' Nor did they provide protection: 'If one felt any danger, so that they might be needed, just then they would all be gone' (St.66). Like many other writers Staiger comes to the conclusion that in this war friends were as bad as foes: 'Our soldiers, as well as the enemy, broke into churches and cloisters, and they pushed about, beat and robbed the people in their houses and in the countryside' (St.148).

9
Priests and Politics

Priests and pastors were more at risk than most in a war in which religion was, at least nominally, a principal issue. This risk was both physical, in that they were often easy targets for robbery and violence from undisciplined soldiery of the opposite persuasion, and political, as their positions and livelihoods were sometimes dependent on which side currently controlled their locality. Some of the pastors lost and regained their livings several times as the war swung back and forth, but other cases were more complex, as the problems and adventures of the Lutheran pastor Abraham Winkler and the Catholic abbot Johann Dressel illustrate. Their stories are worth recounting, as they also demonstrate the disruptive effect of the war on individual lives, giving them a broader representative character even though the particular circumstances are far from typical.

Winkler's text has a curious history. Its author, a well-known preacher in Pirna, near Dresden, fled the town with the retreating Swedish army in 1640, leaving his enemies, jealous of his professional success, to blacken his reputation for posterity. His name was still remembered in 1786, when an archdeacon in Pirna received a visit from some students, one of whom proved to be a descendant of Winkler's from Reval (in modern Estonia), where the latter had eventually settled under Swedish patronage. This visitor produced Winkler's manuscript, and while the students went sightseeing the archdeacon made a transcript, which was published in 1805, although both manuscript and transcript have since been lost.

The text is a form of autobiography in which Winkler describes his upbringing, career and adventures during the Thirty Years War, up to the time he reached Reval in 1642. He wrote it soon afterwards, referring to his arrival there as being 'last April', while in a single paragraph added near the end of his life he notes his subsequent successful career: 'How I have conducted myself up to now, in the sixteenth year of my office as preacher, ... is known to everyone' (Wi.71, 71–2). He adds a pious benediction: 'God grant me health, the blessing of life, and mercy that I may continue to serve him truly to the end of my days' (Wi.72). He mentions his marriage in 1633 and his seven children, three of whom were surviving, only in a brief postscript.

Winkler, who was born near Naumburg, opens his account with a brief factual summary of his parentage, education and early career, but his text becomes a fuller and more descriptive narrative from the time of his move to Pirna in 1628. A pastor who had been asked by the mayor there 'to recommend him a *studiosus* who would be able to undertake the instruction of his children' had 'suggested my humble self and commended me highly' (Wi.49). Winkler took the post, although he was 'minded not at all to stay there, but to take up a country parish in my fatherland' – meaning the area around Naumburg (Wi.50). A suitable opportunity came up in 1631 but by then the situation had changed following the Swedish invasion, so that because 'war was rife throughout the country I changed my mind, preferring to stay on in a well-defended place' until more favourable circumstances arose. In the following months Winkler was inspired by Gustavus Adolphus's reputation and progress; 'Consequently I was ready to leave my fatherland and everything else, and I decided to make my way to the royal Swedish army to become a military preacher, and to find my way into the favour of the most glorious king himself'. Again his plans were frustrated as the main Imperialist forces lay between Pirna and the Swedes; 'Hence I had, against my will, to stay in Pirna, even though the plague was raging there at the time and I would gladly have got away from it again, if only the royal army had come nearer' (Wi.51). Winkler and his pupils escaped the plague but a young deacon died; 'The whole congregation immediately agreed upon my humble person, and I was appointed to this office by due process, confirmed, and on the 4th of November I was invested.' Six years later, in October 1638, a Pirna pastor died and Winkler succeeded to his office 'with the unanimous approval' of the church authorities (Wi.52).

The appointment was a popular one but success created rivalries: 'Where before I had been greatly loved, honoured and rewarded by the whole community, so afterwards I became ever more and more so. Indeed the highest promotion in the town was once or twice promised to me in due course, which gave rise to not a little envy' (Wi.52). Winkler notes that his enemies used against him the fact that 'I was never prepared to endorse the peace of Prague but instead made my disapproval clear, both publicly and in private'. This suggests that he had long been on a political tightrope, as this change of sides from Sweden to the emperor had been made by Elector Johann Georg of Saxony over three years before. 'But God protected me wondrously', he adds, 'until *anno* 1639, on the 23rd of April', when Baner's Swedish army took Pirna by storm (Wi.53).

Although he says nothing of the fighting Winkler devotes much space to his role in saving the citizens of Pirna from the worst consequences of defeat. He reports that 'to my good fortune, and bringing deliverance to many honest people', the colonel in charge of operations against the Pirna garrison, which was holding out in the castle, was a Dresden man and had known Pirna in his youth (Wi.53). In response to the pleas of Winkler's land-lady, who used the latter's presence to claim that hers was 'a house of religion, just as she herself was a preacher's daughter', the colonel provided temporary protection and introduced Winkler to no less a person than 'Major General Wrangel, now Field Marshall' (Wi.54). Wrangel's initial reply to Winkler's petition on behalf of 'the poor sheep' was that if they had wanted mercy 'they should have surrendered on accord', as prescribed in the accepted laws of war (Wi.54, 55). In the course of the discussion he asked Winkler's name, 'and because I was known far and wide for my strong adherence to the principles of Protestantism he had also heard of me, and he looked upon me with favour', with the result that all those who had taken refuge in Winkler's sacristy were spared (Wi.55).

Once the immediate crisis was over Winkler's enemies began to use his high standing with the Swedes against him, sending emissaries, 'a number of whom I could name, but I have long since forgiven them', to denounce him in Dresden. He was in a paradoxical political position, as a good Lutheran supporting his Swedish co-religionists but hence at odds with his immediate ruler, the Lutheran elector of Saxony, who was at the time in alliance with the Catholic Imperialists. 'I used the good disposition of the Swedish commandant and other officers towards me for everyone's preservation, but it didn't help. I was firmly Swedish and I was to die for it, of which I have reliable evidence.' The Swedes too realised that his life would be in danger after their departure, and the general advised him to leave with them when the army moved on in the summer of 1639. For a man of principle caught up in the political and religious cross-currents of a complex war the personal price was high: 'Thus I had to abandon my excellent post, my fine library, my parents-in-law's own house and all the household supplies, and to move to Bohemia, accompanied by my wife and daughter, my parents-in-law, my brother-in-law and two maids' (Wi.56). Friends begged him to stay, but once persuaded of his danger 'they asked me, ... if I saw the field marshall, to plead on their behalf that he should spare the good old town and not have it burned, which I promised them to do and faithfully carried out' (Wi.57).

The significance of this episode for Winkler is evident from the space he devotes to it, about the same as for the following three adventurous years before he reached Reval. The Swedes helped him, and he was employed as a pastor and as a military chaplain and preacher, but the war kept him on the move. His first halt in Bohemia lasted only a few happy months before he had to leave 'with bitter tears and tearing of hair', and his second stay was only a little longer before the Swedish army moved north in March 1640 (Wi.59). Winkler could not go with it as his wife and parents-in-law were all ill, so he was given a pass and assistance to travel to Stralsund, although conditions dictated that this was with military units and by a circuitous route. On the way Winkler himself fell ill: 'I was infected by a fever, but with God's mercy I shook it off with a quick-acting medicine' (Wi.66). His father-in-law died at Hamelin, and his wife and mother-in-law escaped serious injury when their coach overturned, but the latter in turn died shortly before they reached their destination; 'I hurried on to Stralsund, having to travel all night, and tried to find a coffin, but because of the great devastation in the area I couldn't get one' so that she had to be buried without it (Wi.67). In Stralsund his fortunes improved and Winkler was well looked after by the Swedish governor and officers while seeking a permanent post. In January 1641 Torstensson (soon to become the Swedish commander-in-chief) passed through, enquired after Winkler, heard him preach and promptly invited him to accompany him to Stockholm. He was a great success there, moving and preaching in the best circles, including twice for Queen Christina, as a result of which he was 'promoted to the cathedral here in Reval', as well as being handsomely paid. Winkler took this opportunity although there were alternatives: 'His Excellency would have liked to have had me with him on campaign again, as would have the worthy old [Swedish] imperial chancellor' (Wi.69). Even then his adventures were not over, as he first returned to Stralsund, where he again fell sick, before taking ship for Reval and narrowly avoiding shipwreck on the way: 'Between Bornholm and Gotland we suddenly encountered such a strong east wind that the spar on the mainmast snapped in two and the sail warp ripped down the middle' (Wi.71).

The focus of Winkler's representation of the war is its effect on himself and his career, and he gives little wider perspective. He refers only briefly to his own role after the storming of Pirna: 'There I stood among the living and the dead, and had to make an accord to surrender the sacristy, into which the clergy and other good friends, with their wives and children, had fled in order to rescue their lives, goods and honour. ... Meanwhile terrible things were happening in the town' (Wi.53). For the rest his account is mainly one of avoiding the war, adventurous though this proved to be, until he reached the haven of Reval, well outside the war zone. One of his first priorities there seems to have been to write an account of his experiences in order to set out his side of the controversy over his position and actions in Pirna, as much for his own satisfaction as for any practical purpose this might serve.

Dressel's account is another apparently written as a self-justification and answer to criticism. From 1618 until his death in 1637 he was abbot of the Cistercian monastery of Ebrach, between Schweinfurt and Bamberg. This had very large land-holdings, making its wealth a target for the military in their search for contributions, and during the first Swedish ascendency in the area, from autumn 1631 through to 1635, Dressel spent little time in his cloister, seeking by flight to evade their efforts to extort payments from him. His conduct and some of the transactions he was forced into provoked criticism from his own monks, and the account he wrote is clearly intended to give his side of the story. His record commences in January 1632 and ends in substance in November 1633, with brief diaristic notes added until March 1635.

The text provides little firm evidence as to when it was written but style and content give a strong indication. The description of the author's travels and tribulations during 1632 and 1633 forms a coherent story, with future developments foreshadowed by phrases such as 'how it affected me will be set down in the following', while happenings elsewhere are inserted at convenient points, sometimes out of chronology (Dr.26. 80). The continuation is diaristic in style, comprising notes of relatively minor events which occurred up to March 1635 during Dressel's refuge in monastic houses near Koblenz and Cologne. The inference is that he used this period of enforced exile to record and justify his earlier conduct, criticising his critics and supporting his account of events with documentary evidence in the form of the texts of various letters, proclamations and permits which he copied into his manuscript. Later he added contemporaneous notes to his text but he broke off abruptly when circumstances enabled him to commence his homeward journey.

Dressel's problems began soon after the Swedes arrived, when Ebrach was appointed as a muster-place for a colonel commissioned to raise a regiment of cavalry and two regiments of foot. This was a potential disaster, in that undisciplined recruits had to be accommodated and fed for an indefinite period by the host area until each regiment was complete. The colonel, Truchsess, demanded 30 000 taler for an exemption, 'with the threat that if we were not willing to pay him the required sum he would so terrorise the monastery and its unfortunate people that we would wish that we had given him double'. Dressel negotiated a figure of 20 000 taler, entering into a formal agreement as 'the Prelate of Ebrach, Joannes Dresselius von Hollfeld' (Dr.26. 78). This proved easier than raising the money, as the monastery's tenants contributed only 150 florins to the first instalment; 'The others were not prepared to give anything.' Dressel tried to persuade them: 'Indeed I had the feudal tenants called together several times...and warned them to accommodate themselves to it, as such billeting would mainly affect them' (Dr.26. 79). He tried to shift the burden, telling the tenants that 'the monastery had already done its share, finding and paying out the first instalment with great difficulty, so that I would hope that they would also do their part' (Dr.26. 79–80). It did no good: 'They would not agree to it and no-one wanted to contribute a single pfennig. Eventually they came out in favour of the necessary money being borrowed.' Ruefully Dressel reflects:

> Had I taken myself off from the monastery to Bamberg in the first place and allowed the tenants to face billeting and ruin straight away I would have done the best thing, and the 20 000 Reichstaler would have been saved. But nobody told me or gave me any good advice; everyone looked to their own interests. (Dr.26. 80)

Dressel travelled to Schweinfurt, where the colonel constantly pressed him for payment of the agreed sums: 'He sent his servant to me virtually every day to demand the money. I sent back pleas that he should be patient with me; the sums were large and I didn't know how I could raise any cash.' His monks were no help, as he bitterly observes: 'I sent often to the monastery for advice but I got a poor response; I had to sit there and sweat' (Dr.26. 81). Truchsess arranged for him to be arrested but through his contacts he managed to get a pass out of the town, although he had only gone a short distance when a party of soldiers caught up with him and took him back. He came under further suspicion as his route had appeared to be heading not for the monastery but towards Imperialist-held territory, so that his arrest was renewed, lasting for two months: '*Interim*, I sat there under arrest, meditating in the Castenhof as to where I could raise the cash, for the colonel gave me no peace; he wanted his money.' Again he reproaches his colleagues: 'I wrote often to the elders in the monastery, saying that they should think of means whereby Truchsess could be satisfied. They were also affected by the agreement with the colonel, as the matter did not concern just me but the whole monastery and its tenants' (Dr.26. 300).

Others saw their opportunity, including a number of officers who made claims of various sizes and on various pretexts. Dressel resisted the larger ones, although he observes that a smaller claimant 'gave me no peace, until he had thievishly extorted 100 florins from me'. He notes the mood of the time: '*In summa*, everyone wanted to gorge himself on the monastery's possessions' (Dr.26. 559). Among the opportunists were the Schweinfurt city council, who successfully petitioned the Swedish crown for some nearby properties belonging to the monastery, leading Dressel into a long description of how he tried to avert or at least ameliorate this, arguing that the monastery should retain the sheep, and when that failed that they should keep or be paid for the wool harvest as they had wintered the sheep before the transfer of the land. On his arrival in Schweinfurt Dressel had been well received with the customary presents, wine and fish; now when he encountered two of the councillors they were embarrassed: 'They passed by on the other side, just like the Levite, and made as though they didn't see me. And why? Because I had eaten the fish and drunk the wine which they had presented to me a few weeks before, and was their neighbour no longer' (Dr.26. 304).

Eventually Dressel raised the balance of the money by selling monastery property in Nuremberg, commenting wryly when news of completion of this transaction arrived: 'Who was happier than I at my losses?' (Dr.26. 556). Even then the colonel quibbled about the exchange rate and took payment in kind to make up the difference, although for silverware 'worth 300 florins Truchsess allowed only scrap silver value, ... six batzen per half-ounce'. The colonel gave him a full and flowery receipt, which Dressel copied into his record along with the text of an order from Gustavus Adolphus empowering him to raise money from monastery property – 'to mortgage, to pledge, to sell, to alienate, to dispose of, to make and execute the relevant contracts, and also to cede properties completely and hand them over' so far as 'necessary to meet contributions and other burdens of war' (Dr.26. 558). This was evidently the central point of the criticism aimed at Dressel, that he secured his own freedom at the expense of the monastic lands, exceeding his powers on the basis of authority from an alien and Protestant king in temporary military control of the area. Ironically Dressel adds that Truchsess was himself cashiered by the Swedes on account of the money, 'which he later used not for the king's army but for his own benefit' (Dr.26. 560).

Freed from arrest, Dressel left hastily for Würzburg, 'for I had seen enough of a city like Schweinfurt and had been obliged to pay dearly enough for the present they gave me'. On his departure he had to borrow a coach and horses from the despised city authorities, as he had given his own away as a bribe to a senior officer during his confinement. Predictably he was not satisfied with their response: 'They gave me three horses of different colours and a battered old coach which broke down *en route*' (Dr.26. 560).

Dressel's troubles were far from over. In Würzburg he learned that peasants from several Catholic villages near his monastery, including some from its own lands, had banded together and raided their Protestant neighbours, as well as capturing and robbing the Swedish soldiers who had been sent to protect them. The Swedes sought to hold him responsible, involving him in a long self-defence under threat of a new arrest. Eventually he convinced them, whereupon the authorities drafted a proclamation to the peasants under Dressel's name, ordering good behaviour; 'I had no inclination to do that ... and excused myself, saying that if they wanted to have a *mandatum avocatorium* issued they should do it in their own name and not give it out as my command' (Dr.26. 573). Nevertheless Dressel's name was published on the order, an act of apparent cooperation with the Swedish authorities which brought a firm response from the Imperialists: 'The monastery was promptly plundered on the orders of the Friedlander [Wallenstein]' (Dr.27. 102). This added to the monastery's criticism of Dressel, and to his criticism of their response: 'And was it because of me alone, as my dear Fathers and Brothers falsely profess, that the monastery fell into adversity and was plundered? God forgive all those who are living; to the dead I wish eternal joy. Amen' (Dr.27. 103). He concludes a lengthy self-exculpation with the thought that '*in summa*, the fault was not all mine. ... For my own part I have no wish to remain a prelate, if God will only grant me my daily bread as long as I live. Amen' (Dr.27. 104).

Dressel stayed in Würzburg from May to November 1633, during which time demands for contributions from the monastery continued to press upon him. He carefully points out his defence of the monastery's interests, as well as noting that he paid ransoms or other charges for individual monks, although he acknowledges that his efforts were not all successful, the monastery being both taxed and appointed again as a muster-place during this period. He notes more ingratitude, this time from the tenants: 'They would rather have the wickedest nobleman for their lord than the monks.

Ex ore aliorum. That is all the thanks I have had from them' (Dr.27. 113). The monastery was also plundered a second time, on this occasion by Weimar troops, and although Dressel was not there he records the losses, one of his comments reflecting both the riches of the clergy and the lack of discrimination of the soldiery: 'Likewise they cut up the white, flowered vestment, which with the fringe, braid and lining was worth almost 500 Reichstaler, and made caps and jackets out of it for their young curs, which is a great shame' (Dr.27. 377). From the relative safety of the city Dressel complains: 'While I was staying in Würzburg, where I myself had much to suffer and endure, the following Brothers and Fathers came to me: [a list follows]. I gave clothes to almost all of these, keeping a number of them with me for some time and providing for them, but I earned little thanks from many of them'. Mournfully he concludes: 'I never have had any good fortune or a lucky star, for wherever I have been I have always encountered hostility' (Dr.27. 380).

Dressel's departure from Würzburg was occasioned by the news that the Swedish crown had given the monastery lands to a German count holding a high position in their administration, in exchange for a promise of a 600000 taler payment spread over the next four years. Seeing himself effectively dispossessed and also subject to compromising pressure for information about the monastery's affairs from the new owner's steward, Dressel hastily secured a pass and left the city, taking the monastery account books with him. He records his reasoning in deciding upon flight, including his conviction that he had much to fear from his own monks in this situation:

> They will sacrifice you on the butcher's slab like this, and help to make an end of you, crying out on all sides, just as they did before, that you handed over the monastery voluntarily, corresponded with the Swedes, revealed all the monastery's business to them and betrayed it, etc. ... It would have been a thousand times better if I had fled with the rest of them in the first place, and there can certainly be no prelate who has suffered and endured more in this situation than me. Nothing has struck me to the heart more than what I have suffered from my own Brothers, who I virtually brought up, and who have received every kindness from me. (Dr.27. 385)

As he reached Mainz news caught up and he was again arrested, but not before he had hidden the books so that he could deny knowledge of them. He was released some days later after an uncomfortable examination by the Mainz authorities, led by a councillor who had faced Dressel in different circumstances in 1629 when the latter had been a commissioner sent to enforce the Edict of Restitution; 'I recognised him, and vice versa, but he looked at me over the top of the page and said nothing. ... However I heard him say privately to his neighbours: "The Abbot of Ebrach doesn't sneer now as he did at the time when he took the Carthusian [monastic lands] away from my Lord Count"' (Dr.27. 389). Nevertheless Dressel secured a pass to travel on, and this time he reached his destination and refuge safely. In a wry postscript he lists all the various assurances, patents and passes which he and the monastery had received, noting that regardless of who had signed them they were all in the end equally worthless in the prevailing circumstances: 'We all had to go through the mill; there was nothing to be done about it' (Dr.27. 398).

10
Thomas Mallinger's Freiburg Chronicle

No individual account is typical, either in the experience of the war it records or in the approach, style and motivation of the author. The war itself is the common factor, and the specific features of single accounts underlie and shape the overview given by the many. Closer examination of four examples, those of Mallinger, Zembroth, Fritsch and Monro, illustrates the range. They represent the varying times of writing, in that Mallinger maintained a long-running contemporaneous record while the others wrote up their accounts afterwards. In Monro's case this was soon after the events described and while the war was still going on, whereas Zembroth wrote shortly after the war and Fritsch many years later. These same examples span the stylistic range, from Mallinger's impersonal chronicle, through community and military accounts from Zembroth and Monro respectively, to Fritsch's entirely self-centred memoir. The authors were a cleric, a layman and two soldiers, one a German who served the emperor and the other a foreigner who fought with Gustavus Adolphus, while three were Catholics and the fourth was a Protestant. All four accounts have been quoted extensively in earlier chapters, and the following analysis considers the genesis and nature of the texts in order to place their contents in perspective.

Thomas Mallinger wrote a chronicle of events in Freiburg and south-west Germany from 1613 to 1660, an edited version of which was published in 1854 by F.J. Mone. The original manuscript, which is now in the city library at Überlingen, is a quarto volume of 417 pages, but this includes several printed pamphlets bound in and page-numbered by Mallinger, as well as passages copied from similar sources and other short essays which may have been copied or might be Mallinger's own compositions. None of this material is directly related to his account of the war, but it indicates the eclectic nature of his recording, which appears to have been commenced for its own sake, with no apparent central theme or purpose. This attitude is evident in the fair copy of his work which he made – the surviving manuscript – where he filled up many extra pages with lists and dates of popes, emperors, archbishops and others. His approach during the years when the war first affected Freiburg is strikingly different. Here he dispenses with most of the irrelevances and focuses clearly on the task in hand, while he also writes at much greater length than before or afterwards. The rest of his chronicle averages about five pages per year including all the interpolated material, whereas he allocates 31 pages to 1633, almost entirely devoted to the war, and no less than 90 to 1634. After 1634 he wrote less prolifically, although up to 1648 the war continued to provide the bulk of his material, but he reverted to his more random chronicling thereafter. This places his reporting of the war in context. Unlike Zembroth, Mallinger does not begin with the approach of war to the area and nor does his account tail off after its end. The implication is that he was less a chronicler of the war and more a chronicler of his times, which happened to include a major war – a significant difference of emphasis.

Little is known of Mallinger himself other than what can be gleaned from the text. This, although largely diaristic in form and with most entries carefully dated, is in no sense a personal diary. 'Thomas Mallinger' is named from time to time in the later years, but almost always in the third person, most frequently in the context of clerical appointments or elections. Only in the last year, 1660, does he briefly identify himself explicitly as '*ego* Thomas Mallinger' in reporting his part in confirmation services, although in 1655 he does mention other people in personal terms as '*meus discipulus*' and '*meus patrinus*', and in 1660 as '*meus cognatus*', 'my brother-in-law' and 'my cousin' (Ma.612, 609, 612). It is evident from many references that Mallinger was a Catholic priest attached to the chapter of Basle, which had for many years been situated in Freiburg, and that he was still there when he ended his chronicle in December 1660. When he took up this calling is less clear. The first specific references occur between June 1635 and January 1636, when in rapid succession he was first elected as a '*senarius*' of the 'Brotherhood of St John the Baptist', then 'chosen as a *procurator vacantium beneficiorum*', and finally 'selected as an *assisio* and confirmed in this post' (Ma.584). From the very beginning of his chronicle, however, Mallinger interests himself in religious matters, and in March 1624 he refers to the bishop as '*reverend. noster episcopus Basiliensis*', while from that year onwards he frequently records local clerical appointments or deaths. Although tenuous, this suggests that he might have been in the chapter by 1624, and perhaps associated with it earlier as a youth or novice, which is compatible with infirmity or death preventing continuation of his record after 1660.

Scraps of evidence suggest that Mallinger was a local man. His first entry refers to an event 'here in Freiburg' in 1613. This was a shooting contest to which 40 towns were invited but which was won by a Freiburg man, 'steward at St Peter's', his prize being 50 florins. This circumstantial detail suggests the author's personal knowledge rather than report or hearsay, as do fuller accounts of *comediae* performed locally in 1615 and 1616. Of the first, an account of the life of Christ which also took place 'here in Freiburg',

Mallinger says that it was performed 'by several hundred actors, citizens and their children, young and old, women as well as men, ... beginning at four o'clock in the morning and not breaking up until after nightfall'. The second, held in Endingen, 20 kilometres north of Freiburg, was a macabre reenactment of an alleged ritual murder of children in the town 'some time ago' by Jews, who were arrested, confessed and were burned. 'The *cadavera* of those children are still in existence and can be exhibited', Mallinger claims, adding that the event was attended by many thousand people from the neighbouring towns and villages; 'Splendid *instrumentalis* and *vocalis musica* was also performed there' (Ma.529). This same place is mentioned in 1660, when Mallinger refers to '*meus cognatus* from Endingen', who invited him to his daughter's wedding, and in the same year he indicates that he had relatives in Staufen and Breisach, both also within 20 kilometres of Freiburg (Ma.612).

Assessments of when and why Mallinger wrote his account are interrelated. Mone, the editor of the text, believes the extant manuscript to be a fair copy made in 1660, quoting as evidence for the copying both the absence of corrections and the occasional omission of grammatically or contextually necessary words. He fixes the date partly by the time at which the account breaks off and partly by one of the several passages which carry some theme through to its end, well beyond the chronology of the main account, specifically the career history of a particular priest, which is interpolated into the record for 1628 but continues until his election as a canon in 1660. This is not an unreasonable conclusion. Much less acceptable is Mone's contention that Mallinger only began to record events a good many years after the beginning of the war, as it became bigger and long drawn out. He bases this on a note in Mallinger's summary for 1618, '*belli Germanici in Bohemia initium*' (the German war began in Bohemia), quite correctly observing that he could only have known this with hindsight but failing to recognise that he could have inserted the reference into the 1660 fair copy, like the out-of-chronology passages he notes (Ma.528). The only other argument Mone advances is that here and there in the earlier years Mallinger makes mistakes about dates which he would not have made had he been writing at the time. This places too much faith in the accuracy of diarists generally, but also overlooks the fact that the keepers of contemporaneous diaries not infrequently fall behind with their writing and catch up later, with a consequent increased risk of error.

There are much better grounds for believing that Mallinger kept a contemporaneous record from the outset. In the earliest years he gives precise dates for most of the specific events he mentions, and he is even more punctilious thereafter. Without a diary he might much later have remembered the shooting contest of 1613 or the *comediae* of 1615 and 1616, but he is unlikely to have recalled the exact dates, or those of disparate events he records, such as the birth of a son to the elector Palatine in Heidelberg in

1614, a weeping portrait of the Virgin at Endingen in 1615, or the passage of a company of troops through Freiburg in 1617. On 29 November 1618 he mentions the portentous comet of that winter. This was actually visible for a long time, as he himself says, so that the date seems most likely to be that on which he made the entry in his diary, although his description of it as 'a harbinger of all the afflictions of the German nation' is more likely to have been added with hindsight later (Ma.530). It seems similarly unlikely that he would remember unaided the snowy winter of 1614, the water shortage of 1615 or the prices of wine and wheat in 1617, all of which he records with contemporaneous-sounding introductions: 'this winter', 'this summer', 'this year' (Ma.529). He also refers to 'the 1st of July of this current year of 1622' and comments at the end of another passage in the same year that 'what will come of it time will tell' (Ma.531). He might later have researched other sources for his information, but there is no internal evidence to support this supposition nor any apparent reason why he should have done so.

Mone links Mallinger's motive for writing to the war, rather lamely explaining that the account begins in 1613 because the author started with the reign of Emperor Matthias, as the origins of the Thirty Years War lay in that period. Nothing in the entries for 1613 to 1618 supports this claim, and the background to the war is not among Mallinger's principal subjects. On the contrary, the evidence suggests that he conceived his intention to record quite independently of the war, beginning his diary long before it started, maintaining it through the years both before and during which the south-west and Freiburg were affected by war, and continuing it long after the conflict had ended. Although the war greatly increased what he had to record his original motivation must lie elsewhere. The almost total absence of personal material precludes any individualistic purpose in writing, and we therefore fall back upon the desire to record for its own sake which seems to prompt many diarists, in this case perhaps also drawing on the tradition of monastic chronicle-writing and driven by the need for some kind of activity to complement undemanding official duties. There is no indication that Mallinger had a particular – or indeed any – readership in mind, which adds to the impression that his interest lay more in the process of writing and recording than in any purpose this might serve.

This interpretation is supported by the type of record he kept in the periods before and after the war as experienced in Freiburg, that is before 1633 and after 1648, in which a strong external focus is evident. Not only do we learn little about Mallinger himself; we learn little about his work or that of the chapter, or of the daily life of Freiburg and its hinterland. These matters are not entirely absent, but are dealt with mainly in the form of brief notes of events and individuals, mostly connected with the church or the university, and this pattern becomes more pronounced in the latter part of the account. Thus in 1649 we learn of the death of a '*professor ordinarius*'; of the election of a '*praepositus Basileensis*'; that '*hic sacrum officium de s. spiritu*' *solenniter et musicaliter celebratum est'*; and that 'Jodoco Schütz, an *assisio*, held a magnificent banquet in the Baselerhof'. Occasional processions, confirmations, weddings and other humdrum events are recorded in a similarly terse and apparently arbitrary fashion, as one would expect from a casual diarist intermittently noting, without any special pattern or purpose, whatever came to mind as distinguishing one day from another. Regular comments on the weather, particularly storms, snow or lightning striking the cathedral, and on high prices for food and drink, fit in well with this model, as do reports of more notable but essentially mundane happenings, such as that in 1650 'a captain named Joann. Georg Schwartzgater was shot with a pistol by his own servant while in bed at night' (Ma.606). Over and above this Mallinger ranges much more widely but mainly derivatively, both in the information he gives about the war before 1633 and in general outside the war years.

The conclusion is that excluding the war Mallinger's chronicle is a pedestrian record of parochial events and a scrapbook of collected material, unenlivened by any personal insights but diligently maintained over a very long period. This is not particularly unusual, and students of diaries come across many such examples. His account of the Thirty Years War was neither principally motivated by the war itself nor written up *de novo* retrospectively, and thus it does not have an implicit pattern or point of view imposed upon it from the outset. On the contrary Mallinger was in the habit of noting the noteworthy as he saw it and writing it down in plain terms long before he started to record experiences of war. Although in no sense an independent witness he at least did not start with an axe to grind.

Mallinger's account of the hostilities is a war chronicle superimposed on his continuing mundane diary. He persists throughout in noting clerical appointments and deaths, storms, monastic feasts and the occasional wedding, interspersed in his much fuller description of the conflict and its consequences. Here he departs from his diary format of plainly factual entries, brief and frequently in Latin, instead producing a coherent and often quite graphic German text which gives a comprehensive account of the war locally, particularly during the two years 1633 and 1634. This metamorphosis is less surprising if considered in conjunction with the various interpolations earlier in the manuscript, as when viewed as a whole Mallinger's text suggests a man keen to write but casting about for subject matter. The war provided a perfect opportunity and he must have applied considerable effort to this task for the first two years, but a marked change is notable at the end of 1634, after which the text, though still centred on the war, abruptly becomes very much briefer. At the end of 1634 Mallinger summarises events since 1600 and then continues into 1635, commenting: 'This was a year of change, of five times seven' (Ma.583). Mone sees this as a reference to the astrological significance then attached to such years and suggests that Mallinger may have believed that the war would end in 1635, hence making only brief notes until, by 1638, experience proved otherwise. There may be some truth in this but more prosaic explanations are also available. The Swedes evacuated Freiburg on 18 September 1634, in the aftermath of the battle of Nördlingen, and they had withdrawn from much of the area by the end of the year. Although skirmishing continued locally in the following years the focus of the war shifted elsewhere until Bernard of Weimar returned in strength in the latter part of 1637, first threatening and then taking Freiburg early in 1638. Personal factors as well as lack of war-related material may also have reduced Mallinger's writing, as his clerical career progressed rapidly between June 1635 and January 1636, and he probably had less time available.

Although Mallinger provides some descriptions of events and conditions in Freiburg which reflect first-hand knowledge most of his information on the war must have come from other sources, as it concerns military activities in the surrounding area rather than in the city itself. He sometimes strays further afield, often when little was happening locally, but in such cases he almost always implicitly or explicitly acknowledges drawing on outside reports, occasionally referring to a letter which had been received but usually using grammatical constructions which in German indicate hearsay. Conversely when dealing with events within a radius of 20 kilometres or so he uses an impersonal, authoritative style and gives no indication of his sources. He clearly made it his business to be well informed and for much of 1633 and 1634 he reports events day by day, giving considerable detail about troop movements, names of officers and exact times of day. As with other chronicles his numbers are a mixture of the vague – 'many thousand' or 'several hundred' – and the precise – '18 cavalrymen' or '564 head of the best cattle', probably reflecting more what his sources told him than any stylistic trait of his own (Ma.570). It is not easy to judge how much of this could be had from common report in Freiburg at the time, or whether Mallinger cultivated contacts in the military or elsewhere, but his information was generally accurate. Mone confirmed this by checking many entries against the most comprehensive contemporary published chronicle, the *Theatrum Europaeum*, and where he identifies significant errors these are mainly in the reports from outside the area.

It is evident that Mallinger's recording was substantially contemporaneous but that he structured and wrote up his material after a sufficient lapse of time to be able to separate out and describe particular actions coherently where appropriate, rather than always taking one day at a time in a diaristic manner. There are a number of examples where it is evident that he knew the outcome when recording an event. Thus on 7 September 1633 he reports the plundering of Jesuit property 'on the orders of the quartermaster, ... who was beheaded on the 3rd of October on the Münsterplatz in Freiburg'; he then goes on to the events of 8 September. Likewise in mid-April 1634 he records billeting of Mecklenburg cavalry in the city 'from the 15th of April until the 11th of May' before his description of events in early May, while on 13 March 1643 he mentions an influx of refugees from the countryside into the city, 'where they stayed for four months, in direst poverty' (Ma.546, 558, 595). More typically he does not know the outcome at the time of writing, indicating that he has in the main copied up a contemporaneous record without significant later editing. In May 1634 he remarks that strong attacks on Breisach were expected to succeed 'but so far nothing has been achieved', and in giving a report of an attack on Rheinfelden he notes that two hundred wounded were taken to Neuenburg but adds that 'there is as yet no definite news about the dead'. In December 1634 he describes the arrest of a number of leading citizens of Freiburg, who were imprisoned in Breisach until they promised to raise a large contribution from the city. Most were then released but two 'are still being held' (Ma.559, 557, 548). On 14 June 1634 Mallinger includes one of his very rare speculations, describing the later Emperor Ferdinand III outside Regensburg with a large army, while on the other side Bernard of Weimar, Gustav Horn and the Saxons were reported to be seeking to join forces to confront him: 'Should that happen it will come to a bloody battle, and it is to be hoped that an end will thus be made of it' (Ma.562). This was clearly written before the battle of Nördlingen, which it correctly anticipates but which did not bring the war to an end.

Impersonality is perhaps the most striking feature of Mallinger's style. Apart from in passages clearly copied from other writers and the one use of '*ego*, Thomas Mallinger' the first person pronoun appears only in an equally rare expression of opinion, his description of the auxiliaries of the departing Swedes in 1634 as 'those coarse fools and blind apes, the farmers from the Margravate – did I call them soldiers!' His most emotive passages are his descriptions of Freiburg's treatment at the hands of occupying troops, but even here he maintains distance, neither describing his personal experiences nor explicitly or implicitly claiming eyewitness authority for his more general account. He introduces no anecdotes to give colour to his record and only the slightest hints of his personality can be read between the lines in minor asides, such as in his note of the celebratory *Te Deum* after the Swedes left in 1634, where he adds that because they had taken all the ammunition with them 'this was quite inadequately celebrated just by services in the churches' instead of being accompanied by artillery salvos in the customary manner (Ma.574, 576). His wider chronicle betrays little of his feelings, except perhaps when incidents strike close to home; he notes of a Catholic priest held to ransom: 'There he had to lie, amid all the mess, filth and stench, so that he might have wasted away, until such time as he promised to give them 100 Reichstaler, and quickly too'. Even in his report of the atrocious murder of a large force of Catholic peasant irregulars from Kirchhofen after their surrender on accord he limits himself to describing it as godless, unchristian and merciless (Ma.538, 543). This passage is one of a number in which, despite using little other than plain, direct language and factual description, Mallinger produces full and interesting accounts of particular incidents. Another example is his report of the capture of a town in 1634, where he describes stage by stage the hesitations of the defenders over whether to surrender, their negotiation of terms and later retraction when hope of relief appeared, and their eventual compliance and withdrawal from the town, only to be set upon by their own relief column in thick fog, when a hundred were killed.

Although Mallinger sticks to German for these accounts he inserts Latin phrases from time to time, such as *ex desperatione, unanimiter* or *bono contento,* but only very exceptionally does he use imagery, as in his comment on the margrave of Baden-Durlach's visit to Freiburg in 1633: 'After his arrival the old wounds were reopened, as he hacked into the same places again' (Ma.544). Another example is his description of the breaking off of an attack on Rheinfelden 'because the soldiers were retreating all the time and they had to be driven into the attack with blows, just as the butcher does with his animals'. Usually he refrains from imagery or at most uses almost factual similes, for example describing houses as so damaged 'that they can't be compared with real houses any more' (Ma.559). His favourite devices for providing emphasis are to double up phrases or terms, either with the use of 'not only ... but also' or in long sequences of antitheses in a style common in sermons of the period: 'Because this plundering scarcely diminished the unfortunate citizens and feudal tenants, rich and poor, clergy and lay, noble and common, educated and uneducated, began to brood anxiously and to become melancholy, while many lost their senses and succumbed to a serious and severe illness' (Ma.545).

Mallinger's account of the effects of the war on Freiburg itself is far from comprehensive. During those years he was clearly more interested in chronicling military actions than in recording life and circumstances in the city, and he seems to have been better at gathering information from other sources than at observing for himself and describing what he saw. While he records various incidents and provides a number of summaries of conditions these must be seen as indicative rather than as anything approaching a full picture. For example he only once mentions refugees flocking into the city, although on the basis of experience elsewhere this must have occurred on many occasions. Nevertheless it seems reasonable to assume that the information he supplies is representative of the general situation; had things been significantly worse, either overall or at specific times, he would surely have noted the fact.

As in many other places, by far the most catastrophic event in Freiburg during the Thirty Years War was the plague epidemic which reached the city in August 1633. Mallinger's note of this is characteristically impersonal and low-key, but his figures are dramatic: 'Where a year ago there were some 1500 citizens no more than 400 are left, to say nothing of how many women, children, labourers and maids have gone.' Although this death rate of almost 75 per cent seems improbably high Mallinger's figures for the deaths of half – 19 out of 38 – of the chapter clergy are both more precise and comparable with experience in some monastic communities in earlier major plague outbreaks (Hatcher, 1977, pp. 21–5). He notes that 'it has also affected the clergy, so that out of 24 Basle chaplains no more than 13 are left, of ten precentors no more than five, and of four administrators in the parish office not more than one' (Ma.545). Measured against such a calamity – to which Mallinger allots only a brief paragraph – Freiburg suffered relatively little from the direct effects of the war.

11
Gallus Zembroth's Allensbach Chronicle

Allensbach, ten kilometres west of Constance, lies in the part of Germany furthest from Gustavus Adolphus's 1630 landing-point at Peenemunde, and was untouched by the Thirty Years War until the Swedish invasion reached the area two years later. Gallus Zembroth recorded the war experiences of the village and its neighbourhood from 1632 until the final departure of troops in 1649, adding a short continuation dealing with the post-war years, and a few notes were also made after his death by his son. The Karlsruhe archive acquired his manuscript in the 1850s, and it is still there.

Although the editor describes the chronicle as the work of an uneducated farmer, direct biographical information about Zembroth is limited to his son's record of his death in 1662 at the age of 73 and his own statement that he served as mayor of Allensbach in alternate years between 1632 and 1652, in rotation with Christoff Zwy from 1639 onwards. His text is less specific thereafter, but he does mention that he held office again in 1658, while his son notes his own service in 1666. Even in the years when he was not mayor it seems likely that Zembroth was closely involved in the affairs of the village. In 1647 he names Zwy as his deputy mayor and co-negotiator with the garrison commander at nearby Mainau, suggesting joint action whoever held the senior position, while his son, perhaps not distinguishing between levels of office, states that Zembroth 'was mayor here for 30 years' (Z.580). Whether this position derived principally from his personal ability or from his standing as a leading landholder cannot be assessed, but Zembroth appears to have grown grapes, the main crop of the area, on a significant scale, and he mentions on one occasion that after his vineyards had been scoured for firewood by soldiers he had to replace 20000 stakes.

Beyond this Zembroth volunteers little about himself, and although his style is not totally impersonal his explicit direct statements are confined to his role as mayor or to his own observations of war-related matters. Such picture as we can form of him involves reading between the lines and noting the occasional comment which reveals something of the man his son calls 'my faithful and beloved father'. The most prominent theme in his account is the cost to the village of contributions imposed by the military, and while this was clearly a heavy burden the care with which Zembroth repeatedly details the precise levies in cash and kind, as well as his digressions to record agricultural prices, suggest a businessman's mind. Referring to the coinage debasement of the 1620s he notes that he received in effect only 125 florins for wine he had sold for 500 florins, 'and then only tardily'. Listing the supplies they had to contribute during 1635, some of which they had to buy in, he adds: 'As if this wasn't enough the grain was exceedingly expensive' (Z.580, 567, 572). When 70 sick and wounded were billeted on them in 1640 rations were sent from Radolfzell 'but nonetheless they caused us great trouble and expense'. He seems to have accepted as quite natural in relation to his position in the community that he should serve so frequently as mayor, a fact which he normally records without comment although the strain shows through in the worst years; in 1634 he complains that 'I was compelled to hold the office of mayor again', and in 1638 'I served as mayor, with great trouble and danger' (Z.573, 571, 572).

The overall tone of Zembroth's account is factual, with few partisan, personal or emotional intrusions, although he is always quite clear which side he is on. He normally refers to the Swedes and their allies as the enemy, and when Horn's attack on Constance failed he notes that he was forced to withdraw 'amid much derision and with heavy losses'. When Bavarian forces counterattacked he comments that 'this was truly a magnificent success and victory', but when the pendulum swung back he reports Bregenz being taken, 'to the great misery and hardship of the country people' (Z.570, 575, 576). Very occasionally he gives religious expression to his feelings, as after the relief of Constance: 'The city has been preserved with the help of God and through the intercession of his worthy and beloved mother Mary'. Likewise when the island of Reichenau, immediately offshore from Allensbach, was attacked by ships, 'through God's special mercy a north wind suddenly and miraculously sprang up' and drove them back (Z.570, 575–6). Although self-pity is notably absent in Zembroth's description of Allensbach's tribulations he does express pity for others, as when Reichenau was eventually taken and plundered, which 'we on this side of the Rhine had to watch with great sorrow'. More often the hard-headed practical man shows through; briefly describing the deplorable state of Allensbach on the villagers' return after an evacuation, Zembroth notes that 'the grass was growing right into the houses. ... I set the team to mowing, made 14 hundredweight of hay from it, and sold it in Constance' (Z.577, 571). When Überlingen was eventually taken he comments sharply: 'This was due to the negligence and lack of watchfulness of the citizens'. A single comment suggests that he may have had an underlying sense of humour; noting the bad weather in 1642 he reflects that the resulting wine was 'so acid that it could have eaten through an iron helmet' (Z.574).

If Zembroth says little about himself, he is even less forthcoming about his reasons for writing the account or who he envisaged reading it. On the latter point all that can be said with certainty is that his son knew of it at the time of Zembroth's death or soon after. On the former, although he volunteers no explanation some clue is given by his title:

> Short description of all the most important circumstances and notable events which arose and occurred here in Allensbach and in the neighbouring towns and villages during the Swedish war, from *anno* 1632 until *anno* 52, during which 20 years I served as mayor in alternate years. (Z.567)

This wording closely resembles commercially published chronicles and pamphlets describing individual incidents or the war as a whole, so that it is not only probable that Zembroth had read such works (and therefore that he was, if uneducated, at least not unread) but also a fair speculation that he was consciously modelling his account on them, an impression which is strengthened by certain chronicle-like features of his style. This suggests a link between his reading of wider chronicles of the war and his writing of a corresponding local chronicle, in which context the attention he draws to his long service as mayor in his title may be seen as an implicit claim to be an authority on the experiences of the area, or even its official spokesman.

It is also relevant to consider when Zembroth wrote his chronicle. The implication of his title is that this was in (or that the work was completed in) 1652, the first year for which he makes no entry in the text, although he notes nothing of consequence for 1650 or 1651. Logically his account of events 'during the Swedish war' ends in 1649 when the troops finally left, so that his reference to 1652 seems to relate to his writing rather than to the events he set out to record, and his entries for subsequent years thus stand as a continuation rather than as part of his original text. This would be consistent with him having read chronicles of the war as a whole and using these as a model, but it does not rule out the possibility that much of the text was written earlier with the title added on completion in 1652. However the text is not diaristic in form, and at a number of points it looks forward to later events or back to earlier ones. Thus a description of the condition of the village after an evacuation appears at the beginning of 1634, although the logic of events is that the return would have occurred soon after Horn's army withdrew from Constance on 2 October 1633; this is borne out by the mention of cutting the grass for hay, realistic in October but improbable in January or February. He also describes the terms of a contributions agreement the village was forced to make with the enemy garrison at the nearby fortress of Hohentwiel in 1642, noting the immediate payments and adding 'annually thereafter hay, corn and wine to their storehouse, as well as labour service and fortification work, until *anno* 1650'. It seems most unlikely that the original agreement was defined as valid until 1650 and far more probable that this is a reference to the period during which they did in fact have to pay. Commenting on the peace terms and the end of the war in 1648 Zembroth also looks ahead: 'But no sooner had the following year of 49 arrived than it cost us more money than ever before, even though the weapons had been laid aside' (Z.574, 577).

Whenever Zembroth actually wrote his account it is evident that he must have been drawing on contemporary material, whether his own diary or other sources. His detailed recording of contributions year by year in cash and kind and to a range of recipients clearly relies on more than memory, opening up two possibilities. Either he himself kept full notes or – which seems more probable – in compiling his account he referred back to the municipal records. He is also often, but not always, precise about dates. In most years he mentions the weather, particularly events detrimental to the grape harvest such as hail or late frost, and for these he always gives a date; probably as a substantial grower he kept some kind of log to which he was able to refer. He also has dates for most of the occasions when military activity affected Allensbach, whether due to billeting, raids or major troop movements through or near the village. He may have kept a personal note of these in or as well as the farm log, but the relevant information would probably also have been entered in the municipal records, particularly as such events would often have involved public expenditure, either directly or as a later consequence. On other matters his dating is less comprehensive; he dates a meeting he attended in Meersburg in 1632 to discuss contributions but not the one which he and Zwy went to in 1647; he dates the onset and duration of the plague epidemic in 1635–36 but he describes the two full evacuations of the village in 1633 and 1647 without giving dates for either exodus or return. These variations suggest that rather than relying on a comprehensive personal diary as a basis for his account Zembroth may later have extracted dates and factual details from various of his own and municipal records kept principally for other purposes. The same could apply to one other fact which he almost always provides, the name of the commanding officer of troops stationed in or moving through the area. This would have been readily available at the time, as regiments and companies were commonly known by the names of their colonel or captain and these were probably recorded in the municipal accounts for contribution payments.

Although such a conclusion can only be speculation, these features of Zembroth's account open up the possibility that rather than it being the contemporaneous diary of an uneducated farmer it could be a relatively sophisticated piece of historical writing, in which eyewitness memories of earlier events have been supplemented by post-war research in the records. After describing the departure of the troops and the cost of peace contributions in 1649 Zembroth writes in 1650: 'As the soldiers have left the region and there are no more foreign troops about I have not pursued things further, and I don't know of anything of special note that has happened' (Z.578). Precisely what he means by this comment is unclear, but it seems more consistent with him discontinuing researching and writing up his account than with giving up a diary he had previously been keeping. The continuation to the chronicle may give another perspective on his approach. He gives no local information between 1651 and 1658 but he interpolates an account of religious conflicts amounting to war in the Swiss cantons in 1653 and 1656. Zembroth refers mainly to Lucerne, Schwyz and Berne, all some distance from Allensbach and Lake Constance, so that his long (and noticeably more partisan) account is unlikely to be based on personal knowledge, a point confirmed by phrases like 'as I have heard' or 'according to what is said', and his use of the grammatical form which in German indicates hearsay (Z.578, 579). Nevertheless he gives a quite detailed description of the political, religious and military aspects of the conflicts, including the numbers of troops and cannon employed and the names of the mediators eventually appointed, as well as the settlement terms they laid down. Zembroth's inclusion of these Swiss episodes in his chronicle suggests that he was interested in recording for its own sake, even in matters of no direct personal significance, and confirms that he was able to gather and order material from other sources in order to do so.

In his main account Zembroth sets himself clear terms of reference – to describe the Swedish war in the context of Allensbach and the neighbouring places – and he adheres to these quite closely. Geographically he scarcely strays beyond Lake Constance, and seldom outside the narrow triangle of land defined by Constance, Stockach and the fortress of Hohentwiel (near Singen), together with the island of Reichenau. He does not comment on political issues or concern himself with the wider war; if he mentions events further afield, such as the battle of Nördlingen, it is only because of the local consequences. His subject matter is similarly focused, with little that does not stem from or bear upon the war other than the summaries of the year's weather and harvest which he often includes. Within this framework he adopts three distinct narratorial perspectives. In the most personal but least frequent case he reports in the first person singular, either as an eyewitness or through references to his own circumstances, but most of the account is divided between descriptions in the first person plural of what happened in Allensbach or to its villagers and an impersonal voice used to chronicle wider events.

In the latter mode Zembroth is usually brief, factual and dispassionate, as his account of the unsuccessful first Swedish attack on Überlingen well illustrates:

> In spring the enemy immediately advanced upon this area again, and on the 22nd of April Gustav Horn marched up to the city of Überlingen and laid siege to it. After heavy fire had been directed at the Helthor Gate a breach was made and he ordered an assault, but it achieved nothing. Many attacks were beaten off, until eventually, on the 16th of May, he had to withdraw again amid mockery and with the loss of many men who lay dead, just as at Constance in the previous year of 33. (Z.571)

This style of reporting is similar to that employed in contemporary chronicles of the war and is consistent with the hypothesis that Zembroth had read some such publications and was modelling his own account on them. Where entirely external events are concerned he keeps quite strictly to this mode, but because of his narrow territorial focus most of the incidents he reports impinge in some way upon Allensbach. Thus in describing the attack on Constance in 1633 he notes that some of the 25 000 troops approached along the south bank of the Rhine 'but the majority marched by us here'. This digression barely interrupts his account of the siege but it leads into a later paragraph in which his narrative switches to the first person plural to relate the consequences for the village:

> As regards our village of Allensbach, we were driven out and chased right away. Each one sought a way of providing for himself, most going across the lake to Reichenau. The people there took us in and did the best they could for us but anyone who had taken nothing with him found little enough there. (Z.570)

Although Zembroth's style here becomes more personal, reporting a communal experience in which he shared, he remains matter-of-fact about what must have been a traumatic occasion; far from describing it in emotional terms he maintains much of the chronicle style he uses for external events and even reduces the hunger many no doubt suffered to a laconic note.

This is typical of his mode of narrating the experiences of the villagers, in which he combines ostensible first-person subjectivity with a distancing of perspective which often seems to aspire to objectivity. His description of the second evacuation of Allensbach is similarly cool: 'In the above-mentioned year of 47, as the enemy was in the area and there was no hope of improvement, we had to move completely out of our houses and village.' When raiding troops set fire to the village in 1633 Zembroth remains factual, the only hint of emotion arising from his more than customary use of adjectives to describe the destroyed property: 'well-built houses, ... a beautiful helm roof, ... four good bells'. He records the murder of an official of the next village, who he must have known well personally, in the baldest terms: 'There they killed Mayor Übelacker and two other honest men' (Z.576, 570, 569). His descriptions of the plague and famine of 1635–36 contrast sharply with the emotive style of some other accounts. Of the plague Zembroth merely notes that it 'raged fiercely and many people died', of whom he names just two, the then current mayor and a predecessor. Of the famine, after typically detailing the high food prices, he records only that: 'People had acorns ground and baked, and also had to eat bran bread. It was a grim period of great hunger which lasted for five months, although the high prices continued much longer' (Z.572). Even when he wishes to record fear or hardship Zembroth remains low-key: 'which caused great terror to us and the whole district'; 'so we were in the greatest danger'; 'because we had suffered so badly in the previous year and had nothing left' (Z.569, 569, 574). It is tempting to see in this the limitations of an uneducated farmer, but it is evident that he could write more descriptively and emotionally when he let himself go, as in his account of the occupation and fortification of Allensbach in 1640 by troops from his own side, three Spanish regiments:

> They stayed here eight long weeks and created havoc. They tore down some 20 houses and wine-press buildings, and smashed up many others so that they were no longer habitable. ... They used all the hay, of which there was a good quantity, for fodder, and took what there was in the neighbourhood away to Bodman, where a big cargo ship was recently sent from Bregenz. Nevertheless more than 200 horses collapsed from hunger and died. Many tens of acres of vines, together with all the stakes and fences, were burned. Some of the cattle were taken away at the beginning by the soldiers and the rest were slaughtered. There was such devastation that it can scarcely be described, as apart from burning the village nothing else was spared us. (Z.573)

This contrast in styles is consistent with the possibility that Zembroth was consciously aiming at a chronicle mode of writing but that on occasions his feelings intruded, letting his more natural speech patterns show through. Intrusions of another kind occur when he switches to narration in the first person singular, thus implicitly claiming to be an eyewitness. Sometimes he uses his personal experience to reinforce and validate his more general description, as when he quotes the number of vine-stakes he had to replace or the amount of his wine drunk by soldiers, 'more than three tuns'. At other points references to himself arise in his capacity as mayor rather than as author, as in accounts of meetings he attended to negotiate contributions or his observation that he dared not sleep in his house for nine weeks in 1635 'as the warden or mayor of Marggelfingen was caught at night by the Wielers and dragged off to [Hohent]wiel' (Z.572). Among his personal references, however, are some which have no structural relevance to his account. He begins his first paragraph with a description of the 1618 comet, 'which I saw myself', adding a rare glimpse of his own personality in commenting 'foolish though it is to speak of it', and he later describes gunfire damage to the fortress of Mainau, 'as I afterwards saw for myself' (Z.567, 576).

Such overt departures from Zembroth's chronicle style are comparatively rare and may be seen as the self breaking through his aspirations towards a controlled and objective record of events. This may also explain his inclusion of a number of anecdotal accounts of relatively minor incidents which although not narrated in the first person suggest personal experience. Thus he describes how in 1632 villagers acting as militia were helping to guard the newly erected defences at Staringen when the Swedes first reached the area:

> When the above-mentioned corporal saw the enemy so strong and formidable in front of him he ordered the soldiers to retreat, and they started back towards Zell. Farmers and soldiers alike ran away, some throwing down their weapons and others bringing them back with them, so that the redoubt was lost but not a man was killed. (Z.569)

Later in the same year he reports that 'the enemy at Zell had boats fitted out, and these were carefully and completely decked with oak boards so that not a man inside them could be seen'. Soldiers on Reichenau captured one of these, 'which people dubbed "the oven"', he adds (Z.569). In 1645 Allensbach and the neighbouring villages found themselves making contributions to both sides; Zembroth describes how three wagon-loads of their wine *en route* to the garrison at Hohentwiel were ambushed on the orders of the commandant of Radolfzell, and 'it was only with difficulty that we got the wagons and horses back' (Z.575).

Zembroth uses few adjectives and fewer images even in his more personal pieces of narrative, although his writing here does become appreciably more lively. That the style of the main body of his text was consciously modelled on contemporary chronicles can only be surmise, although his brief but accurate opening summary of the Bohemian rebellion again suggests that he was familiar with such accounts. The very fact that he incorporates this summary suggests an effort to relate his own text to chronicles of the war as a whole; the *Kurtze Chronica* of 1650, for example, likewise begins with the Bohemian rebellion and links this with the 1618 comet in its first paragraph. Zembroth does not attempt to describe the subsequent war in full; after Bohemia he briefly notes the conquest of the Palatinate, devotes a longer paragraph to the coinage debasement, and then moves on to 1632 and local experience.

Whether or not his choice of style is deliberate it profoundly influences the overall impression which the text creates on first reading. The largely impersonal chronicle account, the lack of emotive description, the direct and unornamented writing, the emphasis on facts and frequent figures, all convey the air of a plain man recording the plain truth. This is given greater authority by the intermittent eyewitness references and the repeated mention of Zembroth's position as mayor; the author was not only there – he was at the centre of affairs. Further reinforcement is provided by his use of precise dates, names of troop commanders and other circumstantial detail. These features also make it easy to overlook what he does not know or does not record. As noted above he does not accurately date key events such as evacuations of the village and he gives no idea of the number of deaths in the plague epidemic. He often fails to mention numbers of soldiers; when the village was raided or used for billeting he commonly uses phrases such as 'a really strong company', 'a troop of cavalry', 'strong patrols' or 'a corporal with a number of soldiers' (Z.569, 570, 571, 577). In describing resulting losses or damage he is specific only about buildings; he is vague about theft of animals or looting of personal property. That he occasionally names villagers directly affected in some way by the war tends to conceal the fact that usually he does not. These shortcomings are well illustrated in one passage which, although dramatically descriptive at first sight, cries out for more hard information at almost every point on closer reading:

> During this period a strong troop of enemy cavalry raided us and took away what horses and cattle we still had, together with a number of people who had to herd the stolen animals for them; however the majority were safely recovered. (Z.576)

Zembroth's rather pedantic precision elsewhere makes it unlikely that these weaknesses arise from carelessness or lack of interest in detail, a more credible interpretation being that he based his factually well-supported passages on contemporaneous records while the vaguer ones derive principally from his memory.

Although he chronicles Allensbach's experience of many aspects of the war Zembroth is most precise and consistent in his reporting of the extortions of the military. At the same time it is evident from his account that a system of municipal taxation spread the burden of contributions, and despite grumbling he never suggests that the villagers were unable to pay. Even when the contributions required in the first year of peace proved greater than those of the war years a modest loan tided them over:

> *Summa summarum* for this year [1649], 1523 florins and 15 kreuzer, not including the other expenses which had of necessity to be met during the year and further items which fell upon the commune. This was all collected in from taxes on the citizens and others having property here, apart from 300 florins which was lent by His Princely Grace and which was later repaid. (Z.578)

Whether this is quite the picture Zembroth meant to present must be questionable. His resentment of the multiple demands made on the village is apparent, and his chronicle style of focusing on specifics, with little digression into description, has the effect of giving prominence to these financial burdens and to the more direct military interventions in the lives of the villagers. Although his motives for writing remain speculative, somewhere among them must have been a desire to record the hardships experienced by his community, and fortuitously or otherwise the style he adopts serves this end quite well. A first reading of his account does indeed give an impression of the endless burdens of war, and it is only on closer study that it becomes apparent that dire events were few and spread over a long period, that atrocities were virtually non-existent, and that although undoubtedly exploited the Allensbachers were able to keep their heads above water within a functioning economic system throughout the war period.

12
The Memoirs of Colonel Augustin von Fritsch

Augustin von Fritsch spent 31 years, from 1618 to 1649, on active service with the Bavarian army, starting as a common soldier and reaching the rank of colonel. After the war he became military commandant of the fortress of Parkstein and the town of Weiden, where in 1660, two years before his death, he wrote his memoirs of the war, which he entitled: 'A record of all the towns and battles where I was present and took part, from *anno* 1618 to 1644' (F.105). The manuscript, which has since been lost, was clearly incomplete when the Bavarian historian Lorenz Westenrieder printed it in 1792, as the account breaks off abruptly in 1641 rather than continuing to 1644 in accordance with Fritsch's title. Westenrieder reports that there was also a separate note dated 14 May 1652, in which Fritsch summarised his army career on the occasion of his dedication of an altar in gratitude that 'the Most Holy Trinity mercifully protected me and preserved my life' (F.188).

Fritsch confines biographical information about himself strictly to his army career, but Westenrieder adds a few details. Fritsch died in 1662 and was buried in the parish church of St Michael in Weiden. His epitaph records his exact age, so that his date of birth can be fixed as 18 July 1599, but there is no indication of place or of his background. He was probably a native of Bavaria as he was no more than 19 when he joined the Bavarian army, while his enlistment as a common musketeer and slow progress through the non-commissioned ranks suggest modest origins, although his ability to write implies that he did not come from the very lowest levels. In his 1652 summary Fritsch notes that he advanced successively through the ranks of lance-corporal, corporal and sergeant before becoming an officer after some 11 years' service, but he gives no dates for the earlier promotions. The first firm fact is that he was an acting sergeant in 1626, whereafter he was promoted every three years until he reached the rank of colonel. Fritsch is unspecific about this last promotion and his posting as commandant of the town of Amberg, but this may have been in 1644 as this is the end he sets to his battle record, while Westenrieder gives July 1646 as the date of his subsequent appointment as commandant at the town of Waldsassen. He still held this latter post in 1660 but he relinquished the command of Amberg and was discharged from the army at the last stage of the peace implementation. It is not clear in what circumstances he was appointed commandant of Parkstein and Weiden, but this was certainly after 1652 and probably much later in the decade, as he still seems to have been resident in Waldsassen in 1657. Fritsch himself states that he was in the army for 31 years up to his discharge, but his epitaph records 34 years service, suggesting that he might have been recalled for the Parkstein and Weiden post in his latter years.

Westenrieder notes that Fritsch married Marie Salome von Siggenhausen before his move to Waldsassen, by which time they had a daughter, and the baptismal register lists a further five children born to the couple between 1651 and 1656. A chapel votive tablet records that Fritsch had another son, Johann Augustin, presumably also born before his arrival in Waldsassen, who had fallen into the moat from the castle bridge but had escaped unhurt. Nothing in Fritsch's text suggests that he had been married before, so that he was presumably a bachelor during his long years on campaign. It seems that once released from front-line service into a relatively secure post, and with rank, status and the ennoblement which accompanied his promotion to major in 1638 to offer, he made a good but late marriage to a much younger wife and started to raise a family.

Although Fritsch could write, the quality of his text (as printed) suggests no more than a basic education. His spelling is erratic even by seventeenth-century standards, with several variants on the same word not infrequently occurring within a few lines. His use of initial capital letters for nouns and even proper names is equally random, while his punctuation is rudimentary. He employs no paragraphs or subheadings and rarely gives dates, so that his text is a continuous undifferentiated narrative rather than having the format either of a contemporaneous diary or of a written-up retrospective chronicle. Fritsch's language too is plain and straightforward. Although he occasionally uses Latin words this suggests not formal education but that such expressions formed part of the common military parlance of the time, for example '*totaliter* defeated' or '*formaliter* besieged'. He employs almost no imagery, a rare exception being when he complains that Spanish troops failed to provide support 'but left us hanging on the Cross until the blessed night fell' (F.110, 115, 132). Even so his description is sometimes quite colourful. Cannon fire at the battle of Wimpfen created 'such an awful smoke ... that we could scarcely see a pistol-shot in front of us'. His account of an argument is graphic if not over-subtle: 'That made me angry, and I said to him: "You are an idiot, ... that is not true, you good-for-nothing layabout"' (F.110, 155). Although he includes much tedious and irrelevant detail his accounts of skirmishes can be dramatic, lively and realistic:

Each one went for his man, and I took on a fellow in an all-red coat. As soon as I had fired my pistol he brought out a carbine from under his jacket, but once he had got off his shot at me he began to withdraw, and I went after him with my remaining loaded pistol. However as the equerry turned his own horse he saw that mine had been hit, and he rode up to me as fast as he could, shouting: 'Lieutenant, in the name of a hundred devils, get back, your horse has been shot!' At this I looked underneath the horse's front and saw that both shanks and feet were covered in blood. (F.123)

The text has the air of being written by an author for whom composition was not an easy process, and most of it falls into one or other of two distinct styles. Many passages simply recount the movements and actions of Fritsch's unit, and are basic, factual and little more than a string of main clauses or very simple subordinate clauses; they read like military reports written by a poorly educated NCO or junior officer. In other places Fritsch gives extended accounts of incidents, often quite minor in themselves, in which he played a leading personal role, and here his style is much more complex, often becoming convoluted and difficult to follow. He is clearly trying to give a full and graphic description, which one senses that he might do quite well orally, but his writing skills are strained to their limit in the process. This may be significant in assessing the content of his account, the writing of which appears more as a task he set himself, even as a duty, rather than as something he did easily or in response to a deep-seated urge to record or to express himself. In this context his fixity of purpose and narrow focus become easier to comprehend.

Although Fritsch notes that his memoir was written in 1660, long after the events described, its content suggests that he kept a diary of some kind during his military service. He was on the march for the great majority of the 21 years covered by his extant account, 1620 to 1641, passing through a bewildering array of places ranging from Linz to Lorraine, Prague to Maastricht, Rheinfelden to Stade. Up to 40 years later he was able to record these chronologically, adding the apparently exact information that he had been 'at the capture of 75 towns, many of them taken by storm, and also in 12 pitched battles' (F.187). He is frequently able to quote accurate numbers of men or the official strength of an army, and in describing incidents he often includes the names of otherwise inconsequential participants, while he can be precise about the names and ranks of more senior people. The opening passage of his account illustrates both his style and the detail he could recall from 1620:

First we marched out from Linz with the Bavarian army, to Mauthausen, over the Danube and on to Freistadt. From there we went on through the same forest in Austria-below-the-Enns to Drosendorf, which we took. There we joined forces with the Imperialist [General] Comte de Bucquoy and marched together upon Budian [Budweis] in Bohemia, which we besieged and then took by storm. From there we advanced to Brisca, where Captain Schon's steward Julian had his arm shot off as he sat at dinner. On the following day we took the town by storm of hand and killed everyone in it. From there we went with the army to Pilsen, before which we lay encamped for several days. Here Major General von Haslang became ill and set off back to Bavaria, accompanied by my Colonel Schmidt's wife, but they were captured by the Hungarians. (F.105–6)

This passage both suggests that Fritsch kept a contemporaneous diary and indicates the manner in which he may have used it in writing his 1660 account. The content is exactly what a young, not very literate soldier might be expected to note in his pocket book, a mixture of the bare facts of the campaign – where we went, what we did – with odd inconsequential details which seemed interesting, amusing or merely out of the ordinary at the time. Thus the steward losing an arm was probably only noteworthy because he was at dinner when it happened, while the colonel's wife would not have entered the record but for her misfortune in being captured while accompanying the sick general. The style of the passage and the retention of these irrelevances imply that Fritsch may here have done little more than to string together his diary jottings, a possibility which might also account for the simple clausal structure and indeed shed some light on the duality of style in the text as a whole – simple and basic where he was sticking closely to a contemporaneous record and more complex where he was amplifying such notes from memory in order to give a more graphic account. His diaristic passages, essentially march itineraries and lists of actions interspersed with occasional anecdotal details, strongly resemble parts of the contemporaneous diary of the Bavarian soldier Hagendorf, although the latter includes much more personal information and comment on food, drink, conditions and the country through which he passed. The difference probably reflects individual temperament – Fritsch may simply have been a less conscientious or less imaginative diarist in the first place – although it is also possible that he edited out contemporaneous material which seemed inappropriate to his purpose in 1660. Such anecdotes as remain add a little colour to his record: a soldier's trouser pocket shot off and made the subject of a witticism about Bavarian coinage; a lieutenant 'who was shot in a secret place'; troops blundering about in fog during a battle warned of the presence of the enemy only by one of their number who 'had to go off to one side because of his necessity but then came running back with his trousers in his hands shouting: "The enemy! The enemy!"' (F.127, 110). These incidents are not merely regimental jokes; they are specifically related to individuals and occasions, strongly suggesting that Fritsch noted them down at the time. By the same token his fuller, although also anecdotal, accounts of happenings centred around himself have a detailed basis which implies a contemporaneous record, even if this was embroidered later.

Given the assumption of underlying contemporaneous notes the lack of dates in Fritsch's text seems surprising. He quotes the year on only half a dozen occasions, notes the day without year a couple of times ('on the second day of the Whitsun festival'; 'on St Martin's day'), and is only really specific twice, when he dates the battle of the White Mountain in 1620 and his unit's departure from Prague on 1 May the following year (F.122, 173). This makes his chronology hard to follow, although as he usually mentions taking up winter quarters the turn of most years can be identified, while fixed points are provided by the considerable number of major battles at which he was present. Even so this is not incompatible with the kind of pocketbook record he might have made, more a personal *aide mémoire* in which dates were much less relevant than notes of places, people and incidents, rather than a chronicle or a diary kept with any thought that he might later want to write up a full account of his experiences. This feature also suggests that Fritsch relied on his own notes and memory rather than checking from other sources, and the same inference may be drawn from his sometimes specific, sometimes vague quotation of numbers.

Fritsch's reasons for keeping a rudimentary diary are as inscrutable as those of many other people. Like Hagendorf he would have been unusual among the common soldiers in being able to write, and this alone may have prompted him to use his skill. Perhaps he may have seen some professional value in having notes of where he had been and what he had done; certainly his progress from the ranks to colonel suggests more than average ambition and application. On the other hand he has provided a clear and succinct description of his reasons for writing up his account in 1660:

> God the Almighty in his divine mercy preserved me like a father throughout the past war, and further until now as I write this, raising me from the musket to a colonel's command during 31 years on campaign, from *anno* 1618 to 1649. Hence I have compiled and described these things truthfully and with a clear conscience with my own hand, presenting them for eternal remembrance, for the special solace of my children, and for their emulation, so that whether in war or in other service they may conduct themselves equally as faithfully towards every man. (F.105)

Fritsch had good cause to be grateful for having survived active service during the entire Thirty Years War despite being frequently involved in battle and several times wounded, and doubtless he saw the hand of God in this and in his accompanying rise to rank, nobility and fortune. Nor need we doubt the sincerity of the religious dedication of his text, which is in keeping with his erection of the altar in 1652 and with the votive tablet he placed in the chapel after his son survived his fall from the castle bridge. Even so his young family were probably the more immediate cause of his writing, as Fritsch then had several children under ten years of age and perhaps two a little older, while he was himself beginning to grow old by the standards of the time. His references to 'special solace' and 'emulation' surely reflect a perception that he might not be there to guide their development into adulthood, while 'equally as faithfully' defines the moral example he hoped they would draw from his career. Last and not least is the awareness of mortality in his wish for 'eternal remembrance', which is often an implicit if not explicit background to autobiographical writing.

Unlike many of the civilian accounts of the war Fritsch's text is quite specifically autobiographical, although confined to his military career. As such his narrative perspective is straightforwardly first person throughout, either 'we' in recounting his unit's collective activities or 'I' in relating his personal experiences. Occasionally he incorporates third-person anecdotes, but almost always ones describing incidents which he witnessed or which happened in his immediate vicinity. Only rarely and briefly does he comment on matters beyond this horizon; he, not the war, is the principal subject. His treatment of his story is, however, rather unusual. Although he provides a more or less continuous chronological record, much of the time is accounted for in what are little more than itineraries, as in 1632:

> After 14 days we marched away from Stade, leaving it ungarrisoned, moving to Verden and then on to Lemgo, which we besieged and took. From there we went to Herford, which we likewise besieged and took – it was a pretty town – and then on to the strong town of Einbeck, which again we besieged and took, [and on through another dozen towns]. (F.126)

Most of his text is taken up instead with full accounts of a relatively small number of incidents in which he played a leading part. Some of these, particularly in the middle period in which he was a ranking but not yet a senior officer, are descriptions of smaller military actions where he was in command, while others deal with the occasions upon which he was wounded or captured. Later he gives an exhaustive account of his summons to Munich to receive orders from the war council, describing the dignitaries he met and what he and they said to each other, although passing over the assignment they gave him in a few lines. Elsewhere the matters are quite trivial; he describes riding alongside the Imperialist General Piccolomini when the latter sought a volunteer (not Fritsch) to swim a river and set fire to an enemy baggage depot, and he gives considerable space to a dispute with an engineer officer over the correct way to set out trenches at a siege. These episodes give Fritsch's text an interesting quality, illustrating a soldier's life in the war through a series of varied and often colourful sketches rather than in a more even but drier account of the important events in which he took part.

While the basic facts for the extended descriptive sections may also be drawn from whatever diary Fritsch kept, they have in substance the air of often-told tales which many a time enlivened taverns, officers' messes or the dinner table of the commandant at Amberg, Waldsassen or Weiden. Stylistically they resemble transcribed oral narratives rather than written compositions, and they are quite different from the briefly factual passages covering longer periods of time which link the author's more personal experiences. Although he generally maintains chronology Fritsch's style here becomes anecdotal and discursive, tending to ramble, deviate and pursue minor or irrelevant details. In the manner of a typical raconteur he gives emphasis, colour and veracity to his tale through almost verbatim reported speech. Thus when a risky mission arose 'my general called me to him and said: "You like to do this kind of thing. ... Take 30 of the quartermaster's best men and ride there tonight, the whole night through, so that you get to the township before daybreak."' *En route* they passed through a friendly village 'and because the messenger told the people that we were Imperialist they ran to the doors of their houses and called out "God the Almighty give you luck and blessing", and they made the sign of the Cross' (F.139). When quoting what might seem an exaggerated number of enemy cavalry Fritsch interjects in oral fashion 'as true as I am honourable' (F.124). Elsewhere he adds comments in conversational asides: 'and so we had as hot and hard a day as we had ever known in a battle'; 'in as jolly a place as I had ever seen in my life'; 'the infantry was really splendid, and drawn up ready to fight. In all my days as a soldier I never saw a better-executed retreat than this one' (F.131, 151, 172). Even his irrelevances sometimes have the air of a storyteller's devices. Thus when he interrupts his account of the all-night ride mentioned above with a description of resting the horses this would serve orally as a dramatic pause before continuing the action with the dawn descent on the township. In order to stress the difficulties of a particular journey he interpolates the otherwise superfluous fact that 'a woman with her two children, three horses and her manservant were drowned in a ford which I also had to ride across' (F.176). At the siege of Koblenz Fritsch earnestly tells of how a fellow officer was captured and would have been hanged on suspicion of complicity in an earlier broken accord 'if he had not been able to speak French', but he then provides light relief by adding that when the town fell 'I got General Pöse's hat with its three fine feathers' (F.158).

Fritsch's omissions may be as revealing as his actual text. He says nothing of his background or how he came to join the army in 1618, starting instead *in medias res* in 1620. One may surmise that 'Augustin von Fritsch of Moss, Kümmersbruch and Dammelsdorf, his Electoral Highness of Bavaria's appointed colonel, at this time commandant of the town of Weiden and the fortress of Parkstein, also head and chief officer of the jurisdiction of Waldsassen' did not feel it necessary to call attention to his humble origins, instead beginning his account at the point where he first went on active service (F.105). Likewise he does not record his early promotions, perhaps because his initial progress was unremarkable, although also perhaps because his diary or memory were inadequate; there is for example a discrepancy between his 1652 note in which he states that he became a major 'after the battle of Nördlingen', which was in 1634, and his main account in which this promotion was notified while he was in quarters over the winter of 1638–39. Fritsch records here that 'on the same occasion His Imperial Majesty awarded me my patent of nobility as a reward for the storming of Heidelberg', but curiously he provides no description of how he earned this elevation. Easier to explain is the brevity of his description of the major battles at which he was present, which reflects his sharp focus on his own role rather than on wider events; in a full-scale battle the individual soldier or officer is but a cog in the wheel, and such experiences as he might record are likely to parallel those of thousands of other participants. Thus Fritsch dismisses Nördlingen with half a page and the off-hand summary: 'so within six hours the battle was won' (F.187, 169, 149). That he says nothing about the personal side of army life may simply be a matter of his self-set terms of reference, to provide a 'record of all the towns and battles', but it may also derive from his intention that the record of his military career should serve as an example for his young children to follow. The noble and respectable Colonel von Fritsch could scarcely display so naively human a picture of himself as does Hagendorf, and even the sober-sided Monro might sometimes come too near the knuckle for the self-image Fritsch wished to leave to his posterity.

Nevertheless an indication, if not a complete picture, of Fritsch's personality may be gleaned from his memoirs. That he was courageous is evident; he seems often to have been in the thick of the action, where comrades were shot down alongside him, and he himself was three times wounded. Early in his career, in 1621, he took part in the storming of Neckargemünd, 'where Captain Kögler fell down on top of me from a ladder during the assault, and lay dead'. 12 years later, by which time Fritsch was an ensign or possibly already a captain, something similar happened at Rheinfelden, 'where I was the first up the ladder in the assault, with 50 men'; the captain leading the section in the attack was shot dead and Fritsch took command in his place (F.108, 136–7). By 1637 he was a senior captain, temporarily in command of his regiment due to the death or wounding of his superiors, when he led the assault at Paderborn; he was wounded as the attack was beaten off (although the town surrendered the following day), but was rescued by a lieutenant who, 'not knowing whether I was alive or dead, took hold of me by one foot and dragged me away as fast as he could under continuous heavy fire from the enemy. He ran with me to the approach trench and threw me in.' He was still in the forefront at the siege of Göttingen in 1641. By then a lieutenant-colonel, Fritsch was holding a redoubt with a handful of men when the defenders sallied in strength; his text breaks off dramatically just as 700 soldiers were about to overrun his position: 'They leaped out from behind, over the breastwork, whereupon I shot one with a red coat ...' (F.161, 187). An earlier reference makes clear that he was captured here and held prisoner for some time; he had been more fortunate on the occasion of his first capture in a battle outside Wolfenbüttel, where he was exchanged after five days.

Even allowing that Fritsch's account is selective, he appears to have been a competent and resourceful officer, as his promotions testify. At the siege of Höxter with General Pappenheim in 1632 he volunteered to reconnoitre with two men; discovering that the enemy garrison were slipping away from the rear of the town over the river, he sent for another 50 men, approached the gate and successfully talked the mayor into admitting the attackers, an exploit which earned him the nickname 'tall rascal' from Pappenheim, 'as he invariably called me from that time on' (F.128). On another occasion Fritsch was sent out from Rheinfelden to forestall an enemy attack on the village of Altkirch; reaching there in time he forced two successive larger enemy patrols to surrender by allowing them to be admitted through one of the gates which, when closed, left them boxed in between the inner and outer gates under the guns of his concealed soldiers. He captured some 80 men and their valuable horses, and was rewarded by the residents into the bargain. In 1637 he induced a garrison holding a strongly fortified church to surrender by convincing them that he had undermined the building and was about to blow it up, work which would in fact have taken six or seven days. The following year he was sent to hold a bridge, which he realised he could not do as three enemy regiments approached; instead by setting 'two large inns' on the bridgehead afire he forced them to divert to the next bridge, thus avoiding the ignominy of being driven out of his position. The unit at the next place was not so lucky and their captain was killed, Fritsch rather smugly remarking that 'if the good cavalier had only done as I did he might also have come well out of it' (F.165).

This smugness is one of the less lovable traits which emerge between the lines of Fritsch's text. He clearly liked to be right and to be seen to be right; the point of the long account of the dispute with the engineer officer referred to above is that Fritsch got his way, 'so I completed my redoubt before daybreak. In the evening we were relieved as soon as it got dark, and no more than two of my soldiers had been hit by gunfire.' In similar vein he reports that he was in command of a battery of guns at the siege of Nördlingen when no less a person than the later Emperor Ferdinand III sent a complaint that 'I should have them shoot better because there was no dust to be seen rising, to which I answered: "When you see lots of dust, the shots are not going into the soldiers or cavalry", so the general rode back to the King of the Romans and reported the answer I had given.' On his visit to the war council Fritsch also carefully notes down the reported praise of the elector of Bavaria: 'His Electoral Highness himself had a gracious confidence in me because I had always conducted myself well and honourably in the field' (F.156, 148, 175). We may, however, forgive a man who had risen from the ranks his pride at recognition from such a height.

On the other hand Fritsch accepted army life with fortitude and he rarely complains. The pain of his wounds is noted in a matter-of-fact way rather than stressed, and he scarcely mentions other hardships, confining himself even on General Gallas's disastrous campaign in France in 1636 to the briefest description of the sufferings of the army. He appears to have been liked by his superiors, as suggested by Pappenheim giving him a nickname and his colonel's decision to take him with him on a posting 'because he didn't want to have any other lieutenant-colonel from another regiment' (F.169). That he returned this with loyalty is indicated by his brief epitaph for Pappenheim, 'our beloved general', who was killed at the battle of Lützen, and by the most personal passage of writing in the text, recording the death of his long-time colonel, Reinach. The latter had been wounded and Fritsch was under orders to move away:

> Before I set out, however, I rode into the town to see my colonel once again and to say my farewell to him, as everyone readily saw that he would go no further. There he most highly commended and entrusted his children and his estate to me, which duty I promised to carry out diligently. Then I rode out to my unit, but he, my dearly beloved colonel, died that same night, and he was buried with due ceremony on the following morning before the army marched away. (F.134, 171)

For posterity Fritsch's memoirs are on the one hand an interesting collection of vignettes of the professional side of a soldier's life in the Thirty Years War, and also an insight into the scope it provided for a competent but unimaginative man of action to rise from the musket to senior officer status. On the other hand it appears as a frustrating missed opportunity for a wider view of the war to be provided by a well-placed source. Fritsch not only tells us little about himself; he tells us even less about the effects of the war on others. His accounts of his 12 battles are cursory, and of the capture of the 75 towns and cities he usually says nothing more than that they were taken. Occasionally he adds 'and we killed everyone within' or variants such as 'everyone who was found in arms was killed', but even this was a stock phrase of the time which should not necessarily be read literally (F.106, 112). He says nothing of civilians and he makes virtually no mention of foraging, contributions, plundering, burning, hunger or disease, all matters which made a deep impression on other diarists, even military ones such as Monro, Poyntz and Hagendorf. We are left to wonder whether he deliberately excised such things from an account intended for his children, whether his lack of imagination was such that they left no impression on him by 1660, or whether he merely underplays what others exaggerate.

There may be elements of all three in the shaping of the text. While Fritsch makes himself the central character of his account it is by no means a 'warts and all' self-portrait, but a picture appropriate to his status and self-image at the age of 60, a representation of how he wished to be remembered rather than of how he may in his younger days have been. As such he avoids the potentially discreditable and he pays much greater attention to episodes in which he was personally successful or on the winning side, omitting his own failures and playing down his side's defeats accordingly. Although booty was too much a part of the system to be discreditable it was still perhaps not quite gentlemanly to dwell too much on it, and Fritsch rarely refers to his spoils of war; nevertheless by 1638 he had acquired a considerable fortune, enough to lose a wagon and six horses loaded with 'choice tapestries', a whole sackful of silver plate and 5000 Reichstaler in cash at a lost battle (F.163). The only really discreditable episode that Fritsch records is the breach of an accord he made in inducing the defenders of a fortified church to surrender (described in Chapter 3). Here he is careful to point out that a more senior officer gave the order for the prisoners to be killed and that he and his men objected and refused to carry out the executions, but the most interesting point is that he mentions the incident at all. This suggests both that such savagery and duplicity was not a normal and accepted part of the conduct of the war, and also that it affected him to the extent that he did not feel able, years afterwards, to purge it from his account.

13

The Memoirs of Colonel Robert Monro

Few of the participants in the Thirty Years War who kept diaries or wrote accounts of their experiences expected them to be published. Robert Monro is an exception, as he published his own memoirs and observations as a book in 1637. Monro, whose origins were on the Cromarty Firth north of Inverness, was a grandson of the 15th Baron Fowles, and as he is variously reported to have lived until 1675 or 1680 his birth cannot long have preceded his father's death in 1589 (Mackenzie, 1898, pp. 169, 264; Hill, 1869, I, p. 415). Little is known of his early years, before he enlisted in August 1626, probably already in his late thirties, as a lieutenant in the regiment being raised by Sir Donald Mackay for service with the Danish forces in Germany. Monro provides this latter information on the title page of his book, and further on he refers to Sir John Hepburn, commander of the Scots Brigade under Gustavus Adolphus, of whom he says: 'As we were oft Camerades of danger together; so being long acquainted, we were Camerades in love: first at Colledge, next in our travells in France, at Paris and Poictiers, Anno 1615, till we met againe in Spruce at Elben in August 1630' (Mo.II. 75) When and where Monro studied is unknown, but the range of classical and historical references he introduces into his text confirms that he had read widely. He provides only one other snippet of information about his past, describing how he was 'once made to stand in my younger yeares at the Louver gate in Paris, being then in the Kings Regiment of the Guards, passing my prentiship' (Mo.I. 45).

This previous military experience may explain Monro's rapid promotion in Mackay's regiment. Embarking for Germany as a lieutenant in 1626, he was acting major by mid-1627 before being confirmed in this rank and gaining the captaincy of a company in the autumn of that year. Mackay himself was absent most of the time, back in Scotland either recruiting or ill, and Monro almost immediately assumed command of the regiment during the lieutenant-colonel's extended leave. The latter returned in May 1628, commanding during the siege of Stralsund – a matter of weeks – but soon afterwards he 'quit the Regiment' and Monro was promoted to lieutenant-colonel (Mo.I. 82).

Thus within two years he progressed from lieutenant to effective command of the regiment, and in this capacity he negotiated its transfer to Swedish service after Denmark was forced out of the war by Wallenstein. Two years of inactivity in Denmark and Sweden followed before the regiment was shipped to Germany with Gustavus Adolphus's army in August 1630, and Monro was in command throughout the subsequent campaigning although he was only formally promoted to colonel on Mackay's withdrawal in August 1632. In late summer 1633 he returned to Scotland to recruit, building his regiment up to almost 2000 men in 12 companies by 1634, although he himself had not yet returned to Germany when it was effectively wiped out at Nördlingen in September of that year.

That was the end of Monro's direct involvement in the Thirty Years War, and he spent the next few years in Scotland, busying himself trying to found a hospital and gain pensions for old soldiers, and writing his book (Stevenson, 1981, p. 80). His dedication of this work to the young elector Palatine, the son of Frederick V, the 'Winter King' of Bohemia, and his injunction to him to 'come, Noble Sir, unto the field, and fight before us', indicate that he remained loyal to the Protestant cause, but he did not return to the colours in Germany (Mo. Epistle, 4). Instead his recall to military service came in 1639, when he fought in Scotland on behalf of the Covenanters, with the rank of major-general, before going to Ireland in 1642 as nominal deputy but effective commander of a 10 000 strong Scottish army sent to assist in quelling the Catholic rebellion. In December 1643 Parliament placed all the English forces in Ireland under his command, and he continued to serve there and in Scotland until 1648, when he came under suspicion of supporting the Royalist cause, as a result of which he was displaced, arrested, despatched to London and imprisoned in the Tower, where he languished until 1653 (Mackenzie, 1898, p. 263). Monro had made an advantageous second marriage in Ireland, to the widow of the second Viscount Montgomery, and after his release Cromwell intervened to secure him the return of her lands, where he lived in retirement to a ripe old age (Stevenson, 1981, pp. 152, 288).

This biographical information gives some picture of the man who wrote the book, a man who was entrusted with high military command by Gustavus Adolphus, by the Scottish Estates and by the English Parliament. He seems also to have been, at least in part, the model for Sir Walter Scott's Dugald Dalgetty. Scott quotes from Monro's book in his 1829 introduction to the second edition of *A Legend of Montrose*, describing it as 'a work which the author repeatedly consulted while composing the following sheets, and which is in great measure written in the humour of Captain Dugald Dalgetty' (Scott, 1852, VI, p. 173). Other opinions are less favourable. In the mid-nineteenth century Burton described the book as 'unreadable', noting 'the confusion, ambiguity, and verbose prolixity of the narrative', which is 'saturated in a mass of irrelevant erudition' (Burton, 1864, pp. 137, 134, 135). More recently Stevenson comments on Monro's 'lack of ability to discriminate between the useful and the useless, the profound and the obvious', concluding that the picture which emerges is 'one of a conscientious and thoughtful man, skilled in his trade but pedantic and over serious' (Stevenson, 1981, p. 83). It is thus of particular interest to ask what moved this man of action, unusually for the time, to both write and publish his memoirs.

One partial answer is that Monro had time on his hands, but this prompts the question as to why he did not return to Germany either before or after Nördlingen. His reason for visiting Scotland in 1633 is clear; the regiment had been detached from the main Swedish army in order to recruit replacements for its heavy casualty losses, but an attempt to rebuild in Swabia had been thwarted by enemy action, so that returning to recruit in Scotland, as Mackay had regularly done, was both logical and necessary. Nevertheless it may be more than coincidence that Monro decided to make this trip soon after the war had struck heavy blows very close to him. Three Latin epitaphs feature prominently in the introductory pages of his book: to the head of his family, Colonel Robert Munro, 18th Baron Fowles, who died of his wounds at Ulm in March 1633; to his brother Colonel John Monro, killed near Bacharach, also in March 1633; and to his own lieutenant-colonel, John Sinclair, killed in the Upper Palatinate in about July 1633. In November 1632 Gustavus Adolphus, for whom Monro's expressed admiration amounts to hero-worship, had been killed at Lützen, and two months before that Monro had himself been severely wounded at Nuremberg, added to which his horse had fallen on his leg early in 1633 'and being six weekes under cure I continued still with the Armie, on all occasions commanding on horse-back, being unable to travell a foote' (Mo.II. 173). In these circumstances it would not be surprising if a period away from the front were welcome to him, or if he allowed recruiting and family duties to detain him in Scotland for some time.

A year later the regiment was shattered at Nördlingen and reduced to a single company, so that Monro was faced with the need to rebuild from almost nothing. With the loss of so many comrades and members of his clan at that battle adding to the family losses of the previous year his heart may not have been in the task, while the necessary funds may not have been forthcoming from stretched Swedish resources after the near-disastrous defeat. He is also sharply critical of the political and military leadership at that time, commenting that 'before the fall of Kingdomes arise dissensions, that overthrow the confederates more than their enemies, as it happened here in our late warres of Germanie, after the death of his Majestie of Sweden'. He blames 'the suddaine losse of Nerling' on 'discord amongst the Superiours', adding that 'for want of one Supreme Commander, as Gustavus was, they could not agree among themselves' (Mo.II. 197, 197, 198). Problems multiplied for the Swedish cause after this defeat, with Saxony negotiating a separate peace, soon to be followed by Brandenburg, while the Swedish army mutinied in mid-1635 because it had not been paid. Necessity and inclination may have combined to keep Monro away.

Later he appears to have had hopes of returning with a new commission. The introduction and dedication to his book make clear that the dead were still very much in his mind in 1637, and he sets out his aim of 'eternizing their memory', but a more practical objective is also implicit in his formal 'Epistle Dedicatory'. Lengthy baroque dedications to actual or hoped-for patrons were common, but Monro's choice of the elector Palatine is significant. In addressing this dispossessed and impoverished young man he issues a plea to him 'to fight with good lucke and victory, with strength and power, with wisdome and understanding, &c. against your Highnesse enemies'. Monro carefully links together his eulogies of the dead with the aspirations of the living:

> Hoping therefore (for their sakes departed of worthy memory) my paines may be acceptable unto your Highnesse, for their sakes alive (that long for a new Leader) I have beene bold, to send unto your Highnesse at this time, worthy Counsellours, whose counsell your Highnesse may be bold to follow, and their vertues, being most Heroicke and examplary, may be imitated by your Highnesse, in going before us, as our new Master, Captaine and Leader. (Mo. Epistle, 2, 4, 2–3)

Monro refers to 'being at the court of England, attending imployment', and one may imagine that as well as urging the elector to take up arms these counsellors would have been offering his services, seeking for him a colonel's commission to raise a regiment, if not the command of an army (Mo. Epistle, 1). Viewed in this way the book appears to have both a political and a personal dimension. By dedicating to the elector an eyewitness description of the war as conducted by two previous champions of the Protestant cause, Christian IV of Denmark and Gustavus Adolphus, Monro set before him examples to emulate. By drawing attention to his own experience and qualities he may well have been canvassing for employment. Probably such thoughts were not in his mind at the outset, but they may have developed as he progressed, gradually shaping the final text as ideas of using it as a means of reactivating his military career emerged.

While Monro, 'ever in readinesse to fight with our enemies, and to endure all incommodities', may well have had an eye towards his own re-employment, his commitment to the 'good Cause' is evident (Mo.I. 38, 21). His text exudes pride in the achievements of Gustavus Adolphus and the Swedish army, particularly their having 'opened the doores ... of all houses and Churches in the Paltz, that had beene closed ten yeares before', enabling them 'againe to serve God peaceably in their former true, undoubted and onely pure profession of the Faith of Christs Gospell' (Mo.II. 94). Monro probably watched the decline in Swedish fortunes after Nördlingen with the partisan frustration implicit in his wish to be 'avenged of my friends bloud, and mine owne, shed in the quarrell' (Mo.I. 30). His belief in a single, author-itative princely leader is clearly expressed, but by this time most of the credible champions of Protestantism were either dead or defeated, or, like the electors of Saxony and Brandenburg, had hastily made a separate peace with the emperor. Catholic France filled the breach but was hardly to Monro's taste as a militant Calvinist, and the hopes he directed towards his co-religionists of the Palatinate are therefore understandable if politically unrealistic.

Monro's possible personal and political motivations may help to explain the principal idiosyncrasies of his book. In conception its most striking fea-ture is its arrangement into alternating chapters of 'Duties' and 'Observ-ations'. The former comprise a self-sufficient chronological account of his experiences, in line with his stated aim of providing 'a true & simple narra-tion of the principall occurrences which happened in the course of this warre, without omitting one dayes March' (Mo. Epistle, 2). The latter contain amplifications of the story, including Monro's opinions and commentaries on what had happened, together with anecdotes, moralising summaries and a wide range of digressions. There is a significant stylistic difference between the two types of chapter. Within the conventions of the time the Duties are relatively straightforward, informative and readable, whereas the Observations are undeniably tedious. With calculated mock-modesty Monro refers to him-self as a 'rude, and ignorant Souldier', and to his book as 'not adorned with eloquent phrase; but with truth and simplicitie' (Mo. Epistle, 2; To the Reader, 2). The Observations, however, are larded with elaborate expressions and heavy-handed classical allusions, and those on the Swedish campaign in particular are clearly intended (whatever their effect) to create the impression of a well-educated and thoughtful military mind, able to theorise and inter-pret as well as to record events. This may be no more than vanity and intel-lectual pretension on Monro's part, but it could also be partly an exercise in self-presentation, an implicit claim to fitness for higher command and a dif-ferentiation of the author from the many rough-and-ready, man-of-action and not infrequently only semi-literate colonels of the Thirty Years War. These differences in style and content suggest that the Duties and Observations had a different genesis, with the former representing Monro's original narrative account of his experiences and the latter his subsequent attempt to intellec-tualise it for dedication and publication.

It may also be significant that Monro chose to divide his memoirs into two parts. His separation of the Danish and Swedish periods of his service is quite logical chronologically but tends to obscure the centrality of Gustavus Adolphus to the second part. This history of 'Monro his Expedition' is equally a history of Gustavus's expedition to Germany, as indicated by Monro's comment at their parting: 'having bin still both I and our Regiment with his Majesty, on all service of importance, since his Majesties upbreaking from Stetin in Pomeren, till this parting at Donavert on the Danube, the eleventh of October, 1632' (Mo.II. 159–60). Four weeks later Gustavus was dead, and although Monro served a further nine months in Germany these are recorded only cursorily, in a manner quite unlike the preceding full account. There is also a strong thematic unity in Part II between the Duties, which feature the actions of the king prominently, and the Observations, which are essentially a commentary – albeit a highly discursive one – on his character, capabilities and conduct of the campaign. Part I has no such unifying element, the Observations rambling around all kinds of subjects with only the loosest links to the action and containing most of the 'irrelevant erudition' of which critics have complained. While the text provides only thematic and stylistic hints of this kind, it is possible that Monro wrote Part II first, as a tribute to Gustavus Adolphus and a record of his campaign, and that Part I may have followed as time started to hang heavy on his hands.

Stripped of its verbiage the core work reveals a clear pattern. It is essentially an exemplary heroic epic with carefully pointed morals drawn from each episode, written in a style which combines elements of the medieval romance with the rhetoric of the Calvinist sermon. Gustavus Adolphus is – almost literally – the knight on a white charger come to rescue true religion and its oppressed adherents, and Monro and his comrades are his faithful followers. The virtues of piety, courage, honesty and self-sacrifice are praised and rewarded, if not in this world then in the hereafter, and the ungodly or unsoldierly are correspondingly condemned. In Part I Monro makes an unconvincing attempt to fit Christian IV into this mould, even claiming in one eulogistic passage that he was 'for experience in warfare, nothing inferiour to the greatest Captaines we reade of', although he later characterises his service under this king of Denmark as 'where I did learne to make a retreate' (Mo.I. 43, II. 50). The theme of 'a providence ordering all things' runs through his text, and he continues: 'but now being come under another Leader, there Fortune began to change, … we learning under the invincible Gustavus, to advance orderly, never falling off, but ever keeping faces to our enemy' (Mo.II. 174, 50). Part II climaxes with the hero's death, but faith in the cause is maintained and hope placed in a leader yet to come.

Monro often strays into hyperbole in his portrayal of the hero king, 'who was Fortunes Minion, and Mars his equall, Gustavus the Invincible', or 'the Lyon of the North, the Invincible King of Sweden, of never dying memory' (Mo.II. 87, 17). His epitaph for Gustavus sums up his own view of the campaign as a crusade:

> And what he did before his death, for the liberty of Dutch-land, and freedome of the Gospell none but knowes it: he left his owne Kingdome, to bring strangers to freedome in theirs, he set light by his owne life for Dutch-land, that they might keepe theirs, he waked and cared day and night for them, as a father for his children, that at last he might bring peace for them to sleepe sound. (Mo.II. 168)

Nevertheless much of the praise is firmly linked to practical examples. Gustavus's conduct in the period before the battle of Breitenfeld as 'a wise and prudent Generall' is exemplified by his creation of a strongly fortified camp from which he did not stir 'till first he was made certaine by good intelligence, of his enemies designe, counsell and resolution' (Mo.II. 60). His political ability is likewise noted 'in making his friends sure behind him (viz.) the duke of Brandenburg, the Dukes of Pomeren and Machlenburg, from whence his victualls and his supplies must needs come'. In the practical skills of command Monro judges Gustavus as one professional to another. After describing him making a personal reconnaissance at a siege he notes that 'in this point of recognoscing his Majesties judgement was wonderfull, as in all other practicall duties fitting a great Commander', and elsewhere he describes his care in giving orders, when 'hee would not suffer an Officer to part from him, till hee found he was understood' (Mo.II. 56, 92, 16). Sometimes Gustavus's personal courage verged on foolhardiness, but Monro had reason to be grateful for this at Nuremberg in 1632, when despite having 'lost much bloud' from a thigh wound he was leading troops to rescue others pinned down by the enemy in an exposed position; 'His Majesty coming by, and knowing I was hurt, commanded me to retire backe with the party, and went himselfe to make the retreate wonderfully, bringing them off from all Poasts' (Mo.II. 149, 150).

Monro is occasionally critical, even if in a veiled manner. In a difficult strategic situation in the autumn of 1631 he describes Gustavus as 'much troubled in minde and resolution, … not knowing well himselfe what to resolve, the enemie being behind him and before him' (Mo.II. 86). He is forthright about the incautious attack based on faulty intelligence at Nuremberg which led to his own wounding and the deaths of many of his men. Although he charitably attributes this to 'his Majesty having trusted too much to others wrong relation, that did not satisfie themselves', he concludes bluntly that this 'should teach others to be the more circumspect in recognoscing, before they should ingage men in bringing them upon the shamble bankes' (Mo.II. 151). Such exceptions do not detract from Monro's representation of Gustavus as an exemplary heroic figure, as wise as he was brave, summed up in the observation that 'we are instructed, as well by his Majesties politique government, as by his military; He being alike expert in both, discharging the dutie of a King, and a Generall, *Tam Arte, quam Marte*' (Mo.II. 87).

Despite the element of romance in his account many of Monro's comments are hard-headed, and his narration of events is usually direct and sometimes graphic. During his Danish service he describes leading an attack on a village, whose garrison eventually took refuge in the church:

> I thinking to get the Officers prisoners, entred withall, but could not finde them: incontinent perceiving a great quantity of powder spread a

thwart the Church, fearing the blowing up of the powder, I commanded every man upon paine of death to retire, the word not well spoken, the powder blew up, blowing the top of the Church, above a hundred were killed, and a number burnt pitifully. (Mo.I. 51)

His description of the fighting at Nuremberg before he was wounded is direct but evocative:

The service continued in this manner the whole day, so that the Hill was nothing els but fire and smoke, like to the thundering Echo of a Thunderclap, with the noise of Cannon and Musket, so that the noise was enough to terrifie Novices; we losing still our best Souldiers, grew so weake in the end, that the Briggads of foote had scarce bodies of Pikemen to Guard their Colours, the Musketiers being almost vanished and spent by the continuance of hot service. (Mo.II. 148–9)

Monro employs little literary artifice in the Duties, and often his style is plain and military, as in his account of the Swedes digging in hastily as Tilly's larger force advanced upon them: 'But where he did but march with his Army in the day time, we with spades and shovells, wrought our selves night and day in the ground, so that, before his coming, we had put our selves out of danger of his Cannon' (Mo.II. 49). Imagery is rare in the Duties, although in Part I Monro occasionally makes a narratorial address to the reader: 'Yet, gentle Reader', or 'Judge then, judicious reader, ... if we were glad of our owne safeties: I thinke we were' (Mo.I. 11, 28). Only exceptionally does he allow himself a more colourful style, as in setting the scene at Breitenfeld:

As the Larke begunne to peepe, the seventh of September 1631, having stood all night in battaile a mile from Tillies Armie, in the morning, the Trumpets sound to horse, the Drummes calling to March, being at our Armes, and in readinesse, having before meditated in the night, and resolved with our Consciences. (Mo.II. 63)

Monro gives himself much more scope in the Observations, both in content and in style. With a few exceptions those in Part II are clearly linked to specific events in the Duties, taking the form of lessons or morals drawn from them, or meditations of a moral or religious character based upon them. Many use the actions of Gustavus Adolphus, other senior officers, or even the enemy, as military object lessons, often rather obvious ones such as 'the foresight of a wise Commander availes much, in preventing the intentions of our Enemies', or 'Cullions that quit places for feare, not seeing their enemies, are unworthy the name of Souldiers' (Mo.II. 10, 50). These Observations tend to develop into moral or religious lectures, with indiscipline, looting or corruption as frequent targets:

> Nothing is more necessary on a march, then to keepe good discipline, without which there is no order, nor feare of God amongst Officers, that will suffer their Souldiers to grinde the faces of the poore by oppression; ... for where the feare of God is taken away, there the common-weale must needes decay, and then the ruine of the people doth follow. (Mo.II. 48)

Many of Monro's meditations are typically baroque, though particularly appropriate for a soldier. Thus he reflects on transience and inconstancy, observing that 'man is but meerely the ball of time, being tost too and fro', and that 'here below we have no assured estate, from the King to the Clowne, whereof we have frequent examples in Histories' (Mo.II. 174, I. 28). In noting the twists and turns of events he comments that 'we may see the Lords powerfull hand and providence in this, as in all humane affaires', and he advises: 'Let no man therefore flatter himselfe with prosperitie, riches, or honour' (Mo.II. 60, I. 29). Reflections on death follow naturally upon the action, as at the siege of Stralsund in 1628:

> Here our enemies were our pedagogues teaching us vertue, every moment minding us of our duety to God and man: yea minding us both of Death, and of Judgement: here we needed no dead mans pawe before us, to minde us of Death, when Death itselfe never went night or day with his horror from our eyes, sparing none, making no difference of persons, or quality, but *equo pede*, treading alike on all came in his way, whose houre was come. (Mo.I. 66)

The Observations also employ imagery to a much greater extent than the Duties, with expressions ranging from the conventional to the colourful. In shouting during an attack soldiers showed that 'the dogges did barke more than they did bite', while 'the King of Sweden had already too many Irons in the fire', and he manoeuvred his allies 'till in th'end, they were forced to dance after his pipe' (Mo.I. 70, II. 106, II. 36). More strikingly Monro speaks of 'pittie, though she be a downy vertue', of 'darknesse, the enemy of valour', and of 'hanging the Papists by their purse' (Mo.I. 53, I. 18, II. 116). He notes that 'no man that hath his foot in the fire, but would gladly take it out', describes skirmishing parties sent to try to tempt the enemy into the field as going 'to present themselves before Walestines Leaguer, as if they went to borrow a Beare', and cites Gustavus Adolphus as realising that 'the opportunitie of time was like a swift Eagle, which being at ones foote may be taken, but when once he mounts in the ayre, he laughs at those would catch him' (Mo.I. 23, II. 144, II. 129).

In his use of imagery and classical, historical or biblical references, as well as in aspects of the rhetorical style of his Observations, Monro reveals the influence not only of meditations but of sermons, particularly of the erudite type he may have heard in royal company. While his more overtly religious passages could as well have been delivered from the pulpit as in his book, many of what might be termed his secular sermons on the military or human virtues also have this tone and style, as in the peroration to his thoughts on soldierly courage:

> Therefore let resolution be ever present, repulsing force with force; for if thou wouldest be esteemed amongst the number of brave fellowes, thou must resolve to shew thy selfe resolute, couragious, and valiant, going before others in good example, choosing rather to dye with credit standing, serving the publique, than ignominiously to live in shame, disgracing both thy selfe and Countrie. Who would not then at such times choose vertue before vice; glorie, honour and immortall fame, before an ignominious, shamefull, and detestable life? (Mo.II. 93)

Monro was proud of 'the laudable profession of Armes' and of his comrades, and particularly of the large number of his family and of his nation amongst them. He cites five more officers named Monro serving in Mackay's regiment in 1628, adding after Breitenfeld that 'we found the fruits of mortalitie, death having seased more on our kindred, than on any other Family of our Nation, that were employed in this warre'. He misses no opportunity to report praise of the Scots or to add his own praise of 'the Nation, that was ever glorious abroad' (Mo.II. 118, 72, 82). Nevertheless he is realistic, noting that although the Scots were in the forefront of the action 'at other times, on watches, or repairing to their Colours, on Marches or in Garrison, they are more carelesse than others' (Mo.I. 7).

Although his Calvinist beliefs and his view of the war as a crusade on behalf of oppressed Protestantism are evident Monro only rarely lapses into bigotry, speaking of the 'Idolatrous worship of Papists' or of their priests 'that can make the poore ignorant beleeve, that to doe wickedly is the way to heaven', adding rhetorically: 'Who cannot then see, how detestable this Doctrine is, that gives people libertie to commit all villany, and then to assure them of pardon for it?' (Mo.II. 94, 124). More typically he is generous to his Catholic opponents, praising Tilly, 'an old expert Generall, who being 72 yeeres of age, was ready to die in defence of his Religion and Country', and Pappenheim, 'a worthy brave fellow, though he was our enemy, his valour and resolution I esteemed so much of, that it doth me good to call his vertuous actions somewhat to memory' (Mo.II. 118, 136). Calvinism also underlies Monro's frequent tirades about 'covetousnesse, the roote of all evill and dishonesty', and his personal philosophy: 'But for me, let me have health, and glad povertie with credit, for riches I desire not' (Mo.II. 34, 96). The conventions of the time distinguished between legitimate booty and unlawful plundering, but Monro was more puritanical than most: 'And for mine owne part, a few bookes left by my friends, which mine enemy might have burnt, was all the bootie that ever I made: neither doe I repent me of my neglect in this point' (Mo.I. 32).

Monro's stern, Calvinist, soldierly side is balanced by glimpses of a more human and sociable man, able to enjoy marching through the Main valley, 'being one of the pleasantest parts, and wholesomest for ayre', before arriving in Frankfurt, a town 'so pleasant for ayre, situation, buildings, traffique, commerce with all Nations, by water and by land, that it is and may be thought the Garden of Germany' (Mo.II. 89). The evenings *en route* were enlivened by 'the sweete, and sociable society of our countrimen and strangers, the one to season the other, which made our march pleasant' (Mo.II. 88). Such feelings of comradeship are more poignantly expressed at the division of the army in 1632, shortly before the fateful battle of Lützen:

> Being sorry that those who had lived so long together in amitie and friendship, as also in mutuall dangers, in weale & in woe, & fearing we should not meet againe; the splendour of our former mirth was obnubilated with a cloud of griefe & sorrow; which vanished and dissolved in mutuall teares of love, severing from others, as our Saviour did from his Disciples, in love and amitie. (Mo.II. 156)

The man's humanity shows through in a description of the storming of a town in Denmark, in which many of the defenders were cut down:

> For my owne part, I refused not to shew compassion on those, who did beg it of me, and what others did in their fury, I did tolerate, not being powerfull to hinder them: yet truly my compassion was so much, that when I saw the house ordained for Gods service defiled with their bloud and ours, and the pavement of the Church covered over with the dead bodies of men, truely my heart was moved unto the milde streames of pittie, and wept. (Mo.I. 53)

Monro's descriptions of military actions are generally matter-of-fact, and he only rarely reports divergences from the accepted standards of conduct of the time. What today might be regarded as atrocities in victory he accepts, noting indeed Gustavus's 'clemencie towards the Papists, in using no violence against them, save onely, *Jure Belli*, as those who were conquer'd by the sword' (Mo.II. 77). He is indignant when he does report breaches of those standards, predictably mostly by the other side, and as with other writers the most scandalous reports tend to be second-hand. He does describe one incident in which he was directly involved, although in the role of suppressing the perpetrators. When the Danish forces captured the island of Feamer in 1627 the Imperialist garrison surrendered and were granted mercy:

> Neverthelesse, at their comming out, the Country Boores (ever cruell to Souldiers) remembring the hard usage of the Souldiers to them in the

Winter time, seeing them come forth unarmed, ranne violently upon the Souldiers, knocking them pittifully downe, they caused great disorder. ... This insolency of the Boores continued (in killing the poore Souldiers) till by his Majesties charge, I was commanded to put my Souldiers to Armes to suppresse the Boores, which was presently obeyed by my Souldiers, who againe robbed the Boores of that they had taken from the enemy, and withall were well knockt. (Mo.I. 46)

The hostility between peasants and soldiers is mentioned several times in Monro's account, and although his inclination is to take the part of the troops, even enemy troops, he is fair-minded enough to recognise fault on both sides. He also reports two instances of alleged rape of peasants' daughters during the Danish campaign, noting the strict military discipline applied to such offences. In the first case he was himself involved in the judgement and sentence:

To satisfie justice, we called a Councell of warres (having our Auditor with us) of the Regiment Officers; the businesse exactly examined, according to his Majesties Articles, the souldier was condemned to die, and to be shot at a post, to terrifie others by his example from the like hainous sinne. (Mo.I. 41)

The second case followed a skirmish between soldiers and the peasants on whom they were billeted, in which several of the latter were killed. A complaint was then laid, maliciously, Monro believes, accusing three Scots soldiers of rape; despite lack of proof and protestations of innocence the interests of discipline prevailed and the men were shot. Elsewhere Monro notes stern injunctions from both Christian IV and Gustavus Adolphus against soldiers molesting the people of the country through which they passed, and he mentions incidents in which transgressors were whipped for plundering or executed for assault. He speaks of Gustavus's 'good discipline houlden over the Army, horse and foote, not suffering them without great and extraordinary punishment, to oppresse the poore', claiming that this made the populace 'cry for a blessing to his Majesty and his Army' (Mo.II. 68). This is a senior officer's rather optimistic perspective; many offences went undetected and unpunished, but the military authorities at least made efforts to set and enforce standards of conduct.

The difficulty with historical interpretation of Monro's account is assessing the extent to which its central heroic mode influences the detail of the picture he presents. Monro comes over as a decent and honest man with moral and religious standards which would restrain him from deliberate falsification or knowingly selecting his material to present a more favourable image. On the other hand his streak of romanticism and his capacity for hero-worship may have led him to see events, particularly in hindsight, through the proverbial rose-tinted spectacles. Perhaps the best indicator as to the balance is that despite his strongly partisan view of the conflict as a religious crusade he does not blacken his enemies, nor see even Gustavus Adolphus as above occasional criticism. His didactic and moralising Observations are best put to one side, but in his account of events in the Duties he appears to draw on a carefully maintained contemporary record and to keep close to the facts as he saw them. His description of his personal experiences has the ring of the unvarnished truth, and while his wider comments may require more careful evaluation they are probably at least an honest reflection of his perceptions.

14
A 'Myth of the All-destructive Fury'?

The war as reported

Ergang's contention that Grimmelshausen's near-contemporary novel *Simplicius Simplicissimus* influenced the later development of a myth of the all-destructive fury of the Thirty Years War was noted in Chapter 1. As Grimmelshausen had been a soldier in the war the novel has potential eye-witness quality, although the extent to which his fictional account is based upon either observed reality or the common belief of the time cannot now be easily determined. This prompts the question as to how far eyewitness records which are not overtly fictionalised contradict or confirm such a myth, either as a valid representation of actual experience or as a general contemporary perception of the war.

The account which corresponds most closely to the popular image is that of Peter Thiele, an official at Beelitz, near Potsdam, although the individual perception of the war which he conveys is more significant and suggestive than the actual events he records. His text is liberally furnished with anguished but generalised complaints such as 'all the things that have happened in this robber-war can scarcely be described.' Theft by the military is a constant refrain: 'Throughout the country their greatest feats have been no more than robbing, stealing and plundering', he says, adding: 'This is how they waged war in Brandenburg, and this is how they ruined the country' (Th.10, 12, 28). He compares the soldiery to Satan – '*In summa*: the devil in hell could not have done worse' – although he also invokes a religious interpretation, if a somewhat contradictory one: 'God's punishments and torments upon the country have been so numerous that it is truly a miracle that a man has been able to survive; but the good Lord has still helped us, so that he has richly blessed the cultivation of the fields again' (Th.13, 10).

Thiele provides a number of examples which are familiar parts of the war's image. He describes famine in 1636 to 1638:

> The poor people ate outlandish things, which they were forced to do in order to satisfy their hunger. They ground up beechnuts, linseed residues,

cabbage stalks and especially nettles, anno 1636, 1637 and 1638. The people were starving and many died because of these unnatural foods. In Beelitz there were often more than a hundred poor souls on the streets. (Th.10)

Later he refers to depopulation and to fields left uncultivated: 'Because of the numerous enforced collections [of contributions] houses became empty and the town went to rack and ruin'; 'The best farms lay desolate and around a thousand acres, without counting other outlying fields, were left unplanted' (Th.19, 22). Paralleling his account of hunger among civilians he describes starving Imperialist troops in 1639, including alleged cannibalism in the ranks:

The soldiers were so famished that in the Altmark some of them ate human flesh. As they reached Beelitz and marched on around the town they ate dogs, cats and rotting dead horses. Everything that they found in the barns outside they either consumed or destroyed, but the town itself was preserved, thank God. (Th.14)

Thiele reports atrocities perpetrated by soldiers of a passing Imperialist army in 1637, mostly in general terms: 'The shocking things that went on – rape and the like – are indescribable' (Th.15). He amplifies this with emotive but unspecific illustrations: 'They behaved barbarically in Beelitz, despoiling old women, not a few of them 60 years old, to say nothing of the young ones.' In a few cases of violence by soldiers seeking valuables he does name individuals. One man, 'Jürgen Weber, a baker, reliably testified (and had to have medical treatment in Berlin) that these thieves, robbers and murderers stuck a piece of wood half a finger's length into his fistula, *bona venia*, to make him confess where his money was'. They tortured another, 'Adam Rink, a butcher, worse than a hangman, by twisting a rope around his head' (Th.12). He also mentions the notorious Swedish draught but shows his own political prejudices by blaming its invention on the Imperialists:

Nor did they forget the Swedish draught, which our army itself devised, only attributing it to the Swedes to defame them. For this the robbers and murderers took a piece of wood and stuck it down a poor soul's throat, stirring and pouring in water, to which they added sand or even human excrement, thus pitifully torturing the victims for their money. This befell a citizen of Beelitz, David Örttel by name, who died soon afterwards as a result. (Th.13)

Thiele gives a graphic description of the fate of one unfortunate man:

They caught a citizen by the name of Krüger Möller (who perhaps was ill), bound him hand and foot and put him over the fire, where they roasted him for a long time until he was forced to disclose his remaining money.

After these robbers and murderers had taken it and gone another raiding party from the Third Army arrived, and hearing that the first had boasted of grilling 100 taler out of this Möller they took the same man and held him with his face to the fire, hoping to extract more from him. Instead they roasted him for so long that his skin came off him like a butchered goose, and he died. (Th.12)

During these years anxiety about possible raids was ever-present in Beelitz, but for most of the time it was outweighed by the likelihood of billeting and the certainty of extortion of contributions. Thiele writes bitterly about punitive billeting imposed by the Brandenburg military authorities when the town fell behind with contributions:

We were up to our necks with the collection enforcers they set upon us, as numerous as locusts – at times over 40. And we had to give them their rations or subsistence money too, more than 60 taler a day, ... not to mention what they pinched and pilfered from people – cattle, sheep, bread, grain, everything from their farms. ... The field chaplain and the regimental hangman haven't come to extort from us yet, but apart from them practically everyone has been here to enforce contributions from Beelitz. (Th.19)

He sets out a long catalogue of complaints about the behaviour of the Brandenburg soldiery and their officers, describing them levying illegal tolls on the roads, driving off cattle and then offering to sell the owners information as to their whereabouts, recruiting men from the area into the army by trickery or force and making the roads unsafe to travel: 'As regards the enemy one could quite well travel in the country, but on account of our supposed friends, our very own robbers, one often dared not venture outside the gates.' He ends with the wish that 'blessed peace may follow for our offspring and that this misery of war never happens again or falls upon them. May the Eternal God protect us all' (Th.28, 30).

Thiele gives a particularly full account of events typical of the popular view of the war but most of the other civilian writers have examples to add. The personal experiences recorded by these authors (excluding soldiers and those who wrote impersonal chronicles) have been analysed to assess what actually happened to *them*, as distinct from events they report involving third parties or in more general terms. Note has also been taken of specific instances they record of named and known individuals being killed – a hard fact less subject than others to interpretation. The first point to emerge is that three-quarters of the authors were plundered at some time, and since many of the accounts are less than comprehensive and most cover only a part of the war years this suggests that few escaped being robbed in their homes or having horses or farm animals driven off. This is by far the most frequent complaint in the texts, supporting Thiele's description of the conflict as a 'robber-war'. Moreover the experience was often repeated. Renner indicates that by 1634 there had been 61 incursions of troops into his village near Nuremberg, mostly in the previous two years, involving not only plundering but scavenging for anything usable as fuel: 'The aforementioned soldiers played havoc in Vach on account of the scarcity of firewood. They tore down all the fences, barns, gates and buildings, and such beds, chests, tables and trunks as I had left after 61 visitations had this time to be chopped up and burned' (Re.35).

Reports of plundering are very varied, some indicating hasty and less than thorough raids while others were more comprehensive, with the soldiers reported to have taken everything, although this often seems to have been more a reflection of the perception of the victims than a literal truth. Plebanus describes such a raid in July 1637, noting that he had just enough warning to get away to a hiding place overlooking the town, where he could witness what followed:

> Throughout the afternoon cavalrymen and foot-soldiers rode or strode in and out of Wehen; there must have been three or four hundred of them in the town. They plundered and took away all the grain, seed corn and other provisions which the unfortunate people had with great trouble and effort gathered together and hidden. Furthermore they left not a single featherbed, pillow or cushion that seemed worth anything, and they tore the remainder open, shaking the feathers out into the street or wherever. ... They ransacked the castle, finding all that had been left secretly hidden away, and in my room in the new building they ripped everything up and destroyed it. They took away the bedclothes which others had left us, together with the pillows and cushions, as well as various of my best books, two of my wife's chemises, one made of London cloth which cost two Reichstaler an ell, all the food which we had recently bought in Mainz and the bread which had been baked on the previous Saturday. ... This plundering went on from one o'clock into the dark of night. (Pl.284–5)

Some authors also record the burden of more organised military exploitation through contributions, although most say much less about this, possibly because it was not so overtly associated with actual or threatened violence and was therefore less traumatic. The semblance of organisation also made collection less arbitrary and akin to more familiar forms of taxation – burdensome, resented, but nevertheless generally regarded as inevitable.

Specific accounts of violence against civilians are likewise less frequent. Many of the writers mention the common practice of hiding or burying money and other prized possessions, and tales of soldiers torturing peasants to force them to disclose the whereabouts of such concealed valuables feature strongly in the popular perception. This is summarised in Vincent's account of the alleged horrors of the war, complete with appropriate sketches accompanying his description:

> Whom they thought to have hidden gold or other wealth, they have assaied, by exquisite torments to make them confesse. ... They have wound and tied about the heads of such, strong matches or cords, and twisted the same till the blood came out of their eyes, eares, and noses, yea, till their eyes started out of their heads. They have put and tied burning matches betwixt their fingers, to their noses, tongues, jawes, cheekes, breasts, legs, and secret parts. ... The mouthes of some they have opened with gags, and then poured downe their throats water, stinking puddle, filthy liquids, and pisse it selfe, saying; This is a Swedish draught. (V.4, 8)

In the event only Thiele provides any specific report of the more extreme techniques described by Vincent, although Pflummer gives one hearsay example of Swedes extracting 4000 florins by means of torture, albeit in the margin of his manuscript as an addition to the original unvarnished account: 'They put a chain round the under-bailiff's head and twisted it together, putting him to such torment that he was compelled to bring out the cash' (Pf.24).

The Swedish draught appears more often, and this seems to have been something that everyone had heard of happening somewhere else, but specific reports are scarce. Bötzinger claims to have suffered it himself, twice in one day plus much more, but lived to tell the tale:

> Twice within an hour, first on the dunghill in the weird dressmaker's yard and the second time in the gamekeeper's barn, they gave me the Swedish draught, full of manure and water, so that my teeth were almost all loosened. (Bö.354)

A case reported by Lutz, although detailed, is nevertheless hearsay as he was abroad at the time of his brother's misfortune at the hands of militia from a neighbouring town: 'First they gave Bartholl a Swedish draught in Rücksfeld, two pails of filth, and then they took him with them to Steina', where they cut off his beard and threatened him further until he paid them 190 Reichstaler (Lt.20). Freund reports his own experience, but in imprecise terms:

> On 22 August [1633] the Imperialist Croats made another raid, ... ill-treating the people mercilessly, beating, torturing and inflicting the so-called Swedish draught upon them. The like befell me when I fell into their hands, although unrecognised, and I was thus forced to search out my few trinkets and little bit of hidden money and to give them to those barbarians as a ransom in order to preserve my life. (Fr.35)

Threats and less spectacular forms of violence are reported more often, and one in five of the writers record that they themselves were assaulted by soldiers although few appear to have been seriously injured. The major exception was the unfortunate Freund, who died of his injuries, as his successor reports. In 1642 he was making for a nearby town to avoid Imperialist troops but he was captured by Croats, 'tied to a horse's tail and dragged as far as a village near Pegau, where he was badly beaten and tortured in order to extort money from him and eventually left for dead. Charitable people took him from there to the town of Pegau, where he met a pious death' (Fr.44).

Reports of violence towards civilians are almost always associated with robbery, but much robbery also took place without any significant violence, many accounts of plundering recording a wide range of property taken but mentioning no-one being hurt. Preis was robbed in his village by a cavalryman, who 'took from me what I had, but the Lord God granted me the good fortune that he left it at that, and none of the others caught me afterwards' (Pr.121). Cases of highway robbery are frequently recorded, and one in four of the authors describes a personal experience, with violence being more common in such incidents. Typically single individuals or small groups were accosted by a few soldiers, or even by a lone trooper. This may have encouraged the victims to resist or run, provoking a violent response, while the severe military punishments to which the robbers were often liable if brought to account may have encouraged them to be more ruthless. A high proportion of the reports of named civilians being killed are of this type. Büttner records that 'on Wednesday the 7th of November, Anno Domini 1638, the weaver Jacob Vetter was shot through the head in Hertzenauel as he tried to escape from the soldiers in his boat, and he died soon afterwards' (Bt.141). Similar circumstances can be inferred in Gerlach's account of a couple killed while delivering supplies to the military: 'On the 28th of September Crispin Wolf from Albertshausen, who was going to Lindflur to take lard to the cavalry, was shot dead by two troopers, and Ottilie Weiss, who was shot through the mouth, also died' (Ge.14). Sometimes there were efforts to fight back against raiders, and Christoph von Bismarck reports a casualty in a clash during a cattle theft: 'The trusty miller Abraham from Schwarzlosen was hit by a shot, which proved fatal' (Bc.93).

Half of the authors note killings of named individuals probably known personally to them, but other than confirming that such things did happen the random nature of the reporting gives little clue as to their frequency. Although statistically no more significant a better local picture both of the number of such killings and of the range of circumstances is given by eight entries Spiegel made in his two parish registers between 1631 and 1635. These include:

> [1631, Eltersdorf] Margareta, Hans Stauber's wife, who was terrorised and beaten by soldiers from Tilly's army. (Sp.18)

[1632, Eltersdorf] Hans Gürsing, formerly a shepherd, who was ridden down by a cavalryman and died from his injuries. (Sp.27)

[1634, Eltersdorf] Georg Reusch (who received two shot wounds three weeks before during the plundering by Forchheim soldiers) died in the hospital at Nuremberg, and on the following day, 29 May, he was taken out and buried. (Sp.34)

[1635, Bruck] Hans Sümmerlein, a widower, was shot on the road not far from Hersbruck as he was carrying grain. (Sp.47)

Rape plays a prominent part in sensational accounts such as Vincent's, but is much less in evidence in the works of the other authors, certainly when it comes to specifics, although several make generalised or less than precise references. Typically Preis rhetorically asks, when a small town some distance away was raided in 1640, 'how many wives and young girls were dishonoured', but when soldiers raided his own village of Stausenbach soon after 'our Lord God protected the womenfolk, so that they didn't get a single one' (Pr.120, 121). Lang likewise describes a raid on Isny in 1646 in which 'many honourable women were mishandled and beaten', but he records his own wife's good fortune: 'None of us suffered any bodily injury, remarkably not even my wife, who hid for several hours under the hay while they searched for people there by sticking their swords into it' (La.46). On another occasion his wife was held up and robbed but not molested, while Bötzinger's wife reportedly had a narrow escape, but none of the diarists records anyone close to him being raped. There may have been some reticence about this at the time but even so the number of specific rapes noted by these civilian writers is very small, only three, with questions implied in two of them. Gerlach mentions several occasions upon which women were robbed on the highway but he notes only one rape: 'Hannes Trosten's wife was raped by two cavalrymen near the castle wood on her way back from holy almsgiving', to which he adds enigmatically: 'The sheep farmer Hannes Schopf, who was a witness, says she could surely have avoided them' (Ge.14). Spiegel makes a generalised note in his margin in 1637, carefully switching to Latin for the purpose: 'hac septimana stupratae sunt foeminae dure a militibus' (on the seventh of the month the women were pitilessly violated by the soldiers). He also specifically records the birth of the illegitimate son of a servant girl, ascribed to rape although he leaves the matter open: 'The father is said to have been one of the Zuckerbacher cavalry, who according to her account brought about her ruin in Hansen Welcker's cellar, where she had taken refuge and was trying to hide' (Sp.58, 76). In the third case Sautter matter-of-factly records the rape of a farm maid from his village: 'On 28 June they drove off all my cattle, the whole herd, and my maid, along with other girls, had to drive them to Rottenacker, with the unfortunate result that one of them was dishonoured by a soldier in Martin Müller's house at Emmerkingen' (Sa.700).

Personally attested records of more extreme suffering are rare in these accounts. The typical pattern which emerges from the specific events reported from personal knowledge or experience is one of plundering raids and robberies, more or less frequent from place to place, punctuated by a relatively small number of more violent incidents and set against a background of frequent shortages of food which occasionally developed into periods of real but localised famine. There is also a widespread discrepancy between the nature and level of specifically reported experiences and the more generalised descriptions of events and conditions at large given by many of the writers, the portrayals tending to become more terrible the further they move away from the author's direct observation. Walther provides a good example early in the war, when from the relative security of Strasbourg he reports Mansfeld's progress through Alsace in 1621: 'His godless soldiers laid waste to the whole land with stealing, burning and rapine, despoiling it so abominably that the like of it has never been heard before' (Wl.14). 12 years later Schleyss's relatively moderate account of the unpleasant experiences of his own village may be compared with his overwrought descriptions of events outside his personal experience, as when Imperialist troops 'plundered the Margravate of Brandenburg-Ansbach almost totally, abusing the people appallingly and without discrimination or respect of persons, treating the women inhumanly and conducting themselves worse than Turks or Tartars' (Sc.1. 88). His portrayal of Swedish plundering in southernmost Germany is equally comprehensive:

> From that time on the Allgäu ... was plundered through and through. Whole herds of the poor people's livestock were driven off, cows, sheep, pigs, and likewise their horses; *in summa* all the animals were taken. Household effects, linen, bedding, clothes and everything that was worth anything were seized from the people everywhere and sold or carried off. ... *In summa*, from the Danube virtually to Lake Constance the wretched populace has had everything looted and destroyed, so that a Christian heart can only be moved to pity. (Sc.1. 94)

One further example indicates apprehension shaping the description in Hellgemayr's hearsay account of the Swedish advance on Munich in 1632, whereas after they took the city he says nothing of any widespread looting or mistreatment of the citizenry by the soldiers:

> At this time the enemy did enormous damage in the countryside, everywhere butchering, stealing and burning. They took away large numbers of people and animals, repeatedly and distressingly plundering the luckless inhabitants, violating women and girls, doing great evil in cloisters, churches, towns and markets and bringing destruction and misery to the whole country. (Hl.205)

From a broader historical standpoint this discrepancy highlights the importance of taking account only of specifically described events or circumstances authenticated by the author's own experience, observation or well-founded knowledge. The direr but more distant reports are nevertheless relevant as indicators of how the authors perceived both the war at large and their own communities' experiences within that context. As the great majority were recording for private purposes they had no apparent reason to falsify their accounts deliberately, even if some may have tended to exaggerate or to dramatise, and it is reasonable to assume that they themselves believed what they wrote. The discrepancy between the specific and the general reflects a wider perception of the war, derived not only from what they experienced but also from what they heard, implicit within which was the possibility that they might themselves fall victim at almost any moment to the even more terrible events happening elsewhere.

Many of the texts convey a feeling that insecurity, the constant anxiety that something worse might be about to happen, was almost harder to bear than the physical tribulations themselves. In some cases the fear is evident in the anguished pleas that writers confided to their diaries. Reporting an enemy army some distance away breaking camp and moving on, Schleyss adds: 'God grant that they never ever return, neither there nor to us! Amen. For truly we were also in great danger and dread. May God mercifully help and protect us now and henceforth!' (Sc.2. 7). Villagers repeatedly resorted to flight when troops were reported to be in the area, or they slept in the open at such times rather than be caught indoors at night. More than half of the authors report being forced to flee their homes on at least one occasion, and while Heberle lists 30 such flights other writers eventually stopped reporting such common occurrences individually. Insecurity became a way of life. Preis notes: 'We were so afraid and panicky that even a rustling leaf drove us out. ... There were times when for long periods we didn't dare to sleep in our homes at night' (Pr.123). Many writers observe bitterly that friends were as bad as or worse than foes in the treatment meted out to civilians by the military, a further indication of fear and uncertainty in circumstances where the normal expectations did not apply. Paradoxically the same fear underlies the surprise in occasional comments about good behaviour by troops; on one occasion Gerlach notes of a hundred Croat horsemen: 'Didn't hurt anyone; good people', and on another he comments of billeted solders: 'Very well behaved' (Ge.25, 31).

Insecurity took many forms and elicited many responses. Heberle had 'the shoes off my feet' stolen by Imperialist horsemen (He.168). The cunning Preis took precautions when he went out in the morning: 'We dipped our shoes in the manure on our yard so that if some band of soldiers caught us they wouldn't strip us of them.' Preis's wife was not raped as far as we know, but she was press-ganged by soldiers on the streets of Kirchhain and put to work digging fortifications: 'Although she had never thrown a shovelful of earth out of a ditch in her life it made no difference' (Pr.123, 133). When Wetterfeld was evacuated Cervinus prudently waited until he was sure it was safe before resuming residence, although he returned beforehand to preach, presumably to the bolder members of his flock. On one occasion when the village was occupied by an Imperialist regiment he sent schoolboys back daily to sing hymns and to beg from the soldiers 'like poor beggar children, ... as though they didn't belong there', so that they could bring back reports on 'how our homes were being abused' (C.88). Dietwar's wife saw soldiers selling her own household goods in the marketplace in nearby Kitzingen, where Dietwar was also offered his own books. In the relative security of a garrisoned town and with other pastors as witnesses he was able to take a bold line, threatening the soldier with arrest: 'That scared him, so that he gave me the books and made off – but first he had to carry them to my mother's house for me' (Di.77).

As a consequence of constant insecurity and traumatic if occasional experiences, together with stories from further afield which had grown in the telling and which were reinforced by sensational or propagandist press reports, contemporaries probably found it increasingly easy to believe the more lurid accounts of the war at large. A case in point is the recurrent reporting of cannibalism, both in the press and in these private accounts. Ergang quotes a study of these stories which indicates that they are not peculiar to the Thirty Years War, but are typical of longer periods of war and famine, while individual examples can be traced back to roots in history as far as ancient times (Ergang, 1956, p. 17; Julian, 1927). Vincent makes great play with such tales, and references in the *Theatrum Europaeum* were also taken up by later writers, including Gustav Freytag and Ricarda Huch. Raph gives a typical example: 'It is also reliably reported that a mother dug up her buried child two days later and ate it' (Ra.199). This author readily supplies names to authenticate other items in his text but conspicuously does not do so here, suggesting that seventeenth-century 'reliable sources' carry the same weight as modern ones. All these accounts are, almost by definition, hearsay, and it is noteworthy that none of the authors report any proceedings following (in contrast to reports of bestiality where the perpetrators were executed) but their truth is less significant than the fact that they were widely believed as signs of the times. There was also a morbid fascination underlying this topic, as is indicated by the tone of some of the stories. Plebanus gives one in the context of his description of famine and also claims it to have been 'reliably reported':

> This cowherd ... tore and cut pieces from her dead husband, boiled them, and ate them with her children. She also chopped off, washed and cooked her father's thighs, and likewise his head, which she boiled, opened up and ate. When she was asked what it was like she replied that if she had only had a little salt it would have tasted good. (Pl.260)

Perhaps more striking is that such a sober and level-headed recorder as Christoph von Bismarck gives an equally gory and dubious report when describing hungry troops in 1638:

> After the death of his wife a sick soldier in Stendal took the child – who he falsely claimed was also dead – and for lack of a knife tore open its belly with a sharp-pointed nail, took out the heart, lungs and liver, and ate them raw. This he himself admitted in response to the pressing enquiries of several citizens who passed by and saw his bloody mouth. (Bc.86)

The war as perceived

Whatever the nature of the specific experiences they record, most of the writers imply a perception of the war as a whole which is compatible with the later image, which may thus also describe a prevailing contemporary view of the conflict. The title that Raph gives to his text sets the tone:

> An account of what of note has taken place in this town of Bietigheim since 1634, after the battle of Nördlingen, by way of ruinous billeting, everlasting and enormous contributions, murder, robbery, repeated plundering, inflation, famine, death and other misfortunes. (Ra.191)

Piderit gives an overview of the war in the introduction to his chronicle, noting 'the great burdens of war, murder, robbery, arson and devastation which have spread almost throughout the Empire and brought disaster to many lands' (Pi.1. 14). Plebanus encapsulates his perception of the war as 'indescribable misery, ruin and destruction, ... the like of which truly our forefathers never experienced in ten or more previous generations' (Pl.267). Ullmann notes the conclusion of the peace treaty in 1648: 'God be thanked for it – after the war has lasted 30 full years, carried off many hundred thousand souls, swallowed up many hundred million gulden, and produced nothing but afflicted people and desolate towns and villages' (U.334). Ludolph exemplifies a view common among the writers: 'Anyone who has not himself seen and endured such a state of affairs will not believe what I set down here for remembrance' (Lu.53). Perhaps the most comprehensive statement of this contemporary view of the war is given by Grützmann, viewing the wider scene from his village outside Magdeburg in the period following the battle of Lützen in 1632:

> After that it happened time and again. When troops from Saxony marched into the area they ravaged it, captured Magdeburg and stayed the whole summer in camp, destroying all the grain in the fields and driving off the cattle. Soon the Imperialists came, the Lüneburgers, in fact a medley of nations, French and Spanish, so that Germany became nothing

but a looting ground. No-one could stay here, each looking around for a place to head for where he could hold out – Brunswick must have done best. Churches, parsonages and schools were wrecked along with the farmhouses. Church services were forgotten, the land lay waste, and so many fir trees were growing in the fields that from a distance many a village looked like a wood. All the roads were unsafe and the people were fair game, while in the villages neither cats nor dogs were to be seen. Many churches were dens of thieves inhabited by soldiers, and robbery, murder and arson were daily occurrences. The miseries of hunger were widespread; roots, foliage and turnips without bread were the poor folk's nourishment. *Mars et Mors* held sway and many people died of starvation. (Gr.238–9)

An even more highly coloured picture is given by Plebanus in his summary of a letter he had been shown in which the citizens of the town of Wetter described to the Hesse-Darmstadt authorities 'the inhuman tyranny... which was exercised by the troops of the Royal Swedish Field Marshall Alexander Leslie and the Sovereign Landgrave Wilhelm'. This contains allegations of murder, torture, rape, sacrilege, theft and wanton damage, all with the relevant extreme examples. Thus the rapes took place 'in the parsonages, in the churches themselves, in the churchyards and in the schools,...and even 70-year-olds were not spared'. Likewise the murdered included 'the blind, the lame and other unfortunates in the poorhouse, some of whom were shot dead while others had their heads split open with axes'. A newly-delivered mother was 'tipped out of the bed and cruelly beaten', while men were 'tied by their *pudenda* and dragged about, so that foam gathered around their mouths and their eyes started out of their heads' (Pl.273). Among the list of atrocities only the Swedish draught is missing. This report is of course intrinsically unreliable, the writers of letters to the authorities, unlike private diarists, having a clear incentive, probably financial, to exaggerate and falsify their accounts. Nevertheless the fact that Plebanus quotes it suggests that he and other contemporaries found the substance of the letter credible.

A number of the editors of these accounts also reflect the image of the war current in their own times. Thus one writing in 1791 referred to 'the horror of the Thirty Years War ... which so cruelly devastated our fatherland', a view echoed by another in 1886: 'The very term "Thirty Years War" evokes a surfeit of misery which is beyond words, the traces of which have survived into our present [nineteenth] century' (Wo.98; Sc.1. 77). From the standpoint of 1933, shortly after the three hundredth anniversary of the death of Gustavus Adolphus, yet another noted 'the frequent reminders of the Thirty Years War and the obvious comparisons with the World War of our twentieth century', while among more recent editors one summed up the conflict in 1984 as 'the greatest catastrophe ever to befall town and country in recorded history' (Fr.5; Ra.13). Another described conditions around Ulm when peace finally came:

> Especially in the countryside and the villages the war had had a devastating effect. The fields were overrun with weeds and productive ground had become uncultivated woodland. ... The rural population had declined so far because of war, emigration and above all because of the plague that barely enough people still lived in the villages to do the work necessary for regeneration. ... Many places were largely destroyed and the houses stood empty. (He.38)

These perspectives on the war from the three following centuries are not in essence different from those recorded privately by contemporaries. The English soldier of fortune Sydnam Poyntz drew his own contrast between what he saw on arrival in Germany in 1624 and how it seemed when he left in 1636:

> When I wandred out of my owne Country ... wee went, I well remember, thorough many brave Dukes and Princes Countries of Germany full of all things that belonged to mans use and of all things wee had supplies of men and mony as wee passed: for mee that had seene the one now to come to see the contrary was wonderfull, viz. their Countries destroyed, their Townes burned, their people killed. (Po.128–9)

Preis also looked back on the war, before going on to note that the peace was far from bringing an end to the burdens the population of Germany had to suffer:

> To tell of all the misery and misfortune is not within my power, not even what I know and have seen myself. I really can't do it because of my work, as even if I had as many hands now as I have limbs on my whole body they would all have enough to do. And if I did report everything which I have seen and so painfully experienced no-one living in a better age would believe it, but *in summa* the times were awful beyond all measure. (Pr.138)

Preis typifies a view of the war which has endured for most of the last 350 years. If his and other eyewitness personal accounts suggest on analysis that the perception may often have been worse than the experience, many of the events recorded were nevertheless terrible enough for those involved. Individual suffering is not easily represented by statistics or averages, and the debilitating effect of constant anxiety on a generation should not be under-estimated. One conclusion may be clearly drawn from these sources, however. Whether or not the traditional view of the war constitutes a myth, it is not of later origin but is firmly rooted in the well-documented perception of their own times by contemporaries.

Although a number of the authors implicitly or explicitly offer an overview of the war corresponding to the later image, few put forward any personal interpretation of it. Most of those who do view it in religious terms, Minck noting that he wrote 'in order to contemplate previous evil times and to remember the anger of God', while Preis states that the war 'was a great punishment on Germany sent by our Lord God on account of our sins' (Mi.231; Pr.115). Piderit concurs, noting that 'God in his mercy wished to chastise the country' (Pi.1. 14). Saur offers a common perspective:

> For us around the Eder river in Hesse, this [1640] was a devastating and disastrous year. Hunger and sorrow, poverty and misery were the fruits of war and punishments for our sins. Pray God that we do not forget our sufferings and grief. If only our descendants know what we have experienced they will be pious. (Sr.126)

War, famine, disease and other tribulations are commonly linked together in this context, Murr noting that 'we were hard hit this year by God's imposition of his four retributions, war, inflation, hunger and plague' (Mu.83). Beck shares this view, reporting that 'God afflicted us not only with war and the sword of the enemy, but also with the pestilence in 1634 and with a great famine in 1635' (Be.81). Feilinger too links war and natural catastrophes, seeing the hand and punishment of God in them all: 'But now the three rods for our backs accompany one another, *bellum, fames, pestis.*' He laments the shortcomings of man in general terms: 'Oh Germany! Germany! You were not willing to display to other countries what a treasure the beloved peace of body and soul is' (Fe.246, 222). He is specific about the cause of the war, noting that 'the eternal ruling Lord and God' sent war as a punishment 'on account of the terrible self-assurance, pride and arrogance which was again and again apparent, along with contempt for the holy word of God and the true worship' (Fe.237). Renner sets out a paradox common among these writers in his concluding entry for the troubled year of 1632, in which he both interprets the war as God's punishment and places his hopes in God for its end:

> In this year God carried out the threat made to us in Deuteronomy 28. 21, 22, 26, 27 and 35. May he in his mercy take pity on us and make us happy again, after he has tormented us for so long and after we have so long had to suffer misfortune. May he mercifully turn all evil away from us and give us generously of the good. Amen. Amen. Amen. Oh Lord Jesus, Amen. (Re.31)

Apart from Murr's brief characterisation of the conflict as 'a pernicious war of religion' Heberle offers almost the only political assessment:

> With our mouths we were Imperialist and with our hearts Swedish, for we would rather have seen the Swedes win than the emperor on account of

religion and our beliefs. Otherwise the emperor would have been a good sovereign to us. (Mu.74; He.201)

Only Thiele puts forward a more developed interpretation, summing up his perception of the war in one telling observation:

This whole war has been a veritable robbers and thieves campaign. The generals and colonels have lined their purses while princes and lords have been led about by the nose. But whenever there has been talk of wanting to make peace they have always looked to their reputations. That's what the land and people have been devastated for. (Th.11–12)

15
Why did they Write?

The question of motivation – why people wrote – is important in interpreting their resulting texts, but it is also extremely difficult to answer. Two levels or stages of motivation also require consideration, the first underlying the decision to keep some form of contemporaneous record and the second prompting the writing of a retrospective account. This divides the writers into three groups: those who only kept diaristic records, those who kept such records and later made a further decision to write them up into more shaped accounts, and those who wrote such accounts from memory only. These groups correspond to those identified on the basis of time of writing in Chapter 2.

The decision to keep a diary is a relatively commonplace one, given the necessary basic level of education and access to writing materials, albeit both were significant constraints in the seventeenth century. Many of the modern diaries sold in large numbers every autumn are in fact no more than *aides-mémoire* for appointments or things to be done, but others, the large-format, page-a-day type, suggest an expectation of more genuinely diaristic use, some form of contemporaneous recording of the thoughts or experiences of the owner. In this they resemble the German *Schreibkalender* of the Early Modern period, a cheap annual publication, half calendar, half almanac, with spaces left in which the owner could write. The number of these which were on the market indicates their popularity and suggests that the potential intention of recording was at least as common among those in seventeenth-century Germany who were able to do so as it is today, although doubtless then as now far more were sold than were conscientiously filled in. Many people start diaries, often of the 'what I did today' type, but few persevere with them over an extended period, so that the question of what motivated our authors to maintain their records is even more interesting than what prompted them to begin.

Nevertheless beginnings are important. Both the *Schreibkalender* and the modern diary link recording to the passing of time, and particularly to the turn of the year, a time for taking stock of the past and when new beginnings are traditionally made. Although their underlying reasons for recording were probably more complex, many of our diarists may have been prompted actually to begin by no more than the new year, and such a link is also evident in the way in which some of the writers sum up the past year, often coupled with hopes for a better one to come. Particular life events may also have provided the stimulus to start recording. Thus Hagendorf began his diary when he set out for Italy as a young man, while Monro, Fritsch and Poyntz seem to have had contemporaneous records going back to their enlistments to inform the writing of their later accounts. Haidenbucher and Staiger both commenced their diaries at the time of their respective elections as abbess, and Junius refers to her intention to record events since her admission to the convent, although her text was written up later. Preis starts with his purchase of a new farm, while Lang relates writing his memoir to his second marriage, which although clearly not the impetus for his earlier notes is another indication of a link between a perceived turning point in life and the urge to record. Tradition may have provided a starting point for some. Mallinger and Bürster fit into a long history of monastic chronicle-writing, and the penchant of many Lutheran pastors for making wider records in their church registers may contain some echo of this culture as well as being opportunistic use of an available medium. Fashion perhaps prompted others. Krusenstjern suggests that 'keeping a diary was quite usual in the seventeenth century', and even if this is a little sweeping it may be that some, particularly in the professional classes, did indeed start a diary because it was seen as the thing to do (Krusenstjern, 1997, p. 20).

The experience of war often appears as the basis for writing up a retrospective account, but in a number of instances it also seems to have prompted the commencement of a contemporaneous record. Thus Dobel begins with the first incursion of the war into his area of Franconia and Plebanus started writing after he and his parishioners had been driven out of their village by troops in late 1635, while the fact that his first entry is for 1 January 1636 also suggests the influence of a new year. Murr, less personally affected in the greater security of Nuremberg, may have been motivated to start recording by a perception of historic events, commencing his long-running account in March 1619 as the rebellion in Bohemia began to assume significance. One of his first entries notes a meeting of the leading princes of the Protestant Union, which was held in the city and attended by the 'Winter King' of Bohemia, the Elector Palatine Frederick V. Only Heberle makes a specific statement of what prompted his initial decision to keep a contemporaneous record (although others may have done so on opening pages missing from the manuscript, noting that some of the extant texts begin in mid-sentence while others are grammatically complete but lack any form of heading or introduction). Heberle identifies a premonition of great events as his starting point, although that claim was itself made with a degree of hindsight:

What gave me cause and occasion to write this little book is as follows: In *Anno Domini* 1618 a great comet appeared, around the autumn and into

November. This was both terrible and wonderful to see, and it so moved my spirit that I began to write, because I thought that it must mean and bring with it something of great importance – as indeed has happened, which the reader will find amply reported in this book. (He.86–7)

There remains a significant distinction between the initial impetus to begin recording and the underlying motivation to maintain it, the latter separating the few long-term diarists from the many who begin but soon lapse, or those like the Kreuznach wine-grower Wendell, who went through this cycle several times. The abbesses Haidenbucher and Staiger clearly linked their recording to their office, perhaps seeing it as almost a duty, although the former kept essentially a convent record and the latter a more personal diary. The soldiers may have wanted an aid to their own memories, as military service took them to a wide variety of places and into many actions which might soon have blurred without some form of record. Making notes may also have provided a diversion during the many idle periods in camps or billets which were a feature of a soldier's life, particularly in the winter. On one such occasion Monro departed from his strictly eyewitness approach, noting that he felt it 'better to collect at this time somewhat of the actions of others, than to be altogether idle' (Mo.II. 136). Diarists who had been prompted to start writing by the experience of war were probably also sustained by it, although some, such as Ullmann and Gerlach, give the impression of being as much interested in the process of recording as in the war itself. In this they resemble the large remaining group of contemporaneous diarists for whom no clearer motive can be identified than the urge to record for its own sake, their writing and recording appearing important to them as a hobby or pastime, with content a secondary consideration. Some of these, including Mallinger, Schleyss and Hellgemayr, are readily identifiable by the random nature of their entries, with anything of passing interest noted down but no central theme appearing until the war imposed itself on their texts.

Writing up an account retrospectively is a more specific and self-contained task than the keeping of a contemporaneous diary, and in general more specific motivations are perceptible. These are not intrinsically different whether or not the writer had previously kept a diary, although having done so may have made the decision to write an account easier, both because a habit of writing was already established and because the basic material was to hand from the earlier work. More writers indicate reasons for writing a retrospective account than for simply keeping a contemporaneous record, although these cannot necessarily be taken at face value or as comprising the author's total or even principal motivation. Thus Walther states that he wrote his Strasbourg chronicle 'to the honour of God and for the information of my loved ones, … so that they shall see and recognise the wondrous reign of God … and how the good Lord has so often miraculously delivered us from so many great dangers'. Bearing in mind the broad range of his material, some of which the nineteenth-century editor of the text regarded as 'the *chronique scandaleuse* of its time', this seems a less than exact claim, although the relevance of the latter part to the Thirty Years War is un-mistakable (Wl.10, 11). It seems more likely that Walther wrote for his own interest and the employment of his time rather than from any religious motivation or for the benefit of his own posterity, particularly noting the impersonal nature of his record.

Posterity is nevertheless by far the most common and conventional of the reasons authors give for writing. Bürster is among the most specific, and whatever his initial motivation for recording he addressed posterity directly in 1643:

> I write this solely so that if after many years have passed the reader talks or hears speak of these and similar things, through reading this ... he will have some information and knowledge. For after 30, 40, 50 or more years some such person will say: this or that happened in such and such a year. (Bü.2)

He wrote up his final text in the darkest days for the monastery of Salem, which by 1641 was so impoverished that it was forced to dismiss many of its staff and disperse some of the monks, while by 1643 Überlingen was in enemy hands and the remaining monks had to take refuge in Constance or elsewhere. He relates his writing to this situation, suggesting that without it posterity would ask:

> And Salem, long so widely famed and which had been so rich and prosperous, how did they live, that they fell so far and into such poverty that they could no longer support their monks, but had to send them off to strange places far away, [... and had to] lay off all their officers, officials, staff and servants, etc. Why then was nothing written? Why is there nothing about it to be read? What kind of lazy, dilatory people were they, that they wrote absolutely nothing? (Bü.2)

In this Bürster displays a clear historical sense and intent, seeking to provide both an accurate record and some explanation of events rather than merely offering the account of tribulation given by other writers. The latter approach is made equally explicit by Junius in her introduction, where she states that she wrote 'so that when pious Sisters come after us who know nothing of these distressed and difficult times, they can see what we poor Sisters suffered and endured, with the grace and help of God, during these long years of war' (J.7).

As celibates, Bürster and Junius obviously aimed to reach posterity at large rather than their own descendants, although Junius's reference to successor nuns has something of the latter quality about it. Götzenius makes explicit a motive for writing which is implicit in many other accounts: 'so that our posterity may retain some measure of knowledge of how long this town has been burdened with military garrisoning' (Gö.147). Several other writers, though setting out their purpose less specifically, had posterity in general in mind, Thiele, Plebanus and Minck all mentioning descendants, while the monk Hueber makes a direct request for the prayers of readers of the short account which he bricked up in the foundations of a wall. Yet others thought more directly of future generations of their families or of their own offspring, among them Hartmann, who refers to his children, and Bötzinger, who addresses his directly by name in the course of his account. Oberacker speaks of his family, and Lang too mentions his children, already born or yet to come, in setting out his motive for writing:

> What happened from the beginning of my first journey away in my youth (which was in my fifteenth year) up until about the time of my marriage is briefly recorded in this book, and if the Lord God grants me grace what happens in my coming married state will also be entered here-after. This information may perhaps be of service to my children, those God has given and any yet to be granted to me. (La.6–7)

Lutz may have been looking not only to his own children but to subsequent generations: 'I wanted to leave this little [record] with the little I leave to my descendants. God grant them that they are not terrorised and afflicted by men in the way that we were' (Lt.26). Heberle goes further than this general reference to descendants or Bürster's 30 to 50 years to demonstrate the longest of family perspectives:

> This little book of mine will please and be dear to all my descendants. When they find it after I am gone I have no doubt that they will take pains to keep and preserve it on my behalf, both on account of the rela-tionship and for the chronicle which is written and recorded in it, ... for as long as the Heberle lineage lives, even if it survives until the Day of Judgement. (He.86)

By way of introduction to their texts two elderly pastors set out reasons for writing in terms which are both religious and personal, while also mention-ing posterity. Dietwar opens by quoting Psalm 66: 'Come and hear, all ye that fear God, and I will declare what he hath done for my soul.' He continues:

> In emulation of David's holy example, as a memorandum for myself and my family, and as the thanks due to God the Almighty, I, Bartholomäus Dietwar, in this year of 1648 pastor at Segnitz, will give an account of my arrival in this world and of my further life history, together with those other things which I found noteworthy in the time of my vanity. (Di.3–4)

There is a distinction between this view of posterity in personal terms and Cervinus's wider address:

> Since the good Lord in his exceptional mercy has for so long preserved me, an undeserving servant of the church, here in the sight of my fellow men in the praiseworthy lordship of the Counts of Solms Laubach, and has permitted me to experience much, I have in my simplicity thought it good and advisable to set a part of this down on paper, to the honour of God and as a record for others, in the hope that it will be well received and interpreted. (C.23)

Posterity as a motivation is most directly suggested by those writers identified as having written or rewritten their accounts later in life, but at a time when they had young families. Six of Hagendorf's children died in infancy or soon after, so that when he rewrote his diary in 1647 his four-year-old son was the first prospective survivor, and he was taking a great interest in his education, while Fritsch, who first married and had a family towards the end of the war, had several growing children by the time he wrote in 1660. Both men perhaps saw their texts as a means of relating their complicated life stories and experiences in the war to their own offspring, but even so it is clear that they started recording very much earlier, when children were not an immediate consideration.

It remains open to question how far references to posterity, particularly those made formally in the introductions to accounts, really represent the motivation of the authors, as opposed to being conventional and acceptable reasons to offer for writing. While posterity may have been a significant factor for some writers and at least a contributory one for others it is probable that in most cases more directly personal motives were involved, although the address to posterity as a form of aspiration for some small degree of immortality should not be overlooked; Heberle's ambition not so much to inform as to be remembered by future generations is plain in the passage above.

Written-up accounts can be divided into two broad groups according to whether the author's apparent centre of interest is himself or the war. The distinction is illustrated by accounts written retrospectively by four soldiers. Fritsch and Augustus von Bismarck deal almost exclusively with the war but their texts are nonetheless self-centred; they are accounts of the authors' careers, which, as they were soldiers, were bound up with the war. Monro, on the other hand, gives a description of the war as he saw it, in which his own experiences naturally feature but are secondary to his purpose. In the last analysis the same is true of Poyntz; the interest of his friends in the 'thinges of most importance which happened' was principally as an account of the war rather than in him personally (Po.45). It is also notable that most accounts which were written up after the end of the war are more autobiographical in character, whereas those composed during the war years are centred mainly on the war itself. This suggests that for authors closer to events the experience of war was a principal motivation, whereas from a greater distance it was only one of the diverse contributory factors underlying autobiographical writing.

Many of those writing accounts centred on the war perceived their experience as one of exceptional tribulation and therefore worthy of recording. Minck's observation that 'our descendants will never believe what miseries we have suffered' may reflect as much his own difficulty in coming to terms with the experience as a desire to transmit knowledge of it to posterity (Mi.231). At the same time such authors often seem to be saying that posterity *ought* to know what they suffered – Junius, quoted above, is another example – thus turning the apparent intention of informing posterity into a self-centred attempt to impose upon posterity a duty to remember. Thiele sums up this attitude in representing his account as a warning to future generations: 'Our descendants can discover from this how we were harassed, and see what a terribly distressed time it was. May they take this to heart and guard themselves against sin, begging God for mercy so that they may be spared such dread' (Th.22).

The style and tone adopted by some of these authors suggests that they may have been writing as part of a personal process of coming to terms with their experiences, an exercise in which writing was itself the point irrespective of any potential readership. Bötzinger gives a highly dramatic account of his repeated mishandling by soldiers and his remarkable escapes, and if this is factually correct he could well have been traumatised by the experience and have needed some means of working through it afterwards. Likewise the contemporaneous entries which Feilinger made in his church register appear to be more an expression of his inner tensions and fears than a record of events. Plebanus offers no explicit reason for keeping his diary but the background and content suggest that he felt the need to record his period of exile and tribulation as much for his own benefit as for that of future generations, both being implicit in the pious wish which summarises his view of the war: 'God grant that [my children's] descendants never ever experience such indescribable misery' (Pl.267). Schuster's use of the municipal records to preserve his personal observations for posterity implies not only the urge to record but also the belief that the future should know of the experiences of this troubled era, while indications that he drew earlier notes together into a more comprehensive record suggest a desire to reappraise events and to close a chapter. Maul's overwhelming sense of grievance over his losses is never far from the surface and he evidently wrote in large measure to record and lament his financial decline. For Thiele the dominant emotion seems to have been anger, and his style suggests that he was more interested in getting things off his chest in a series of bitter recollections set down much as they came to him than in producing an authoritative record of events.

In some cases defensive or self-justificatory motives for writing can be postulated. Winkler and Dressel both complain about criticism of their conduct and blackening of their reputations and set out to put the record straight. Vitzthum's diary also has a strongly self-righteous tone; his central theme, criticism of the conduct of the Saxon campaign in Brandenburg, carries throughout the corollary that if his advice had been followed the outcome would have been better. Grützmann prefaces his text with a critical commentary on his predecessor, who during his 20 years in office 'was seen more in his fields than in the church' and who 'left behind him a despicable name for preachers, which here means *avaritia*, meanness and self-interest' (Gr.232, 233). His repeated references to the ingratitude of his flock and his persistent air of robust defensiveness suggest that he may himself have been subjected to criticism as a too-worldly priest, possibly explaining why he goes to some lengths to describe the presumably greater worldliness of the previous incumbent. Spiegel makes repeated references to flights from the villages in his parish, either directly or in the context of poorly attended or abandoned church services, and many of his notes have an apologetic air. He represents himself as a man doing his best in impossible circumstances, as when in 1634 he excuses the long period since he had 'been to the children's classes and helped to catechise them, because in these times I have been unable to keep anything in my parish in order owing to the dispersal of the congregation' (Sp.45). He also explains away potential shortcomings in his baptismal register arising from christenings during flights from the village:

> That is why, if sooner or later someone who was baptised in these times wants to know his date of birth but this information cannot be provided to him from this book, the blame should not be placed on the pastor, particularly if no-one had contacted him and arranged for him to enter children who had been baptised in the city into this register. (Sp.34)

More individual reasons for writing may be discerned in one or two texts. Büttner himself commenced the parish register in which he later wrote his account, suggesting a wider concern with the process of recording. Zembroth sets out in his title the intention of describing not his personal experiences but those of his community, the noteworthy events in and around Allensbach, which he immediately links to his office as mayor, perhaps hinting that he saw chronicling the burdens of war as a form of public responsibility. The miller-woman Wolff's account is notable for its religious quality, with verses from hymns and quotations from the Psalms interpolated, and it may be that the recording of her remarkable escape when the Imperialists took Schwabach had an element of devotional duty about it. This is further suggested by her addressing it late in life, at a time when she was very conscious of mortality, particularly as she makes clear her view of the attack on the town as divine retribution: 'Thus did our good Lord inflict his punishment' (Wo.102).

Ludolph was not the only one who wrote without a clear motive, but he is unusual in appearing puzzled by this himself. He incorporated an account of local conditions into his baptismal register each year from 1640 to 1642, but he ends the last with the note that 'I must cease to describe this state of affairs, not only because it is impossible to describe but also because I did not intend to write a chronicle of Reichensachsen but to compile a *catalogum baptizatorum et copulatorum'*. One may speculate that he began his account in the enthusiasm of a new ministry but later tired of the task, as is suggested by his failure to maintain the register of deaths, for which he offers the excuse that 'I have had to give up keeping a register of deaths for lost in such miserable times. I have had a great deal to do, and I am glad that I have so far been able to keep up the baptismal and marriage registers, which are the most important' (Lu.53, 54).

The few of these accounts which were published at the time had a more public purpose, such as Götzenius's sermon after conclusion of the peace or Vincent's polemical work, which espouses the Protestant cause and appeals for financial help for pastors and parishes in Germany. 'Onely the thing I desire', he claims, 'is to move thy Christian heart to compassionate the estate of thy poore brethren, so lamentable, and almost desperate' (V. To the Reader). Monro prefaces his book with a note that he wrote in memory of his dead comrades, and he concentrates on recording what he himself experienced in their company, 'having bin an eye-witnesse of the accidents most remarkable, which occurred in Germany, during those seven yeares warres'. Implicit in this is an inherent diarist's urge to record, but nevertheless his lost comrades, including his brother, were very much in mind when he published the book 'to expresse my love, and thankfulnesse to my country, and to my deere Camerades, Britaines, Dutch and Swedens' (Mo. Epistle, 1–2).

In his foreword Monro states that he wrote to enable the 'noble and worthy minded Reader...to follow the Traces of those worthy Cavaliers mentioned in my Observations' (Mo. To the Reader, 2). Implicit in this is the obvious expectation of an author publishing a book that there will be readers, even though he may not know precisely who. The vast majority of our authors neither published their texts nor anticipated that they would be published, raising the question of what, if any, readership they envisaged when writing. While those authors who mention posterity may in fact have been writing mainly for personal reasons, such references are probably indications of expected readership within the writer's own family and descendants. The monks and nuns may have read their works to their contemporaries, a practice in some cloisters, but they also expected their manuscripts to be preserved in the archives and to be available to future members of their orders, as Junius makes clear and Bürster implies. Those who took advantage of church or town registers to insert their own observations will likewise have foreseen retention and continuation of the substantive records and anticipated that at least some of their successors in office might refer back and read their entries. Even so, with the exception of a few such as Heberle with an almost dynastic view of family, most cannot have expected a wide or long-term readership, a point

confirmed by the fact that so few of the writers even refer to prospective readers. Wolff is unusual in directly addressing a putative reader at intervals
through her text, an otherwise unidentified 'good soul' or 'dear Christian',
whereas Heberle does so only in his foreword, which he begins: 'Worthy, honourable and especially well beloved friend' (He.86). This again suggests that for
the majority writing may have been much more a personal process than
deliberately targeted at readers, a reversal of the general case in which writing
is first and foremost a medium of communication.

Nevertheless there is evidence that at least some of these accounts were
read by posterity before later coming to the notice of the editors who published them. In most cases the history of the manuscripts is unknown, and
survival for many may have been largely a matter of chance. Some, however,
were carefully preserved by descendants for a century or more, although this
may often have reflected respect for a half-remembered grandfather or
merely respect for a notebook as a family heirloom, rather than an evaluation of the account itself. The most direct evidence of descendants' interest
in the text concerns Oberacker, who had two daughters, one of whom married Wolfgang Gruner and took over her father's mill. Some three hundred
years later the rebuilt mill was still in the Gruner family, while Oberacker's
manuscript was owned by a relative in Constance. At an unknown date part
of the original was lost, but it was rewritten by a descendant, who added a
note: 'I have only been able to write this because we had often read it before,
and the whole manuscript is no longer here. I am called Jakob Gruner the
fourth' (O.110). Likewise a descendant added a note to the end of Preis's manuscript: '*Anno* 1690. Heinrich Preis of Stausenbach, to whom this book is very
precious, and whoever takes it from him is a thief, be he whom he may'
(Pr.186). In a number of other cases descendants either continued or added
notes to the account. Various of Wendell's posterity made entries intermittently in his notebook, the first being a record of his death on 24 March 1647
made by his son-in-law, and the last dating from 1758, 111 years later, while
the Schleswig farmer Sierk's descendants also made entries in his notebook
from time to time, the last in 1782. Freund's chronicle was continued up to
1698 by his son and grandson, and the manuscript is a fair copy of the whole
by the latter, while the editor of the text in 1933, Max Freund, was a descendant of the original authors. Other manuscripts were retained and read
although not added to. Sautter's manuscript remained in the parish archives
and was copied out by a successor priest in 1736, while in 1786 a descendant
of Winkler's brought his manuscript back from Reval to Pirna, where a transcript was made. Heberle's manuscript remained in family ownership in his
village of Neenstetten until the mid-eighteenth century, and notes in the
margin indicate that it was read intermittently in the nineteenth century by
local people, mostly also shoemakers, even if his vision of informing his posterity up to the Day of Judgement was a little ambitious.

16
Historical Sources or Ego-documents?

> The historian has traditionally approached autobiography with the attitude of a prosecuting attorney examining an ageing witness with a record of numerous convictions for perjury. (Barkin, 1976, p. 84)

As the above quotation indicates, historians have long regarded autobiographical writing, including memoirs and retrospective eyewitness accounts, as suspect, and this has been particularly the case in Germany. The view of the Thirty Years War derived from sources of this kind in the preceding chapters therefore needs to be qualified by an assessment of the basis and validity of this suspicion. It is also relevant to look at the standing and reception of such texts in the context of genre studies of diaries, memoirs and autobiography, and in the light of the recent wider interest in ego-documents or *Selbstzeugnisse* (literally 'self-evidence'), terms which are used to describe all forms of personal writing which reveal something of the author's self.

To begin with German historiography, Briesen and Gans sum up their paper, 'Concerning the Value of Contemporary Witnesses in German History', with the observation that 'not the human subject but the historical totality was the traditional goal of German historicism'. They note that the emphasis which developed in the eighteenth century, not only upon source-based history but upon the type and quality of sources, was re-emphasised by Ranke and Droysen and remains influential in Germany today; 'The historical-critical method, and with it the differentiation between surviving material and tradition as sources, therefore appears to represent the unquestioned consensus of historical science' (Briesen and Gans, 1993, pp. 2, 20). In this context 'surviving material' broadly refers to official, controlled or functional documentary records, the preferred sources, whereas 'tradition' embraces the range of more subjective material, particularly suspect among which are memoirs or anything else which may have been written with an eye to posterity. Noting this suspicion, Motzkin comments that 'the uneasiness that memoirs create in the historian stems not only from their position midway between reality and the imagination, between history as truth and fiction; it also derives from the significant inca-pacity of historians to decide whether memoirs are primary or secondary sources.' This he attributes to the often considerable time gap between expe-rience and writing, thereby implicitly distinguishing memoirs from truly contemporaneous diaries, as retrospection introduces the problem of 'the unstable position of memory between truth and fiction, between reality and the imagination' (Motzkin, 1994, pp. 106, 105).

Schulze observes that 'autobiographical texts were previously subjects for research into cultural history, or in the literary-historical branch of literary science' rather than material for the historian (Schulze, 1996, p. 16). Even here, however, the types of text discussed in this book have received rela-tively little attention. There is indeed a considerable body of academic research on true autobiography, but the principal focus has usually been the autobiographer rather than his account of events. The more texts concern themselves with things that happened – as all of these accounts of the Thirty Years War do – the less interest they attract from this standpoint, so that there has been a notable scarcity of theoretical work on memoirs and eye-witness accounts as a class. Diaries have been more researched, although much of the better analysis is quite old, but even so a 1986 review indicated that genre studies were far from plentiful, a conclusion which is still valid (Rendall, 1986). Wuthenow made the same point in a German context, noting that 'hitherto diary literature has astonishingly rarely been taken seriously or treated in its own right as a separate genre' (Wuthenow, 1990, p. ix). Moreover, as with autobiography much of the scholarly interest in diaries has been in style and in accounts of the self rather than of events. Typical in this respect is Hocke's massive work on the European diary, in which he notes that 'there are factual documentary diaries as well as self-centred subjective ones from all periods since the Renaissance', but he places at the centre of his study '"real", that is to say subjective diaristic elements', and diaries 'which have a clear personal confessional character' (Hocke, 1991, pp. 34, 18, 19).

Academic perceptions are changing. In 1976 Barkin commented:

> As long as historians continue to be concerned primarily with political, diplomatic, and military history in the traditional manner, the value of autobiography for scholarship will be marginal. But this eventuality increasingly appears to be a remote one. (Barkin, 1976, p. 86)

Twenty years later the editors of a collection of papers on ego-documents could confidently assert that 'interest in historical autobiography has been increasing for some years, and self-perceptive testimonies have proved to be key historical sources' (Lehmann *et al.*, 1996, p. 7). Two complementary trends have brought about this change, namely the development of the concept of microhistory and the growing interest in ego-documents. Microhistory needs no further introduction here, but the approach is well summed up by Krusenstjern and Medick in the passage quoted in Chapter 1, reflecting what Schulze describes as 'an immense new interest in the behaviour of the individual person in history, a swing away from the big structural questions' (Schulze, 1996, p. 13).

Although it has echoes elsewhere, much of the enhanced interest in personal writings in recent years stems from northern Europe. The term 'ego-document' was coined in 1958 by a Dutch historian but it became better known as a topic for study and discussion in the 1980s and 1990s, particularly in Holland and Germany. The collections of papers referred to in this chapter and in Chapter 1 testify to the stimulating effect this has had on research activity in the field, but perhaps inevitably it has also sparked off a debate about terminology. At its simplest, Schulze defines ego-documents as any source 'in which a person gives information about himself or herself', but he also goes further, noting that this applies 'irrespective of whether this was done voluntarily – for example in a letter or an autobiographical text – or whether it was necessitated by other circumstances' (Schulze, 1996, p. 9). In this latter category he includes all kinds of officially required information, such as witness statements, court hearings, tax returns and so forth, which others distrust. Pleading instead for the use of the term '*Selbstzeugnis*', Krusenstjern rejects involuntary material and specifies that such sources must be 'self-composed and as a rule also self-written (or at least dictated) as well as self-motivated'. This would include all the accounts of the Thirty Years War discussed in this book, but Krusenstjern echoes the earlier attitude by insisting that 'the most important criterion is that the writer should treat himself or herself thematically. ... In other words the author appears in person in the text, either as subject or object of the action, or otherwise makes explicit reference to himself or herself' (Krusenstjern, 1994, pp. 470, 463). Thus she specifically excludes Mallinger's text from her bibliographic register of *Selbstzeugnisse* on the grounds that it belongs to the class of 'records in which the explicit self has only a very marginal role to play' (Krusenstjern, 1997, p. 19).

Two more quotations summarise the growing interest in personal writing as a source for the study of history at the level of the individual, together with its specific application to the Thirty Years War:

> Particular attention has been attracted, both in international research and among the interested public, by popular autobiography, personal writings from the lower and middle classes. The existence of such texts was previously barely known, but precisely these have proved to be indispensable for all attempts to reconstruct social usage and the pattern of experience of the world in which people lived. Personal writings open new approaches to showing participants in history as feeling, perceiving, acting and suffering individuals. (Lehmann *et al.*, 1996, p. 7)

The Thirty Years War counts as one of the most traumatic events in the German past, and in contrast to other wars of the Early Modern period the sufferings of the people, as they have been transmitted in diaries, autobiographies and parish chronicles, play a major part in its analysis and description, alongside political, diplomatic and military history. However in the past these sources were used predominantly for illustration rather than as a particular opportunity to access the range of personal perceptions and interpretations of the war, together with the corresponding individual strategies for dealing with it. (Wunder, 1995, p. 84)

The texts discussed in this book typify the general problem which genre analysts have with personal writings, in that few of them fit easily into a particular definition. The only true contemporaneous diaries are those of the unknown soldier and of Peter Hagendorf, and even these seem to be the authors' own fair copies, so that the possibility that they edited or revised them to some extent cannot be ruled out. Other texts have an autobiographical framework, probably modelled on the self-written life histories prepared with one's funeral sermon in mind which were popular in Germany at the time. Dietwar's account is of this type and a number of others approximate to it, for example those of Lang, Cervinus and Winkler. All, however, depart radically from the pattern when they describe the author's experience of the war, altering their focus from the self to external events, so that the resultant works are far from typical examples of the genre. Many of the accounts could be loosely described as memoirs and some as chronicles, but the majority override such boundaries and have characteristics of more than one type, or shift between types under the pressure of circumstances.

Pascal, whose 1960 study of autobiography remains one of the best, attempts to clarify the distinctions. Autobiography, he states, 'is a review of life from a particular moment in time, while the diary, however reflective it may be, moves through a series of moments in time. The diarist notes down what, at that moment, seems of importance to him.' Diaristic writing may, however, be belated or retrospective, so that it assumes some of the characteristics of a memoir, or even of autobiography. Pascal says that no clear line can be drawn between these latter genres:

> There is no autobiography that is not in some respect a memoir, and no memoir that is without autobiographical information; both are based on personal experience, chronological, and reflective. But there is a general difference in the direction of the author's attention. In the autobiography proper, attention is focused on the self, in the memoir or reminiscence on others. (Pascal, 1960, pp. 3, 5)

Henning agrees, but draws the distinction more between self and events than between self and others: 'The memoir writer remains in the background, behind his description of the events in which he was involved. The objective is not a self-portrait of the author, but a picture of an epoch' (Henning, 1994, p. 109). In the light of these definitions many, if not most, of the eyewitness accounts qualify as memoirs. Those of a more contemporaneous nature may be classified as diaries, the essential feature of which, according to Fothergill, in another old but still useful study, is that they should have been 'written in the first person as a discontinuous series of more or less self-contained responses to the writer's present situation and recent experience', although elsewhere he admits that '"diary" means what you think it means; moreover its usage appears to be indistinguishable from that of "journal"' (Fothergill, 1974, pp. 48, 3). Wuthenow echoes this latter point, observing that 'diary literature is so extensive and multifarious' that it is impossible 'to contemplate a valid and clear-cut definition' (Wuthenow, 1990, p. ix).

Analysts of the genres all agree that the reasons why people write are important, although without arriving at any very precise assessment of the range of potential motives or the consequences likely to flow from them. They tend instead to fall back upon neat but essentially unhelpful encapsulations such as 'no two diarists are prompted by identical impulses; at the same time no diarist writes for reasons unique to himself'. Often the simplest answer seems to be the best, an urge, probably inexplicable even to the writer, to record for its own sake, or to be a chronicler of the times, to which, appropriately in the present context, Fothergill adds 'the onset of Historic Events, especially a war, which confer on the diarist the self-important role of eyewitness' (Fothergill, 1974, pp. 94, 16). Most, however, agree that the author's own explanation can rarely be taken at face value, and Delany comments that in seventeenth-century works in particular 'these stated motives are usually half-truths, attempts to make the writing of an autobiography look respectable or to fit it into some accepted tradition' (Delany, 1969, p. 113).

The previous chapter put forward various possibilities as the impetus for writing particular accounts of the Thirty Years War, and these correspond to suggestions in more general studies and to specific examples from other places and times. Among the most obvious is the desire for an aid to recollection in later life. Bacon regarded a journal as a means of observing and remembering more accurately; 'Let diaries therefore be brought into use', he advised young men off to see something of the world in his essay 'On travel' (Bacon, 1959, p. 50). Velten identifies the same idea in sixteenth-century Germany, referring to a systematic approach to travel 'in which keeping a diary, at the least, was strongly recommended. ... Diaries had the principal functions of prompting the memory and of recording important experiences and observations'. He goes on to link this to more personal writing, observing that 'like the travel journal, the personal diary can also have subjective and autobiographical passages' (Velten, 1995, pp. 60, 61).

Personal recollection often leads to thoughts of posterity, as it did for Sir John Bramston (1611–1700). Feeling himself, in his seventy-second year, to be potentially 'on the brinck of the grave', he notes:

> I may well take occasion [...to] call to remembrance the yeares that are passed, what I have done, and how I have spent (I hope not wasted) my time. That posteritie, therefore, (I meane my owne descendents,) may know somethinge of my father and my selfe, beside our names in the pedegree or line of descent, I have set downe some thyngs (tho' few) done by my selfe not unworthy. (Bramston, 1845, p. 4)

From recording for posterity it is only a small step to wishing to be remembered by posterity. Boswell's view of his diary, like Heberle's, suggests an aspiration to vicarious immortality: 'My wife, who does not like journalizing, said it was leaving myself embowelled to posterity – a good strong figure. But I think it is rather leaving myself embalmed. It is certainly preserving myself' (Boswell, 1963, pp. 174–5).

There may also be parallels in accounts of the Thirty Years War to cases where people wrote as a means of exorcising the ghosts of past trauma, as suggested by Davis's observation that 'turning a terrible action into a story is a way to distance oneself from it' (Davis, 1987, p. 114). Likewise Young observes of Holocaust diaries:

> It is almost as if violent events – perceived as aberrations or ruptures in the cultural continuum – demand their retelling, their *narration*, back into traditions and structures they would otherwise defy. ... For once written, events assume the mantle of coherence that narrative necessarily imposes on them, and the trauma of their unassimilability is relieved. (Young, 1987, p. 404)

In the context of motivation a note about the particular circumstances of the seventeenth century is warranted. Although there was some autobiographical writing in medieval times this was mostly of a spiritual nature, analysing and recording the individual's inner progress towards God, both as an aid to the self and as an example to others – or a warning, as they often dwelt on shortcomings. The Renaissance brought a gradual change in approach, so that by the seventeenth century individuals were readier to write autobiographies which dealt with their worldly lives, although still tending to be somewhat apologetic about it. Delany regards the Civil War as a significant stimulus to memoir writing in England, although 'it was the gentry or aristocracy who were both more assertive in their daily affairs and more likely to have the experiences of travel, military command, or political office which helped to arouse the autobiographical urge' (Delany, 1969, p. 109). Among the Thirty Years War eyewitnesses this description perhaps fits the three colonels

Monro, Vitzthum and Fritsch and the lawyer Pflummer, but many of the others came from further down the social scale, providing support for Amelang's opposing contention that the Early Modern period was marked by 'the expanding resort to formal literary expression by writers of humble extraction'. The era, he says, 'not only saw the rise of autobiography. It also witnessed, more specifically, the rise of *popular* autobiography' (Amelang, 1993, p. 32). Again Velten confirms this from a German perspective, referring to 'the middle-class autobiography which developed in the second half of the sixteenth century … in which the life of the author stood at the centre and determined the limits of the description' (Velten, 1995, p. 70). Peters agrees, but like Delany he identifies historical break points as providing impetus: 'It cannot be a coincidence that particularly ambitious forms of popular writing … developed during the Thirty Years War, in the years after the French Revolution, and in the time of radical change following the agricultural reforms of the nineteenth century' (Peters, 1993, p. 241).

The popularity of funeral sermons in seventeenth-century Germany referred to above, particularly in Lutheran areas, was another potential encouragement for autobiographical writing, and I have discussed elsewhere the influence of this and other models of writing on these accounts of the war (Mortimer, 2000). Such sermons commonly included a life history of the deceased, and it was not unusual for the more literate people to prepare a draft – in effect an autobiography – in advance for the preacher. Large numbers were printed and published, so that this type of personal writing will have been familiar to many of those writing accounts of the war period. They may not have considered their work autobiographical, however, regarding themselves as recorders of a communal experience rather than as focusing unduly on their own lives.

Nevertheless a certain defensiveness in this respect remained, exemplified by Monro's claim that he wrote in memory of his comrades who died in Germany, 'and not for the world, for which I care not' (Mo.I, To the Reader, 2). This is also evident in the explanation for her autobiography offered by an English contemporary, Margaret Cavendish, Duchess of Newcastle (1625–74), in which despite her claim to write for herself she clearly had posterity's view of her in mind:

> I hope my readers will not think me vain for writing my life, since there have been many that have done the like, as Caesar, Ovid, and many more, both men and women, and I know no reason I may not do it as well as they. … It is true, that 'tis to no purpose to the readers, but it is to the authoress, because I write it for my own sake, not theirs. Neither did I intend this piece for to delight, but to divulge; not to please the fancy, but to tell the truth, lest after-ages should mistake, … for my Lord having had two wives, I might easily have been mistaken, especially if I should die and my Lord marry again. (Cavendish, 1886, pp. 317–8)

This recalls the question discussed in the previous chapter of what audience or readership the authors of the eyewitness accounts envisaged as they wrote. Monro published his own work, but few of the others could either have intended or foreseen publication. But how many truly wrote 'for my own sake', and if they did to whom were they divulging and telling the truth? The question is important, as consciousness of an implied reader inevitably shapes what is written. Such considerations may well have influenced what the officer memoirists reveal about their own or their comrades' behaviour – the common soldier Hagendorf is notably more forthright than his superiors in reporting his taking of girls as booty – and a corresponding reticence may have inhibited the civilians in recording rape of their own womenfolk. Wuthenow comments that 'distortion and falsification can also be explained by the fear that someone else might come to see the entries, ... or conversely misrepresentations may be made specifically in the hope that someone else will read them' (Wuthenow, 1990, p. 5).

This leads on to the question of the self-presentation of the author, and how much he knowingly or unwittingly reveals of himself, noting that, try as he may, he can never efface himself completely:

> Everyone who writes also writes about himself. Even if the facts, events, thoughts and feelings which are presented seem to permit of no bio-graphical conclusions, so the writing self still allows itself to be perceived through the choice and treatment of subjects, through the form of the presentation, and through the style of what is presented.... The self expresses itself, and as it does so at the same time it with-holds itself. (Götz, 1993, *Vorwort*, first page)

Literary theories of fictional narrative distinguish between the real author, the implied author and the narrator or narratorial voice. For eyewitness memoirs these might be assumed to be one and the same, but this is not necessarily so, as in controlling information about himself the real author effectively creates an implied one who is not identical. The resulting autho-rial persona contains elements both of the writer's self-image and of the image that he wishes to present, or is prepared to expose, to the implied reader. The Nuremberg chronicler Murr's decision to write a record in which he as author is almost invisible is as definite and personal a narratorial stance as Poyntz's corresponding choice of a lively and anecdotal tale with himself at the centre, and this influences the selection and shaping of the material in the text. At the most obvious level, depending upon where he has placed himself along the spectrum from apparently external narrator to central character, the author may minimise or exaggerate his own involve-ment and experiences, together perhaps with those of his comrades or com-munity. More subtly, he may implicitly craft his text in accordance with his personal stance or interpretation of events and wider circumstances; for example the underlying attitude of civilian chroniclers to the war ranges from a religious acceptance of punishment from God to a bitter condemnation of the evils of man, or of one party among men.

Such shaping of the account can go further, leading to what I have elsewhere described as fictionalisation (Mortimer, 2001b). This implies not any deliberate falsehood or exaggeration on the part of the author, but that the process of writing itself, the ordering of events into a narrative, can create a misleading impression of the underlying reality. Other analysts sound similar cautionary notes. Jancke observes:

> To analyse the recorded facts simply into categories of true or false, complete or incomplete, would therefore certainly not exhaust the actual information content of such reports. For beneath every communication of facts there lies a perception and a concept which inform the choice, arrangement, connection, weighting, evaluation and interpretation of the particulars. (Jancke, 1996, p. 76)

Henning goes further, suggesting that in memoirs such selection may sometimes be purposeful: 'It has also to be taken into account that an author may not have wanted to represent the truth up to the limit of what was possible for him, but may have been pursuing certain specific intentions in his recording' (Henning, 1994, p. 112). Even more fundamentally, Wuthenow adds that 'the process of remembering is itself, in a sense, an invention' (Wuthenow, 1990, p. 2).

As discussed in Chapter 2, the time at which the text was written is significant. Where diary entries are made contemporaneously the writer can at most shape them on the basis of the story so far; if memoirs are written later the writer knows, if not the outcome, at least a great deal more of the course of events and can fashion the account accordingly. Bernheiden notes that 'with regard to a process of recollection, and such a process forms the basis of autobiographical writing, [it seems appropriate] to speak not of truth in the sense used by the historian, but of correspondence to the truth' (Bernheiden, 1988, p. 32). Moreover circumstances at the time of writing are likely to be uppermost in the writer's mind, influencing his interpretation of earlier recollections. Chateaubriand took many years over writing his memoirs, during which he experienced sharp fluctuations in fortune, causing him to observe that 'the varied events and changing forms of my life thus enter into one another. It occurs that, in prosperous moments, I have to speak of the time of my misfortunes and that, in my days of tribulation, I retrace my days of happiness' (Chateaubriand, 1947, *Préface*). Krusenstjern warns that with seventeenth-century personal accounts 'one is dealing predominantly with reworkings, extracts or fair copies made by the author himself, versions for posterity, so to speak' (Krusenstjern, 1997, p. 11). Such editing implies selecting material with the benefit of hindsight rather than in response to the degree of importance it appeared to have at the time, and also consciously or unconsciously moulding the resulting narrative in accordance with an emerging pattern or story. Poyntz and Monro both refer to making notes on campaign but they wrote their memoirs after returning home, Monro placing 'the valiant king Gustavus Adolphus' and 'the good cause' at the centre of his account whereas Poyntz wrote a romance with himself as hero (Mo.II. 169, 67).

Enough has been said to offer some support for the general caution of historians towards memoirs, but having entered these caveats to taking eyewitness personal accounts of the Thirty Years War at face value as historical fact, what do they then have to offer? Essentially they are concerned with perception, how people of the time felt and interpreted their experiences, and how they attempted to represent them through the medium of writing. History is not – or should not be – concerned just with events. A generation living in constant or recurrent fear of what might be about to happen is also historically significant and a valid part of human experience, as is the reaction of people to what actually did happen. The very fact that the authors of these accounts were moved to write and to record shows the significance they attached to their experiences; the question is how successfully they have been able to transmit this, and to evoke in the reader the feel of the times as human reality. The value of these eyewitness records lies in the extent to which they help to answer not only the factual question: 'What happened?', but also the evaluative one: 'What was it like?', and how far they enable us 'to get to know a period from the perspective of the author, who was a part of it' (Henning, 1994, p. 114).

Appendix: Authors, Occupations and Locations

A	Ackermann	Soldier*	Kroppenstedt (Magdeburg)
Be	Beck	Pastor	Emtmannsberg (Bayreuth)
Ba	Bismarck, A.	Soldier	on campaign
Bc	Bismarck, C.	Landowner	Briest (Tangermünde)
Bö	Bötzinger	Pastor	Poppenhausen
Bü	Bürster	Monk	Salem
Bt	Büttner	Pastor	Altenheim
C	Cervinus	Pastor	Laubach
Di	Dietwar	Pastor	Kitzingen
Do	Dobel	Baker	Virnsberg (Ansbach)
Dr	Dressel	Monk (abbot)	Ebrach
Er	Ernst	Nun	Villingen
–	Eschlinsperger	Warden	Überlingen
Fe	Feilinger	Pastor	Schlüchtern
Fr	Freund	Pastor	Lucka (Leipzig)
F	Fritsch	Soldier	on campaign
Ge	Gerlach	Schoolmaster	Albertshausen (Würzburg)
Gö	Götzenius	Pastor	Friedberg
Gr	Grützmann	Pastor	Bottmersdorf (Magdeburg)
G	Guericke	Engineer	Magdeburg
Ha	Hagendorf	Soldier	on campaign
Hd	Haidenbucher	Nun (abbess)	Chiemsee
Hr	Hartmann	Boy*	Bad Wildungen
–	Hartung	Steward	Fulda
He	Heberle	Shoemaker	Neenstetten (Ulm)
Hl	Hellgemayr	Court chorister	Munich
Hn	Henrici	Pastor	Friedberg
Hu	Hueber	Monk	Eichstätt
J	Junius	Nun	Bamberg
La	Lang	Army supplier*	Isny
Lu	Ludolph	Pastor	Reichensachsen (Kassel)
Lt	Lutz	Innkeeper	Salmünster (Hanau)
Ma	Mallinger	Priest	Freiburg im Breisgau
Ml	Maul	Tax official	Naumburg
Mi	Minck	Pastor	Biberau (Darmstadt)
Mo	Monro	Soldier	on campaign
Mu	Murr	Unknown	Nuremberg
O	Oberacker	Soldier's boy*	on campaign
Pf	Pflummer	Lawyer	Überlingen
Pi	Piderit	Pastor	Blomberg
Pl	Plebanus	Pastor	Miehlen (Koblenz)
Po	Poyntz	Soldier	on campaign
Pr	Preis	Farmer	Stausenbach (Marburg)
Pn	Prinz	Merchant	Magdeburg

Ra	Raph	Town clerk	Bietigheim
Ry	Raymond	Soldier	on campaign
Re	Renner	Pastor	Fürth
–	Rotenburger	Copper engraver	Bietigheim
–	Rüger	Gun captain	Coburg
Sr	Saur	Pastor	Besse (Kassel)
Sa	Sautter	Priest	Unterwachingen (Ulm)
Sc	Schleyss	Pastor	Gerstetten (Ulm)
Sh	Schuster	Town clerk	Strausberg
Sk	Sierk	Farmer	Wrohm (Schleswig)
–	Simmern	Salt merchant	Colberg (East Pomerania)
Sp	Spiegel	Pastor	Erlangen
St	Staiger	Nun (prioress)	Eichstätt
S	Strampfer	Baker	Bad Windsheim (Ansbach)
Th	Thiele	Tax official	Beelitz (Potsdam)
T	Turner	Soldier	on campaign
U	Ullmann	Estate officer	South-west Silesia
Uk	Unknown	Soldier	on campaign
V	Vincent	Army doctor (?)	on campaign
Vi	Vitzthum	Soldier	on campaign
–	Volhard	Town clerk	Friedberg
Wa	Wagner	Cloth merchant	Augsburg
Wl	Walther	Artist	Strasbourg
We	Wendell	Wine-grower	Sponheim (Bad Kreuznach)
Wi	Winkler	Pastor	Pirna
Wo	Wolff	Miller	Schwabach
Za	Zader	Pastor	Naumburg
Z	Zembroth	Wine-grower	Allensbach (Constance)

* Ackermann later became a land owner, Hartmann, an innkeeper's son, became a pastor, and Oberacker became a miller. Lang was a cloth-finisher by trade.

Map: Homes of Civilian Eyewitnesses
(with locations of the most important battles)

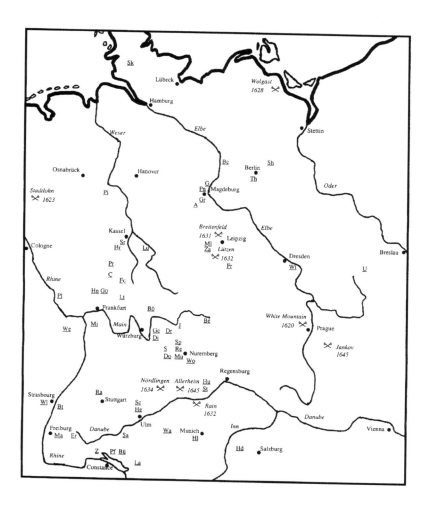

Bibliography

Further reading

As there is such a vast general literature on the Thirty Years War all that can be given here are a few suggestions as to where to look further. The best and most readable comprehensive account of the war remains C.V. Wedgwood's *The Thirty Years War*, which has been widely translated and is still in print even though it was first published in 1938. Geoffrey Parker's *The Thirty Years War*, dating from 1984, covers the same ground in less depth but summarises the modern scholarly approach to the subject. Parker's wide-ranging bibliographic essay also provides an invaluable starting point for further study, with a large number of relevant works listed thematically for ease of reference.

Most of the more recent specialist work is in German, and the collections of articles cited in Chapters 1 and 16 bring the subject up to date for the expert, particularly as regards the growing interest in microhistory and ego-documents. Relevant volumes are those edited by Schulze (1996), Kroener and Pröve (1996), Lademacher and Groenveld (1998), and Krusenstjern and Medick (1999), while some of the individual articles also have useful bibliographies.

There is remarkably little secondary literature on the specific subject of eyewitness accounts of the war. All the examples quoted in this book have been published, and many of the more recent editors of individual texts, as well as a notable few of the earlier ones, researched them in depth. Hence some provide useful commentaries and supplementary information, but almost always focusing sharply on the particular account and location concerned. A number of what appear to be wider studies prove to be based on misleading use of the terminology. Thus Hoffmann's 1927 doctoral thesis on accounts of English eyewitnesses 'from the age of the Thirty Years War' (often used as a catch-all title in German) draws on material extending over more than a century, with only a short chapter on the actual war period. More than half of Krügel's 1911 study is taken up with lengthy excerpts from clearly fictional sources, notably Grimmelshausen, the rest being limited to three genuine accounts and extracts from commercial chronicles. More recently Jessen's 1963 book, *The Thirty Years War in Eyewitness Reports*, takes its material either from contemporary publications (a quarter coming from the *Theatrum Europaeum* alone) or from the reports and letters of principal participants, rather than from essentially private accounts. The latter are now starting to attract more attention and are mentioned increasingly frequently in articles such as those comprising the collections referred to above, but specific studies remain the exception. Three examples are Erdmann on Mallinger's chronicle (1995), Burschel on Hagendorf's diary (1999), and Woodford on the nuns' accounts (1999), while Pröve also deals in part with Hagendorf (1997). Full publication details for these and other works mentioned in this bibliographic note are listed below.

Source eyewitness accounts

These are listed alphabetically by name of the original author, followed by the reference codes used in the text. Where there is no reference code this indicates that the source concerned formed part of the original study but is not mentioned in this book. Krusenstjern (1997) notes the location of many of the extant manuscripts, and as some of the published texts are hard to find library shelfmarks are given below in most cases, principally in Berlin or elsewhere in Germany, but also in the British or Bodleian Libraries where known to be available, using the following codes.

AGB	Amerika-Gedenk Bibliothek, Berlin
BOD	Bodleian Library, Oxford
BL	British Library, London
FU	Freie Universität, Berlin, Central Library
FU/M	Freie Universität, Friedrich-Meinecke Institut
HAB	Herzog August Bibliothek, Wolfenbüttel
HUM	Humboldt Universität, Berlin, Central Library
HUM/G	Humboldt Universität, Zweigbibliothek Geschichte
KAR	Landesbibliothek, Karlsruhe
LIP	Lippische Landesbibliothek, Detmold
KON	Konstanz-Bibliothek
REG	Universitätsbibliothek, Regensburg
SBB	Staatsbibliothek, Berlin
VGB	Bibliothek des Vereins für Geschichte Berlins
WÜR	Württembergische Landesbibliothek, Stuttgart
ZWI	Ratschulbibliothek, Zwickau

Ackermann (A) Volkholz, R., ed., *Jürgen Ackermann, Kapitän beim Regiment Alt–Pappenheim: 1631* (Halberstadt: Schimmelburg, 1895). SBB.Ry.6219.

Beck (Be) Holle, ed., 'Abschrift aus der Emtmannsberger Pfarrregistratur aus den Jahren 1632 und 1641', *Archiv für Geschichte und Alterthumskunde von Oberfranken*, 3 (1846), 79–85. SBB.Sf.5732.

Bismarck, Augustus von (Ba) Zahn, W., ed., 'Die Memoiren des Junkers Augustus von Bismarck', *Jahresbericht des Altmärkischen Vereins für vaterländische Geschichte und Industrie zu Salzwedel*, 23 (1890), 90–105. FU/M.6.Ms.10.

Bismarck, Christoph von (Bc) Schmidt, G., ed., 'Das Tagebuch des Christoph von Bismarck aus den Jahren 1625–1640', *Thüringisch–Sächsische Zeitschrift für Geschichte und Kunst*, 5 (1915), 67–98. FU.28.74.1258(X)5; BL.Ac.7345.4.

Bötzinger (Bö) Krauß, J.W., ed., 'Extract aus Hr. Martin Bötzingers ... Vitae Curriculo', in *Beyträge zur Erläuterung der Hochfürstl. Sachsen–Hildburghäusischen Kirchen–, Schul– und Landes–Historie*, Theil 1 (Greitz, 1750), pp. 341–68. SBB.Ss.6032.

Bürster (Bü) Weech, F. von, ed., *Sebastian Bürster's Beschreibung des schwedischen Krieges 1630–1647* (Leipzig: Hirzel, 1875). SBB.Ry.5976; BOD.246.e.276; BL.9435.dd.1.

Büttner (Bt) Kappus–Mulsow, H., ed., 'Trübe Jahre im Ried nach dem ältesten Kirchenbuch Altenheims', *Die Ortenau: Mitteilungen des historischen Vereins für Mittelbaden*, 14 (1927), 140–54. SBB.Si.4255.

Cervinus (C) Solms–Laubach, F. Graf zu, and W. Matthaei, eds, *Wetterfelder Chronik: Aufzeichnungen eines luth. Pfarrers der Wetterau, welcher den dreißigjährigen Krieg von Anfang bis Ende miterlebt hat* (Giessen: Ricker, 1882). SBB.Sk.9130.

Dietwar (Di) Wirth, V., ed., *Bartholomäus Dietwar: Leben eines evangelischen Pfarrers im früheren markgräflichen Amte Kitzingen 1592–1670, von ihm selbst erzählt* (Kitzingen: Stahel, 1887). HUM.B.36787; BL.4888.b.62.

Dobel (Do) Rechter, G., ed., 'Der Obere Zenngrund im Zeitalter des Dreißigjährigen Krieges', *Jahrbuch für fränkische Landesforschung*, 38 (1978), 83–122 (pp. 109–14). SBB.Zsn.3628.

Dressel (Dr) Hüttner. F., ed., 'Memoiren des Zisterzienserabts Johann Dressel von Ebrach aus den Jahren 1631–1635', *Studien und Mitteilungen aus dem Benediktiner- und dem Cistercienser-Orden*, 26 (1905), 76–85, 294–305, 551–73; 27 (1906), 102–13, 368–99. SBB.Cg.4500.

Ernst (Er) Glatz, K.J., ed., 'Ein gleichzeitiger Bericht über das Wirtembergische Kriegsvolk vor der östreichischen Stadt Villingen vom Jahre 1631 bis 1633', *Württembergische Vierteljahrshefte für Landesgeschichte*, 1 (1878), 129–37. SBB.Sh.250; BL.Ac.2432.4.

Eschlinsperger (–) Harzendorf, F., ed., 'Ueberlinger Tagebuch aus dem Schwedenkrieg: Die Aufzeichnungen des Spitalpflegers Johann Heinrich Eschlinsperger', *Bodensee-Chronik*, 27 (1938), 50–2, 57–8, 62–3, 67–8, 70–1, 74–5, 80. KON.G.4104.y.

Feilinger (Fe) Rullmann, J., ed., 'Die Einwirkungen des 30jährigen Krieges auf die Stadt Schlüchtern und ihre Umgegend, aus Kirchenbüchern zusammengestellt', *Zeitschrift des Vereins für hessische Geschichte und Landeskunde*, n.s.6 (1877), 201–50. SBB.Sk.161.

Freund (Fr) Freund, M., ed., *Die Freund'sche Chronik von Lucka: Die Schicksale einer kleinen deutschen Stadt im Jahrhundert des 30jährigen Krieges* (Lucka: Berger, 1933). REG.NR.6750.I.941.F8.

Fritsch (F) Westenrieder, L., ed., 'Tagbuch des Augustin von Fritsch (Obersten und Commendanten der Stadt Weyden) von seinen Thaten und Schicksalen im dreyßigjährigen Kriege', in *Beyträge zur vaterländischen Historie, Geographie, Staatistik, und Landwirthschaft*, ed. L. Westenrieder, 8 vols (Munich: Lindauer, 1788–1806), IV (1792), pp. 105–91. SBB.Sf.114.4; BL.P.P.3548.a.

Gerlach (Ge) Zimmermann, H., ed., *Das Tagebuch des Schulmeisters Gerlach in Albertshausen 1629–1650* (Würzburg: Memminger, 1924). SBB.Sf.7019.

Götzenius (Gö) Waas, C., ed., 'Joh. Philipp Götzenius: Die Kriegsereignisse und Einquartierungen 1620–50', in *Die Chroniken von Friedberg in der Wetterau*, ed. C. Waas (Friedberg: Bindernagel, 1937), pp. 146–51. SBB.Sk.6037.181; BL.09327.ddd.4.

Grützmann (Gr) Hertel, G., ed., 'Nachrichten über Bottmarsdorf während des dreißigjährigen Krieges', *Geschichts-Blätter für Stadt und Land Magdeburg*, 29 (1894), 232–61. SBB.Te.7448.

Guericke (G) Hoffmann, F.W., ed., *Otto von Guericke: Geschichte der Belagerung, Eroberung und Zerstörung Magdeburg's* (Magdeburg: Baensch, 1860). SBB.71419.

Hagendorf (Ha) Peters, J., ed., *Ein Söldnerleben im Dreißigjährigen Krieg: Eine Quelle zur Sozialgeschichte* (Berlin: Akademie Verlag, 1993). SBB.HsLs.CM.1056; BOD.M93. F09368; BL.YA.1995.a.19939.

Haidenbucher (Hd) Baumann, M.W., and A. Mitterwieser, eds, 'Tagebuch der Aebtissin Maria Magdalena Haidenbucher von Frauenchiemsee (1609–1650)', *Heimatbilder aus dem Chiemgau*, 54 (1928), 307–22; 56 (1929), 339–54; 58 (1929), 371–86; 60 (1930), 403–13; 61 (1930), 419–34; 62 (1930), 435–50; 66 (1932), 499–514. Quotations are taken from the foregoing publication, but there is also a more recent edition of the same manuscript: Stalla, G., ed., *Geschicht Buech de Anno 1609 biß 1650: Das Tagebuch der Maria Magdalena Haidenbucher (1576–1650), Äbtissin von Frauenwörth* (Amsterdam: Holland University Press, 1988). KAR.88.A.13429; BL.YA.1991.a.13656.

Hartmann (Hr) Uckeley, A., ed., 'Aufzeichnungen über das Geschick der Hartmannschen Familie im Jahrhundert des dreißigjährigen Krieges', *Geschichtsblätter für Waldeck und Pyrmont*, 7 (1907), 14–56. SBB.Sn.1502.5.

Hartung (–) Haas, T., ed., 'Die chronikalischen Aufzeichnungen des Fuldaer Bürgers Gangolf Hartung (1607–1666)', *Fuldaer Geschichtsblätter*, 9 (1910), 49–171. SBB.Sk.6181.

Heberle (He) Zillhardt, G., ed., *Der Dreißigjährige Krieg in zeitgenössischer Darstellung: Hans Heberles 'Zeytregister' (1618–1672): Aufzeichnungen aus dem Ulmer Territorium* (Ulm: Kohlhammer, 1975). SBB.Ser.6431.13; BL.X.700.18021.

Hellgemayr (Hl) Leuchtmann, H., ed., 'Zeitgeschichtliche Aufzeichnungen des Bayerischen Hofkapellaltisten Johannes Hellgemayr aus den Jahren 1595–1633', *Oberbayerisches Archiv*, 100 (1975), 142–229. SBB.Zsn.3341.

Henrici (Hn) Waas, C., ed., 'Johannes Henrici: Aufzeichnungen aus seinem Leben und seiner Zeit (1592–1656)', in *Die Chroniken von Friedberg in der Wetterau*, ed. C. Waas (Friedberg: Bindernagel, 1937), pp. 231–6. SBB.Sk.6037.181; BL.09327.ddd.4.

Hueber (Hu) Radspieler, H., ed., 'Wer dises lesen wirt ...', *Historische Blätter für Stadt und Landkreis Eichstätt*, 20 (1971), 18–20.

Junius (J) Hümmer, F.K., ed., 'Bamberg im Schweden-Kriege', *Bericht über Bestand und Wirken des historischen Vereins zu Bamberg*, 52 (1890), 2–168; 53 (1891), 169–230. SBB.Sf.5741.

Lang (La) Pfeilsticker, K., ed., *Tagebuch des Hans Conrad Lang, Bürgers von Isny ... aus den Jahren 1601–1659* (Isny: the author, 1930). WÜR.ACH.1923.

Ludolph (Lu) Kürschner, W., ed., 'Aus dem Kirchenbuch von Reichensachsen (und Langenhain) von 1639–1653', *Archiv für hessische Geschichte und Altertumskunde*, n.s.9 (1913), 48–55. SBB.Sk.1520.

Lutz (Lt) Scherer, K., ed., 'Die Hauschronik des Johann Lutz von Salmünster', *Fuldaer Geschichtsblätter*, 3 (1904), 17–27, 59–64, 110–15, 137–9, 157–60, 161–6. SBB.Sk.6181.

Mallinger (Ma) Mone, F.J., ed., 'Thomas Mallingers Tagbücher', in *Quellensammlung der badischen Landesgeschichte*, ed. F.J. Mone, 4 vols (Karlsruhe: Macklot, 1848–67), II (1854), pp. 528–615. SBB.4º.Si.90; BOD.240.h.165–168.

Maul (Ml) Hoppe, F., ed., *Johann Georg Mauls Diarium aus dem Dreißigjährigen Kriege* (Naumburg: Sieling, 1928). SBB.Tf.2667.

Minck (Mi) Kunz, R., and W. Lizalek, eds, 'Die Biberauer Chronik (1579–1654) des Pfarrers Johann Daniel Minck', in *Südhessische Chroniken aus der Zeit des Dreißigjährigen Krieges*, ed. R. Kunz and W. Lizalek (Lorsch: Verlag Laurissa, 1983), pp. 229–88. SBB.Ser.25.925.6; BL.YA.1992.a.4650.

Monro (Mo) Monro, R., *Monro, His Expedition with the Worthy Scots Regiment (Called Mac–Keyes Regiment)* (London, 1637). BOD.K.4.10.Art; BL.600.K.6.

Murr (Mu) Murr, C.G. von, ed., 'Hanns Hieronymus von Murr: Chronologische Nachrichten vom Zustande der Reichstadt Nürnberg während der Zeit des dreyßigjährigen Krieges', in *Beyträge zur Geschichte des dreyßigjährigen Krieges, insonderheit des Zustandes der Reichstadt Nürnberg, während desselben*, ed. C.G. von Murr (Nuremberg: Bauer und Mann, 1790), pp. 1–117. HAB.Gl.3320; BL.9325.c.16.

Oberacker (O) Teichert, H., ed., 'Aus der Chronik der Familie Gruner, Ittlingen: Ein Schicksal aus dem Dreißigjährigen Krieg', *Kraichgau*, 1 (1968), 106–10.

Pflummer (Pf) Semler, A., ed., 'Die Tagebücher des Dr. Johann Heinrich von Pflummern 1633–1643', 2 vols, *Beihefte zur Zeitschrift für die Geschichte des Oberrheins*, 98–9 (1950–51). SBB.Zsn.751; BL.P.P.3543.a.3.

Piderit (Pi) Anon., ed., 'Der dreißigjährige Krieg. Nach einer Piderit'schen Handschrift', *Blätter für lippische Heimathkunde*, 1 (1900), 14–15, 22–3, 31, 38–9, 46–7, 55–6, 62–3, 69–70, 77–8, 85–7, 93; 2 (1901), 7–8, 14–15, 22–3, 31–2, 38–9, 47–8, 55–6, 66–7, 78–9, 84–6, 93–5; 3 (1902), 6–7, 15–16, 22–3, 28–30, 39–40, 45–7, 51–3. LIP.LZ.37.4º.+3.

Plebanus (Pl) Heymach, F., ed., 'Aufzeichnungen des Pfarrers Plebanus von Miehlen aus den Jahren 1636/37', *Annalen des Vereins für nassauische Altertumskunde und Geschichtsforschung*, 38 (1908), 255–85. SBB.Si.7048.

Poyntz (Po) Goodrick, A.T.S., ed., *The Relation of Sydnam Poyntz 1624–1636* (London: Camden, 1908). BOD.K.6.1.182; BL.Ac.8118.7.

Preis (Pr) Ruhl, J.A., ed., 'Stausenbacher Chronik des Kaspar Preis, 1637–1667', *Fuldaer Geschichtsblätter*, 1 (1902), 113–86. SBB.Sk.6181.

Prinz (Pn) Volkholz, R., ed., *Jürgen Ackermann, Kapitän beim Regiment Alt–Pappenheim: 1631* (Halberstadt: Schimmelburg, 1895), pp. 19–29. SBB.Ry.6219.

Raph (Ra) Bentele, G., ed., *Protokolle einer Katastrophe: Zwei Bietigheimer Chroniken aus dem Dreißigjährigen Krieg* (Bietigheim–Bissingen: Stadtarchiv, 1984). SBB.4.43.SA.1144.1; BL.YA.1989.b.463.

Raymond (Ry) Davies, G., ed., *Autobiography of Thomas Raymond* (London: Camden, 1917). BOD.K.6.1.196; BL.Ac.8118.7.

Renner (Re) Großner, R., and Freiherr B. von Haller, eds, '"Zu kurzem Bericht umb der Nachkommen willen": Zeitgenössische Aufzeichnungen aus dem Dreißigjährigen Krieg in Kirchenbüchern des Erlanger Raumes', *Erlanger Bausteine zur fränkischen Heimatforschung*, 40 (1992), 9–107. VGB.C.246.

Rotenburger (–) Bentele, G., ed., *Protokolle einer Katastrophe: Zwei Bietigheimer Chroniken aus dem Dreißigjährigen Krieg* (Bietigheim–Bissingen: Stadtarchiv, 1984). SBB.4.43.SA.1144.1; BL.YA.1989.b.463.

Rüger (–) Karche, P.C.G., ed., *Coburgs Vergangenheit: Jahrbücher der Herzogl. Sächs. Residenzstadt Coburg 741–1822*, 2nd edn, (Coburg: Blume, 1910), pp. 527–63. SBB.1A.72.088.

Saur (Sr) Bätzing, G., ed., 'Auszüge aus den ältesten Kirchenbüchern von Besse aus der Zeit des 30jährigen Krieges', *Zeitschrift des Vereins für hessische Geschichte und Landeskunde*, 83 (1972), 97–135. SBB.Zsn.4904.

Sautter (Sa) Anon., ed., 'Die Schweden in Schwaben', *Historisch–politische Blätter für das katholische Deutschland*, 104 (1889), 688–707. SBB.Ac.7125; BL.P.P.86.

Schleyss (Sc) Dieterich, H.A., ed., 'Leben und Leiden einer Albgemeinde im dreißigjährigen Krieg', *Blätter für württembergische Kirchengeschichte*, 1 (1886), 77–80, 82–8, 92–5; 2 (1887), 4–8, 15–16, 46–8, 53–5, 61–3, 69–71.

Schuster (Sh) Seiffert, B., ed., 'Zum dreissigjährigen Krieg: Eigenhändige Aufzeichnungen von Stadtschreibern und Ratsherren der Stadt Strausberg', *Jahresbericht des Königlichen Wilhelms–Gymnasiums zu Krotoschin*, 48 (1902), Beilage, 1–47. SBB.Ah.15736.

Sierk (Sk) Mensing, O., ed., *Die Bauernchronik des Hartich Sierk aus Wrohm (1615–1664)* (Flensburg: Kunstgewerbemuseum, 1925). SBB.So.298.1.1; BL.9335.a.23.

Simmern (–) Hanncke, R., ed., 'Cosmus von Simmerns Bericht über die von ihm miterlebten Geschichtsereignisse zur Zeit des Wallensteinschen und Schwedischen Kriegsvolkes in Pommern', *Baltische Studien*, 40 (1890), 17–67. SBB.Zsn.9910; BL.Ac.7380.2.

Spiegel (Sp) Großner, R., and Freiherr B. von Haller, eds, '"Zu kurzem Bericht umb der Nachkommen willen": Zeitgenössische Aufzeichnungen aus dem Dreißigjährigen Krieg in Kirchenbüchern des Erlanger Raumes', *Erlanger Bausteine zur fränkischen Heimatforschung*, 40 (1992), 9–107. VGB.C.246.

Staiger (St) Fina, O., ed., *Klara Staigers Tagebuch: Aufzeichnungen während des Dreißigjährigen Krieges im Kloster Mariastein bei Eichstätt* (Regensburg: Pustet, 1981). REG.75/BO.5250.S.782.

Strampfer (S) Kerler, ed., 'Schicksale der Reichstadt Windsheim in der zweiten Hälfte des dreißigjährigen Krieges: Aufzeichnungen des Johannes Andreas Strampfer 1634–50', *Jahresbericht des historischen Vereins für Mittelfranken*, 52 (1905), 31–6. SBB.Sf.5950.

Thiele (Th) Elsler, B., ed., *Peter Thiele's Aufzeichnungen von den Schicksalen der Stadt Beelitz im 30jährigen Kriege* (Beelitz: Schneider, 1931). AGB.Bran.155/Bee.3a.

Turner (T) Turner, Sir J., *Pallas Armata: Military Essayes of the Ancient Grecian, Roman and Modern Art of War* (London: Chiswell, 1683). BOD.L.22.Art; BL.8825.f.31. Quotations are taken from Turner's foregoing book. His memoirs were published later: Turner, Sir J:, *Memoirs of his Own Life and Times* (Edinburgh, 1829). BOD.GA.Scotl.4º.13.26; BL.Ac.8248.28.

Ullmann (U) Grünhagen, G., and J. Krebs, eds., 'Quellenmäßige Beiträge zur Geschichte des 30jährigen Krieges: Jeremias Ullmanns jährl. Anmerkungen sonderbarer Geschichten von 1625–1654', *Zeitschrift des Vereins für Geschichte und Alterthum Schlesiens*, 20 (1886), 319–35. SBB.Zsn.5631.

Unknown soldier (Uk) Lehmann, R., ed., 'Bruchstück eines Tagebuches aus der Zeit des 30jährigen Krieges', *Neues Archiv für Sächsische Geschichte und Altertumskunde*, 40 (1919), 171–8. SBB.Sq.593.

Vincent (V) Vincent, P., *The Lamentations of Germany* (London: Rothwell, 1638). BOD.8º.V.68.1.Art; BL.1077.c.19 & G.6312.3.

Vitzthum (Vi) Budczies, F., ed., 'Der Feldzug der sächsischen Armee durch die Mark Brandenburg im Jahre 1635 und 1636: Aus dem Tagebuche eines Zeitgenossen', *Märkische Forschungen*, 16 (1881), 303–86. SBB.Tc.336; BL.Ac.7325. Quotations are drawn from the foregoing publication. Another section of the same manuscript was published earlier: Budczies, F., ed., 'Aus dem Tagebuche des Obersten Vitzthum von Eickstädt', *Geschichts–Blätter für Stadt und Land Magdeburg*, 10 (1875), 280–5. SBB.Te.7448.

Volhard (–) Waas, C., ed., 'Aus dem Tagebuch der Stadtschreiberei von 1645 bis 1647, geführt von Dr. Johannes Volhard', in *Die Chroniken von Friedberg in der Wetterau*, ed. C. Waas (Friedberg: Bindernagel, 1937), pp. 196–230. SBB.Sk.6037.181; BL.09327.ddd.4.

Wagner (Wa) Roos, W., ed., 'Die Chronik des Jakob Wagner über die Zeit der schwedischen Okkupation in Augsburg vom 20. April 1632 bis 28. März 1635', *Wiss. Beigabe des Jahres–Berichts über das Kgl. Realgymnasium zu Augsburg im Schuljahre 1901/1902* (Augsburg: Haas & Grabherr, 1902). SBB.Ah.20851.

Walther (Wl) Reuss, R., ed., 'Strassburg im dreissigjährigen Kriege (1618–1648): Fragment aus der Strassburgischen Chronik des Malers Johann Jakob Walther', *Protestantisches Gymnasium zu Strassburg – Programm auf das Schuljahr 1879–1880*, 3–41. SBB.Ah.20072.

Wendell (We) Guthmann, O., ed., 'Burgsponheimer Aufzeichnungen (Memorial) des Sebastian Wendell von 1639–1646', *Bad Kreuznacher Heimatblätter*, 7–10 (1973–74), 25–7, 31–2, 35–6, 37–9.

Winkler (Wi) 'W.', ed., 'Merkwürdige Lebensgeschichte Abraham Winklers, eines Pirnaischen Predigers, aus dem dreißigjährigen Kriege', *Blätter aus der Sächsischen Schweiz zur nützlichen Unterhaltung für allerlei Leser*, 3–5 (1805), 39–47, 49–59, 65–72. ZWI.Ad.13.

Wolff (Wo) 'D.E.', ed., 'Fragment einer Handschrift aus den Zeiten des dreissigjährigen Kriegs von einer Frauensperson aufgesetzt', *Fränkisches Archiv*, 3 (1791), 98–120. SBB.Sa.9030.

Zader (Za) Opel, J.O., ed., 'Die Städte Naumburg und Zeiz während des dreißigjährigen Kriegs, aus Zader: Naumburgische undt Zeizische Stiffts–Chronica', *Neue Mittheilungen aus dem Gebiet historisch–antiquarischer Forschungen*, 9.2 (1860), 22–68. HUM/G.Ab.403.

Zembroth (Z) Mone, F.J., ed., 'Allensbacher Chronik von Gallus Zembroth', in *Quellensammlung der badischen Landesgeschichte*, ed. F.J. Mone, 4 vols (Karlsruhe: Macklot, 1848–67), III (1863), pp. 566–81. SBB.4º.Si.90; BOD.240.h.165–8.

Other works referred to

Amelang, J.S., 'Vox Populi: Popular Autobiographies in Early Modern Urban History', *Urban History*, 20 (1993), 30–42.

Bacon's Essays, ed. J.M. McNeill (London: Macmillan, 1959).

Barkin, K.D., 'Autobiography and History', *Societas*, 6 (1976), 83–108.

Benecke, G., 'The Problem of Death and Destruction in Germany during the Thirty Years War: New Evidence from the Middle Weser Front', *European Studies Review*, 2 (1972), 239–53.

Bernheiden, I., *Individualität im 17. Jahrhundert: Studien zum autobiographischen Schrifttum* (Frankfurt am Main: Peter Lang, 1988).

Boswell: The Ominous Years 1774–1776, ed. C. Ryskamp and F.A. Pottle (London: Heinemann, 1963).

Bramston, Sir J., *The Autobiography of Sir John Bramston, K.B., of Skreens, in the Hundred of Chelmsford* (London: Camden, 1845).

Briesen, D., and R. Gans, 'Über den Wert von Zeitzeugen in der deutschen Historik', *Zeitschrift für Biographieforschung und Oral History*, 6 (1993), 1–32.

Burkhardt, J., *Der Dreißigjährige Krieg* (Frankfurt am Main: Suhrkamp, 1992).

Burschel, P., 'Himmelreich und Hölle. Ein Söldner, sein Tagebuch und die Ordnungen des Krieges', in *Zwischen Alltag und Katastrophe: Der Dreißigjährige Krieg aus der Nähe*, ed. B. von Krusenstjern and H. Medick, (Göttingen: Vandenhoeck & Ruprecht, 1999), pp. 181–94.

Burton, J.H., *The Scot Abroad*, 2 vols (Edinburgh: Blackwood, 1864).

Cavendish, M., Duchess of Newcastle, *The Life of William Cavendish, Duke of Newcastle, to which is added the True Relation of my Birth, Breeding, and Life*, ed. C.H. Firth (London: Nimmo, 1886).

Chateaubriand, F.R.A. de, *Mémoires d'Outre–Tombe*, ed. Levaillant, 4 vols (Paris: Flammarion, 1948). The translation of the passage quoted is given by Pascal (see below), p. 12.

Davis, N.Z., *Fiction in the Archives: Pardon Tales and Their Tellers in Sixteenth–Century France* (Stanford CA: Stanford University Press, 1987).

Delany, P., *British Autobiography in the Seventeenth Century* (London: Routledge & Kegan Paul, 1969).

Erdmann, E., 'Der Dreißigjährige Krieg im Spiegel der Tagebücher des Thomas Mallinger: Handlungsweisen der Bevölkerung', *Zeitschrift für die Geschichte des Oberrheins*, 143 (1995), 515–27.

Ergang, R., *The Myth of the All-destructive Fury of the Thirty Years War* (Pocono Pines, PA: The Craftsmen, 1956).

Fothergill, R.A., *Private Chronicles: A Study of English Diaries* (London: Oxford University Press, 1974).

Franz, G., *Der Dreißigjährige Krieg und das deutsche Volk: Untersuchungen zur Bevölkerungs– und Agrargeschichte*, 4th edn (Stuttgart: Fischer, 1979).

Freytag, G., *Bilder aus der deutschen Vergangenheit*, 2 vols (Berlin: Knaur, 1927). First published 1859–65.

Götz, B., O. Gutjahr and I. Roebling, eds, *Verschwiegenes Ich: Vom Un–Ausdrücklichen in autobiographischen Texten* (Pfaffenweiler: Centaurus, 1993).

Hatcher, J., *Plague, Population and the English Economy 1348–1530* (London: Macmillan, 1977).

Henning, E., 'Selbstzeugnisse', in *Die archivalischen Quellen: Eine Einführung in ihre Benutzung*, ed. F. Beck and E. Henning (Weimar: Böhlaus, 1994), pp. 107–14.

Hill, G., ed., *The Montgomery Manuscripts (1603–1706)*, (Belfast: Archer, 1869).

Hocke, G.R., *Europäische Tagebücher aus vier Jahrhunderten* (Frankfurt am Main: Fischer, 1991). First published as *Das europäische Tagebuch* (Wiesbaden: Limes Verlag, 1963).

Hoffmann, I., 'Deutschland im Zeitalter des 30jährigen Krieges: Nach Berichten und Urteilen englischer Augenzeugen' (unpublished doctoral thesis, University of Münster, 1927).

Huch, Ricarda, *Der Dreißigjährige Krieg* (Frankfurt am Main: Insel, 1974). First published as *Der große Krieg in Deutschland* (1912).

Jancke, G., 'Autobiographische Texte – Handlungen in einem Beziehungsnetz. Überlegungen zu Gattungsfragen und Machtaspekten im deutschen Sprachraum von 1400 bis 1620', in *Ego–Dokumente: Annäherung an den Menschen in der Geschichte*, ed. W. Schulze (Berlin: Akademie Verlag, 1996), pp. 73–106.

Jessen, H., *Der Dreißigjährige Krieg in Augenzeugenberichten* (Düsseldorf: Rauch, 1963).

Julian, F., 'Angebliche Menschenfresserei im dreissigjährigen Kriege', *Mitteilungen des historischen Vereins der Pfalz*, 45 (1927), 37–93.

Kroener, B.R., and R. Pröve, *Krieg und Frieden: Militär und Gesellschaft in der Frühen Neuzeit* (Paderborn: Schöningh, 1996).

Krügel, Gerhard, *Aus dem großen Krieg: Schilderungen und Berichte von Augenzeugen* (Leipzig, 1911).

Krusenstjern, B. von, and H. Medick, eds, *Zwischen Alltag und Katastrophe: Der Dreißigjährige Krieg aus der Nähe* (Göttingen: Vandenhoeck & Ruprecht, 1999).

Krusenstjern, B. von, *Selbstzeugnisse der Zeit des Dreißigjährigen Krieges: Beschreibendes Verzeichnis* (Berlin: Akademie Verlag, 1997).

Krusenstjern, B. von, 'Was sind Selbstzeugnisse?', *Historische Anthropologie*, 2 (1994), 462–71.

(*Kurtze Chronica*) – *Von dem dreyssigjährigen Teutschen Krieg, Kurtze Chronica, welcher sich im Jahr 1618 angefangen, und durch Gottes Gnade im Jahr 1648 geendet hat* (1650). A copy of this early pamphlet history of the whole war is held in Cambridge University Library at Acton.d.34.631.2.

Lademacher, H., and S. Groenveld, eds, *Krieg und Kultur: Die Rezeption von Krieg und Frieden in der Niederländischen Republik und im Deutschen Reich 1568–1648* (Münster: Waxmann, 1998).

Lehmann, H., A. Lüdtke, H. Medick, J. Peters, R. Vierhaus, 'Geleitwort zur Reihe "Selbstzeugnisse der Neuzeit. Quellen und Darstellungen zur Sozial– und Erfahrungsgeschichte"', in *Ego–Dokumente: Annäherung an den Menschen in der Geschichte*, ed. W. Schulze (Berlin: Akademie Verlag, 1996).

Mackenzie, A., *History of the Munros of Fowlis* (Inverness: Mackenzie, 1898).

Mortimer, G., 'Perceptions of the Thirty Years War in Eyewitness Personal Accounts' (unpublished doctoral thesis, Oxford University, 1999).

Mortimer, G., 'Models of Writing in Eyewitness Personal Accounts of the Thirty Years War', *Daphnis*, 29 (2000), 609–47.

Mortimer, G., 'Did Contemporaries Recognise a "Thirty Years War"?', *English Historical Review*, 116 (2001a), 124–36.

Mortimer, G., 'Style and Fictionalisation in Eyewitness Personal Accounts of the Thirty Years War', *German Life and Letters*, 54 (2001b), 97–113.

Mortimer, G., 'Individual Experience and Perception of the Thirty Years War in Eyewitness Personal Accounts', *German History*, 20 (2002).

Motzkin, G., 'Memoirs, Memory, and Historical Experience', *Science in Context*, 7 (1994), 103–20.

Parker, G., *The Thirty Years' War* (London: Routledge & Kegan Paul, 1984).

Pascal, R., *Design and Truth in Autobiography* (London: Routledge & Kegan Paul, 1960).

Peters, J., 'Wegweiser zum Innenleben? Möglichkeiten und Grenzen der Untersuchung popularer Selbstzeugnisse der Frühen Neuzeit', *Historische Anthropologie*, 1 (1993), 235–49.

Pröve, R., 'Violentia und Potestas. Perzeptionsprobleme von Gewalt in Söldnertagebüchern des 17. Jahrhunderts', in *Ein Schauplatz herber Angst: Wahrnehmung und Darstellung von Gewalt im 17. Jahrhundert*, ed. M. Meumann and D. Niefanger (Göttingen: Wallstein Verlag, 1997).

Rendall, S., 'On Diaries', *Diacritics*, 16.3 (1986), 57–65.

Repgen, K., 'Seit wann gibt es den Begriff "Dreißigjähriger Krieg"?', in *Weltpolitik, Europagedanke, Regionalismus: Festschrift für Heinz Gollwitzer*, ed. H. Dollinger and others (Münster: Aschendorf, 1982), pp. 59–70.

Repgen, K., 'Noch einmal zum Begriff "Dreißigjähriger Krieg"', *Zeitschrift für historische Forschung*, 9 (1982), 347–52.

Roeck, B., *Als wollt die Welt schier brechen: Eine Stadt im Zeitalter des Dreißigjährigen Krieges* (Munich: Beck, 1991).

Schmidt, G., *Der Dreißigjährige Krieg* (Munich: Beck, 1995).

Schulze, W., 'Vorbemerkung' and 'Vorüberlegungen für die Tagung "Ego–Dokumente"', in *Ego–Dokumente: Annäherung an den Menschen in der Geschichte*, ed. W. Schulze (Berlin: Akademie Verlag, 1996), pp. 9, 11–30.

Scott, Sir W., *Waverley Novels* (Edinburgh: Black, 1852).

Steinberg, S.H., *The 'Thirty Years War' and the Conflict for European Hegemony 1600–1660* (London: Arnold, 1966).

Stevenson, D., *Scottish Covenanters and Irish Confederates* (Belfast: Ulster Historical Foundation, 1981).

Theatrum Europaeum, 21 vols (Frankfurt am Main: Merian). The first six volumes cover the Thirty Years War period, with first edition publication dates between 1633 and 1652.

Theibault, J., 'The Rhetoric of Death and Destruction in the Thirty Years War', *Journal of Social History*, 27 (1993), 271–90.

Vasold, M., 'Die deutschen Bevölkerungsverluste während des Dreißigjährigen Krieges', *Zeitschrift für Bayerische Landesgeschichte*, 56 (1993), 147–60.

Velten, H.R., *Das selbst geschriebene Leben: Eine Studie zur deutschen Autobiographie im 16. Jahrhundert*, Frankfurter Beiträge zur Germanistik, 29 (Heidelberg: Winter, 1995).

Wedgwood, C.V., *The Thirty Years War* (London: Pimlico, 1992). First published 1938.

Williams, E.N., *The Ancien Régime in Europe: Government and Society in the Major States 1648–1789* (London: Bodley Head, 1970).

Woodford, C., 'Women as Historians: The Case of Early Modern German Convents', *German Life and Letters*, 52 (1999), 271–80.

Wunder, H., in *Bericht über die 40. Versammlung Deutscher Historiker in Leipzig, 28. September bis 1. Oktober 1994* (Leipzig: Leipzig Universitätsverlag, 1995), p. 84.

Wuthenow, R.R., *Europäische Tagebücher: Eigenart, Formen, Entwicklung* (Darmstadt: Wissenschaftliche Buchgesellschaft, 1990).

Young, J.E., 'Interpreting Literary Testimony: A Preface to Rereading Holocaust Diaries and Memoirs', *New Literary History*, 18 (1987), 403–23.

Index of Eyewitness Authors

General Index

Printed in Great Britain
by Amazon

61754991R00131